W. B. YEATS – DRAMATIST OF VISION

IRISH LITERARY STUDIES

W. B. YEATS
DRAMATIST OF VISION

A. S. Knowland

with a preface by
Cyril Cusack

Irish Literary Studies 17

1983
COLIN SMYTHE
Gerrards Cross, Bucks.

BARNES AND NOBLE BOOKS
Totowa, New Jersey

First published in 1983 by Colin Smythe Limited
Gerrards Cross, Buckinghamshire

British Library Cataloguing in Publication Data

Knowland, A. S.
    W. B. Yeats, dramatist of vision—(Irish literary
    studies, ISSN 0140-895X; 17)
    1. Yeats, W. B.—Dramatic works
    I. Title   II. Series
    822′.8   PR5908.D7

    ISBN 0-86140-117-4

First published in the United States of America
in 1983 by Barnes & Noble Books, Totowa, N.J. 07512

Library of Congress Cataloging in Publication Data

Knowland, A. S.
    W. B. Yeats, dramatist of vision.
    (Irish literary studies, ISSN 0140-895X; 17)
    Includes index.
    1. Yeats, W. B. (William Butler), 1865-1939—
    Dramatic works. I. Title. II. Title: WB Yeats,
    dramatist of vision. III. Series.
    PR5908.D7K68   1983   822′.8   83-12274
    ISBN 0-389-20407-2 (Barnes and Noble)

Produced in Great Britain
Set by Grove Graphics, Tring, Hertfordshire,
and printed and bound from copy supplied
by Billing & Sons Ltd., Worcester

CONTENTS

Page numbers in *Collected Plays* are given after the play.

ABBREVIATIONS

Books by Yeats

A	*Autobiographies* (1955)
AV(B)	*A Vision* (1937)
CP	*Collected Poems* (1933, 2nd ed., with later poems added, 1950)
CPl	*Collected Plays* (1934, 2nd ed., with additional plays, 1952)
DWL	*Letters on Poetry from W. B. Yeats to Dorothy Wellesley* (1940)
E	*Explorations* (1962)
E&I	*Essays and Introductions* (1961)
FPFD	*Four Plays for Dancers* (1921)
L	*Letters,* ed. Allan Wade (1954)
M	*Mythologies* (1959)
PAIT	*Plays for an Irish Theatre* (1911)
PC	*Plays and Controversies* (1923)
PPV	*Plays in Prose and Verse* (1922)
VPl	*The Variorum Edition of the Plays of W. B. Yeats,* ed. Russell K. Alspach assisted by Catherine C. Alspach
WB	*Wheels and Butterflies* (1934)

Other books

ADM	Barton R. Friedman, *Adventures in the Deeps of the Mind* (1977)
AL	Lady Wilde, *Ancient Legends, Mystic Charms and Superstitions of Ireland* (1887, re-issued 1971)
CNPlJ	Fenollosa and Pound, *Certain Noble Plays of Japan* (1916) Intro. by W. B. Yeats
Comm.	A. Norman Jeffares, *A Commentary on the Collected Poems of W. B. Yeats* (1968)
Comm.Pl	A. Norman Jeffares and A. S. Knowland, *A Commentary on the Collected Plays of W. B. Yeats* (1975)
DC	Michael J. Sidnell, George P. Mayhew, David R. Clark, edd., *Druid Craft. The Writing of 'The Shadowy Waters'* (1972)
DWBY	Richard Taylor, *The Drama of W. B. Yeats* (1976)
ICL	Birgit Bjersby, *The Interpretation of the Cuchulain Legend in the Works of W. B. Yeats* (1950)

IDE	Katharine Worth, *The Irish Drama of Europe from Yeats to Beckett* (1978)
IDM	Una Ellis-Fermor, *The Irish Dramatic Movement* (1954)
IT	James W. Flannery, *W. B. Yeats and the Idea of a Theatre* (1976)
IY	Richard Ellmann, *The Identity of Yeats* (1954)
HT	T. R. Henn, *The Harvest of Tragedy* (1956)
LT	T. R. Henn, *The Lonely Tower* (1950; rev. ed. 1965)
MLD	John Rees Moore, *Masks of Love and Death* (1971)
ND	Liam Miller, *The Noble Drama of W. B. Yeats* (1977)
OIT	Lady Gregory, *Our Irish Theatre* (1913, re-issued 1972)
PCA	William H. Pritchard ed., *W. B. Yeats,* Penguin Critical Anthologies (1972)
PY	James Hall and Martin Steinmann edd., *The Permanence of Yeats* (1961)
RI	Frank Kermode, *Romantic Image* (1957)
S	Mark van Doren, *Shakespeare* (1941)
S&S	Thomas R. Whitaker, *Swan and Shadow* (1964)
TCP	Reg Skene, *The Cuchulain Plays of W. B. Yeats* (1965)
TD	Leonard E. Nathan, *The Tragic Drama of W. B. Yeats* (1965)
WMA	Georgio Melchiori, *The Whole Mystery of Art* (1960)
Y	Harold Bloom, *Yeats* (1970)
YCE	D. E. S. Maxwell and S. B. Bushrui edd., *W. B. Yeats 1865–1939 Centenary Essays (1965)*
Y&GI	Donald T. Torchiana, *Yeats and Georgian Ireland* (1966)
Y&T	F. A. C. Wilson, *Yeats and Tradition* (1958)
YCI	B. Rajan, *Yeats. A Critical introduction* (1965)
YI	F. A. C. Wilson, *Yeats's Iconography* (1960)
YN	Hiro Ishibashi, *Yeats and the Noh: Types of Japanese Beauty in Yeats's Plays* (1965)
YSC	Thomas Parkinson, *W. B. Yeats, Self Critic* (1951)
YT	Robert O'Driscoll and Lorna Reynolds edd., *Yeats and the Theatre* (1975)
YTDR	David R. Clark, *W. B. Yeats and the Theatre of Desolate Reality* (1965)
YTP	Peter Ure, *Yeats the Playwright* (1963)
YV	Helen Hennessy Vendler, *Yeats's Vision and the Later Plays* (1963)
YVP	S. B. Bushrui, *Yeats's Verse Plays: The Revisions 1900–1910* (1965)
YW	Curtis Bradford, *Yeats at Work* (1965)

PREFACE
Cyril Cusack

To word a questionable paradox – or is it a 'Bull'? – my approach as an Irish actor to Yeats the dramatist began by way of a retreat. Hardly would I mean 'Retreat' in the religious sense – or do I? From a student production of *The Pot of Broth* as the Tramp in the holy precincts of Newman House, seat of the old Catholic University in St. Stephen's Green, to *Purgatory,* alternately playing the Boy and the Old Man, on the stage of the Abbey Theatre and thence to Oxford and the University of Lille was, for me, the labyrinthine way offering meditative pursuit, in the wake of the poet-playwright's progress, of Yeats in search of Yeats.

The playwright's verdict on *The Pot of Broth* – 'trivial'! Nevertheless, with the delicate hand of Lady Gregory gently fluttering in authentic rhythms of native dialect it rings forth sounds of reality. Then, with the first production of *Purgatory* in 1939, on the fall of the curtain the poet was heard announcing from the stage that in this play, elegantly shaped in remorseless verse, was contained his whole philosophy. If so – whatever of the American clergyman's protest that night from the auditorium – was it, allowing the dramatist's particular vision of our purgatorial torments, such a digression from Christian belief?

Vide:
> The souls in Purgatory . . .
>
>   Re-live
> Their transgressions, and that not once
> But many times; they know at last
> The consequence of those transgressions
> Whether upon others or upon themselves;
> Upon others, others may bring help;
> But when the consequence is at an end
> The dream must end; if upon themselves,
> There is no help but in themselves
> And in the mercy of God.

ix

Well – but is there omission of the possible efficacy of prayer for the undefended dead?

Time-switches (down the arches of the years – all fifty of 'em!)

The bourgeois comedy over, I opened the stage-door on to a rainy night. Suddenly, like the génie in pantomime erupted on to centre-stage, aflame and sizzling from the rub of the magician's lamp, a figure confronted me – Yeats, towering, glowering. The wetted pavement all a-dazzle from the laneway light conjures up for me the 'floats' and 'foots' of touring theatre, with a flashing mind's-eye glimpse of that other Yeats, friendly brother 'Jack', in his Fitzwilliam Square studio magically brushing on to canvas the glisten and glow of the beloved 'fit-ups'.

Luciferian or avenging angel, 'Where's Dolan?', the poet cried, eyes and voice providing lightning-flash and clap of thunder.

With my hand still clutching the door-handle I heard it in the tone of that Old Man to the loveless Boy in *Purgatory* – 'Stop! Sit there upon that stone.' I stopped and like an angry wind he plunged past me into the interior darkness of the theatre. What terrible judgement was to be passed on poor Dolan, actor-producer of a harmless domestic comedy? But later it was given out that Yeats, perhaps at a time when his several Muses were squabbling for possession, was put out of humour by the play.

It was my one and only close encounter with this Yeats of another kind, Yeats of the Abbey Theatre. It placed me in immediate opposition to the idolators.

Again but from afar, eyeing the poet pontifical, foyer centre-piece opposite the stained-glass windows of the old theatre, as he stood there loftily grandiloquent over the heads of uncomprehending patrons, mentally I joined the mob.

So early on I became aware of the theatreman Yeats and for long I remained wary. There were the actors' tales too, of course: the great F. J. McCormick, once catching sight of Yeats, alone, descending the stairway from the dressing-rooms . . . 'And his eyes were *pink*!', cryptically the actor said, darkly suggesting diabolism; and O'Donovan, with his description of Yeats perambulating the Greenroom, sweeping back the mane of hair as he addressed the ladies of the company, with John Millington Synge, tucked behind a Gordon Craig screen, uneasily tinkling a cup of tea and fiddling with a piece of Lady Gregory's famous Gort cake . . . 'Afraid of his life,' said O'Donovan, 'someone might speak to him.'

And what has all this to do with Professor Knowland's book,

W. B. Yeats — Dramatist of Vision? Scarcely an affable Introduction, to be sure, but in the end, peripherally if not placatorially, at least it may prove indicative. For there was I busily building up around me my walls of bias and objection: dramaturgy dizzied in convolutions of thought and symbolism, halted with scatterings of social comment; creative acting, when revelation should come through the pores of the skin, fettered in the Mask, symbol of untruth; gone the boundlessness in the mirror of the eye; rigid versification interrupting the poetic underflow of natural speech; mysticism falling into confusion before a coterie of dabblers in parlour-games and room-lighting — a dehumanized drama.

Scene-changes:

Yes, and there is Anne Yeats kneeling with her brushes on the floor of the Abbey paint-room. She looks up at me in smiling challenge.

'Listen to Daddy to-night on B.B.C.,' says she, ' — on poetry!'

I listened. The trumpets are at my walls. Poet and playwright are as one in Yeats. What has all this incantatory sound, this heavily pounded out 'sovereignty of words' to do with theatre? Where the light and shade, the infinite variability of tone, the subtler interior processes of 'common' speech, where, in this mannered chanting alien to meaning in the reality of our times? I am under seige within my fortress.

Yet, playing as cast, I serve my reluctant apprenticeship to the dramatist, Yeats, passing, but with gathering experience and lessening certainty, along *Baile's Strand* into *Shadowy Waters* till at last, belatedly I come to the feet of *Cathleen Ni Houlihan* — to a vision.

Once again I hear the Abbey gong's awesome threesome — à le théâtre francais — 'In the Name of the Father and of the Son and of the Holy Ghost'. Peering through a gash in the flimsy present I espy these graceful shades, myself a youthful 'Patrick' amongst them, floating strangely, incandescently in the luminosity of an amber-lit dream. I await that perfect curtain-line poised in the air with theatrical precision:

> *Peter (to Patrick, laying a hand on his arm).* Did you see an old woman going down the path?
> *Patrick.* I did not, but I saw a young girl, and she had the walk of a queen.

. . . that virgin voice of unconquerable innocence, the voice to be raised again over the tumult of Dublin city's crumbling bones and stones through the Easter Rising of 1916.

> Did that play of mine send out
> Certain men the English shot?

And my fortress, without foundations, is swaying before that reddened wind from the past.

What then?

Once more in Newman House, the full half-century later and Professor Augustine Martin, with a sidelong caring look of reproach, saying, 'Why do not actors like Gielgud and Cusack give their talent to the drama of Yeats?'

I was indeed flattered.

But 'The characters lack interiority,' was the actor's glib reply, which Knowland's thesis easily disproves.

And then?

Professor Ronsley, of McGill University: 'Will you consider brining your Irish company to Montreal with some Yeats plays this coming year?'

I have always mistrusted academic forays into the professional theatre and is it now unconditional surrender to the playwright of Academe? But no, here come the millionaires! The World Business Council sits in Killarney. There, to a display of Yeats theatre blending voice, music, Celtic costume, and ballet, the group reacted with statuesque stillness and silent emotion, bearing out the Knowland dictum that 'The visual effects in Yeats's drama should never be underestimated.'

'We were greatly moved,' said chief organizer, Mr Weaver.

From millionaires and academics, more recently to London cab-driver and old 'lag', 'Jimmy' sitting at the wheel – unrestrainedly, as we drive round Trafalgar Square, he bursts out, 'Y'know, I 'as a record of this 'ere Yeats, and every time I plays it, Gawd, it brings tears to me eyes!' Thus, what I thought was my fortress comes toppling down, no more than a paper cell.

Comes Professor Knowland bearing precious gems, extract of Yeats, reflecting the mysteries of creation and death, the interweaving of time and timelessness, of change and changelessness, the congress of 'circumference and centre', the presence of 'non-rational truth' . . . 'Atishoo! Atishoo, we all fall down! – and my paper bag is blown away!

It may be that at the wedding-feast in Oxford when first we met, Professor Knowland sensed in me, old Abbey man, the traditional rebel and, self-challenging, invited this Introduction. Whether or no, whether or not I am the new-found convert, with this tireless yet far from idolatrous pursuit and brooding analysis of the visionary

Yeats, Professor Knowland I see as liberating attendant on a spiritual quest, leading down the labyrinthine ways towards the dawn-light of the dramatist's vision.

And now, remindful of the warning given to me by the great Abbey comedian, Barry Fitzgerald – 'Let analysis but enter and acting flies out the window,' shall I, penitentially, as an 'act' of renunciation, cease to be an actor?

INTRODUCTION

Like most readers of Yeats I came to the plays from the poetry. At one time even the poetry was viewed in some quarters as a tangle of gyres and pernes in which figures like Maud Gonne and others with unpronounceable names, and occasionally swans, got caught up, but at least it could be, and it was, read. But you could rarely see a professional performance of the plays. They were dismissed or ignored as impenetrably obscure and cliquish. Yeats himself, with his élitist distrust of the commercial stage, encouraged this view. For years the plays were submerged in neglect, both critical and theatrical. Now, the critical neglect has been remedied and there have been signs recently of theatrical recognition too, largely, I think, because the extent and variety of the appetite for drama has been increased by the theatre-going public's acceptance of styles and forms of drama that have broken out of traditional moulds. The time has come when the characteristic features of Yeats's plays − mask, dance, stylization of language and movement − may not seem quite so strange. But we have still not had the opportunity of eating enough to prove the quality of the pudding.

In the pages that follow I have tried to keep my analysis of the plays' meaning related to their effect in performance. But it is a performance which, alas, has all too often to be imagined. I have tried to treat them not as appendages to or extensions of his poetry, or as expressions of his 'philosophy', but as viable theatrical experiences, offering insights to audiences with and without previous acquaintanceship with his work. In this aim I have treated each play as an individual unit, as a theatre-goer would encounter it in the theatre. My approach has been broadly chronological, though with an author who revised so much and over such long periods, that term cannot be treated too strictly. It seemed to me that this was the best way of pointing to the main steps that Yeats took in the development of his dramatic craftsmanship. The fact that he did revise so much, and often as a result of experience in the theatre, the degree of his involvement in the practical details of stage presentation − set-design, lighting, décor, costume − revealed in the work of such scholars as Liam Miller, James Flannery, Katharine Worth and Karen

Dorn, should help to dispel the view that his was only a kind of closet-drama.

What follows could not have been written without the discoveries, the perceptions and understanding of previous Yeats scholars. To mention them individually would be to repeat the names of all those authors the titles of whose books appear in the list of abbrevations, but I am happy to acknowledge my debt to them here, if it is not already apparent in the body of the book. Thanks must also be given to all those, amateur and professional, whose efforts to bring the plays to life on the stage I have witnessed, even though their labour has not always been backed by the resources that the plays require for their full realization. In this context, I hope it will not seem invidious if I single out the Sligo Drama Circle, whose work at the annual Yeats International Summer School at Sligo has brought Yeats's drama to the attention of an ever-widening circle of people. In my view scholarship is co-operative and accumulative, and I hope I have added a pebble or two to the cairn of our appreciation of Yeats the dramatist.

But above all I must, of course, thank Michael and Anne Yeats, Macmillan London Ltd., and the Macmillan Publishing Company Inc., for permission to quote from the dramatist's work, I must also pay a special debt of gratitude to Cyril Cusack, whose Preface brings a genuine and welcome whiff of the green room to the groves of academe, and finally to Anne Knudde, without whom this book would not have been printed.

A. S. Knowland

EARLY STAGES

The Countess Cathleen, The Land of Heart's Desire, Cathleen ni Houlihan, The Pot of Broth, The King's Threshold, The Shadowy Waters.

It should not be a matter for surprise that so much of Yeats's energy, both practical and creative, was expended on theatre, for the simple reason that his imagination was essentially dramatic. Just as in his lyrical poetry he was to find a way of embodying his conviction that conflict is at the root of life, so in his drama he was to develop techniques that enabled him to shape his vision into actable form. In that process he discovered that that vision itself demanded expression in a dramatic mode that was unlike anything being written in English at the time. That is the extent of Yeats's achievement as a dramatist – something that is only now beginning to be realized. Yeats made himself into a powerful dramatist, whose mature work, unique to his vision and innovative in its techniques, can stand by itself.

He began to learn his techniques in the place where so many dramatists have learned theirs – in the theatre. His juvenile works, *The Island of Statues, The Seeker, Mosada, Time and the Witch Vivien,* were all written without any experience of the practicalities of theatre, and it was not until he moved with his family, to Bedford Park in London, that, through John Todhunter, he gained any practical experience of the stage. As he explained in *Autobiographies*:

Bedford Park had a red-brick clubhouse with a little theatre that began to stir my imagination. I persuaded Todhunter to write a pastoral play [*Sicilian Idyll*] and have it performed there.

[*A* 119]

This experience, his contact with the actress Florence Farr, who, with her 'incomparable sense of rhythm and . . . beautiful voice' [*A* 121] confirmed in practical terms his belief in the primacy of words in drama, and Professor Dowden's suggestion that he should 'write a poetic drama with a view to the stage' [*L* 108] set him on his path in drama. He grasped at the outset that the first task was to learn the art of effective drama construction. As he wrote in *Samhain 1903*:

1

If we do not know how to construct, if we cannot arrange much complicated life into a single action, our work will not hold the attention or linger in the memory.

[*E* 108]

His belief in the sovereignty of words led naturally to his rejection of illusionist drama, which for him lacked 'beautiful and vivid language' [*E* 166], and so to his search for a drama that would break through the barriers of time and place into an experience that is eternally valid, where what matters is not particularity but passionate intensity. For this the most suitable verbal medium is verse. His second task, therefore, was to fashion an effective poetic language. This meant that 'the poetry' should not be mere ornament but integral to action, theme and character. He realized, too, that the reforms he was demanding in plays and language also involved reforms in acting style, particularly in gesture and movement, and in stage settings. Action, language, movement and décor were all to be pressed into the service of a total drama, in which all these aspects of the dramatic vocabulary combine in the expression of meaning. His early plays, *The Countess Cathleen, The Land of Heart's Desire, The Pot of Broth* (though this is mostly Lady Gregory's work), *The King's Threshold* and *The Shadowy Waters,* all show him moving slowly and hesitantly towards competence in dramaturgy.

In terms of construction there is a progressive improvement. *Cathleen Ni Houlihan* and *The Pot of Broth,* being little more than dramatized anecdotes, present no problems. *The Land of Heart's Desire* is a definite improvement on *The Countess Cathleen. The King's Threshold,* a much more complex play than any of its predecessors, with many more thematic lines of development to be woven together, is the most dramatically coherent of them all. *The Countess Cathleen,* for all its revisions – some the product of his experience in the theatre, others of the exigencies of the Abbey Theatre stage – remains jerkily episodic. The love scene between Cathleen and Aleel in the first part of Scene ii merely interrupts the main story without being satisfactory in itself; scene iv adds nothing to narrative whatsoever, and the theatrical climax of Aleel's vision in scene v is a mere appendage to the narrative climax, the death of the Countess herself.

The construction of *The King's Threshold* is much more logical and therefore more dramatically convincing. The first scene, up to the King's departure [*CP1* 110], announces the situation, from which everything else develops. The first episode, between Seanchan and the Oldest Pupil, constitutes Seanchan's first temptation, but it also expands the theme, in that in rejecting the temptation Seanchan's language establishes his uncompromising stand not simply on his personal situation but on the value of poetry itself. The second temptation, to compromise with politics and the state, and, through Brian, with the claims of family, develops from the first. The third episode, which begins with the arrival of the Chamberlain, who has come on stage to quell the uproar at the end of the previous episode, is much more complex, but all its constituent elements are dramatically justified. The Monk represents not so much a temptation as an attack on art and beauty from a base of ascetic puritanism. The attack is related both to the sensuousness of the girls, with their stroking of the Soldier's hand, their love of dancing and hurling, and also to the theme of the nature of the imagination. The Soldier's temptation, though weakly motivated, is in the event dramatically effective, in that ironically it results in the strengthening of Seanchan's imagination. In rejecting Chamberlain, Monk and Soldier, Seanchan widens the issue from the banishment of one poet from the King's Council to the threat posed to the creative imagination itself by political authority, religion and social convention. At the same time it prepares for the extension of the theme to the dangerous properties inherent in the imagination itself.

The fourth episode, of the Princesses, who have been sent for by the King, develops the idea of hysteria latent in the imagination and relates it to the hysteria which is the product of Seanchan's increasing physical weakness, so that when the Cripples enter for the second time their entry is justified thematically. They externalize the sickness in Seanchan's imagination. In the final episode Fedelm appears because she has been sent for by the Mayor in the second. At the end of the episode, as Seanchan pushes the bread away with her hand, and as she associates herself with his refusal, she is linked both visually in the stage picture and verbally – 'We have refused it' – to the theme of Seanchan's heroic defence of the creative imagination and the analysis of it. Visually and thematically she is linked to Seanchan's heroic defence of the creative imagination and also to Yeats's analysis of it. The play demonstrates Yeats's growing power of dramatic construction and his Aristotelian understanding of the importance of the action. He made the point in a letter to Arthur Symons in September 1905:

. . . *The King's Threshold* has been changed and rehearsed and then changed again and so on, till I have got it as I believe a perfectly articulate stage play. I have learned a great deal about poetry generally in the process, and one thing I am now quite sure of is that all the finest poetry comes logically out of the fundamental action.

[*L* 460]

He was to say much the same thing in 1928 in the letter to Sean O'Casey in which he rejected *The Silver Tassie*:

Dramatic action is a fire that must burn up everything but itself; there should be no room in a play for anything that does not belong to it.

[*L* 741]

And he said it again towards the end of his career, in 1937, in *An Introduction for my Plays:*

I had begun to get rid of everything that is not, whether in lyric or dramatic poetry, in some sense character in action; a pause in the midst of action perhaps, but action always its end and theme.

[*E&I* 530]

The Pot of Broth is the only one of the early plays to lack any symbolic resonances or overtones of meaning. All the others in one way or another attempt to cope with the problem of the extension of the naturalistic into the symbolic. All these early plays – with the exception of *The Shadowy Waters,* which is to some extent a special case anyway, because Yeats at this point in his development was convinced that an Irish Dramatic Movement should be grounded in Irish material – are located in space and time, but there is a movement in each play away from this naturalistic framework. In *The Countess Cathleen* the famine is actual enough and most of the characters are set in its context: Oona, Shemus, Teigue, Mary, the Steward. But both Aleel and the Countess are outside it. For them the famine becomes spiritualized. There are other uncertainties of dramatic level, some glaring and unacceptable. What, exactly, is Aleel's social position? Why does not Cathleen recognize her own house? And surely anyone, half-starved or not, would have some suspicions about the sudden and inexplicable appearance of two men dressed as Eastern merchants. At this stage Yeats was uncertain how to blend naturalistic illusionism with symbolism into an effective dramatic unity.

There is uncertainty too in the social placing of the Bruin family in *The Land of Heart's Desire,* and, more dangerously, in this, the first of the plays in which Yeats handles the theme of the irruption of the supernatural into the natural world, in the theatrical effectiveness of the Child as the agent of the supernatural. A figure resembling that of Beardsley's poster for the play, reproduced in Liam Miller's *The Noble Drama of W. B. Yeats,* would have been much more effective, but Yeats was constrained by his commission to write a vehicle for Florence Farr's eight year old niece: Dorothy Paget. There is no reason, however, why present-day performances should be so constricted and should not find a way, more effective theatrically, of suggesting the cold, ruthless power of the supernatural.

Cathleen ni Houlihan, the most precisely located in place and time – actually at Killala in 1798, the year of the French landings in support of Irish nationalism – is much more effective in the way it moves out from naturalism. This extension is achieved naturally and without strain, first through verbal means within the framework of naturalistic prose – the Old Woman's mention of strangers (with its connotation of English foreigners), the land that was taken from her and her four beautiful green fields, then through the heightened language of the first song, again naturally introduced; then through the build-up of Michael's tightening attention, the old woman's second song, and finally the growing intensity of her prose:

It is a hard service they take that help me. Many that are red-cheeked now will be pale-cheeked; many that have been free to walk the hills and the bogs and the rushes will be sent to walk hard streets in far countries; many a good plan will be broken; many that have gathered money will not stay to spend it; many a child will be born and there will be no father at its christening to give it a name. They that have red cheeks will have pale cheeks for my sake, and for all that, they will think they are well paid.

[*CPl* 86]

The King's Threshold attempts most and achieves most. In it the dramatic boundaries are extended from the natural to the symbolic. The theme is extended from individual poet to poetry, to the creative imagination itself, thence to the contradictory qualities inherent in the imagination, and finally to the climactic paradox of tragic joy. This extension is achieved both by the progressive development of the plot and by the relevance of the language to the theme. The poetry is in the drama.

In the Acting Version of *The Shadowy Waters* there is not so much an extension from a naturalism to symbolism as a juxtaposition of these two elements, a juxtaposition that destroys the play's dramatic coherence. There is a good case to be made out for the view that it would have been better left in its poetic version as a dramatic poem. As it is, the attempt to get more dramatic naturalism into it, however superficially effective the result may be, makes it less credible. The contrast between naturalistic Sailors speaking in Kiltartanese prose and the metaphysical protagonists speaking in poetry is so great as to make it questionable whether these two elements can inhabit the same imaginative world. The removal of the secondary symbolism does indeed make for clearer dramatic intelligibility but the fundamental problem remains: what, precisely, is the nature of the experience that Forgael and Dectora in the end aim at together?

The clearest advance in the handling of stage setting and in the use of stage space is to be found in *The Land of Heart's Desire* and *The King's Threshold*. In *The Countess Cathleen* there is no consistent treatment between exterior and interior scenes, house and wood. The Countess, who rejects material wealth, occupies a palace that is no less real than the house of Shemus and Teigue who pursue it. There is no convincing naturalistic reason why the Eastern merchants should make Shemus Rua's house their first port of call, and still less why their appearance should raise no remarks – the 1892 version, in which they come as travellers to a hostelry, is more acceptable. Nor is there any justification for the merchants being Eastern. *Cathleen Ni Houlihan* makes a much clearer distinction between selfish bourgeois middle-class ideals, represented by the dowry- and career-conscious Peter Gillane, and the self-sacrifice both demanded by patriotic nationalism, and given to it, as represented by the Poor Old Woman and Michael. The constricting cottage is contrasted with the open fields and the lonely roads which are the territory of the patriotic martyr. The point is made visually, in the stage setting. In *The Land of Heart's Desire* this contrast is made all the more effective by Yeats's use of the stage space, which, with its domestic setting that allows for a glimpse of the mysterious wood through the open door, underlines the theme, and gives added point to much of the dialogue. In *The King's Threshold* the physical threshold itself is a key symbol. It is the place where the interior action, the clash of opposing values, is worked out. *The Shadowy Waters* suffers from the same defects inherent in the contrast between the use of prose and verse. Forgael's spiritual voyage in the ship of life, for which poetry is indeed the appropriate medium, simply does not fit in with the Sailor's prosaic search for plunder. He never gets within leagues of becoming even a metaphysical Captain Hook, who could command the allegiance of a crew of roughnecks. And in spite of Lady Gregory's help their prose is far from convincing. But then Yeats always admitted that he never got the hang of the Irish countryman's language. Some of Forgael's and Dectora's language, in which ecstatic lyricism rises to a pitch of dramatic intensity, is, however, apt and memorable.

Indeed much the hardest task for the poet-dramatist is to hammer out an effective poetic language for himself, and it is a task made all the harder for the twentieth-century dramatist by the ghost of Elizabethan blank verse breathing down his neck. It is not until Yeats found ways either of keeping the ghost at a distance by offsetting it with lyric or other metres as in the dance plays, or, as in *Purgatory,* exorcizing it altogether, that he created his own distinctive music. The early plays are uneven in the degree to which language is integrated with character and theme. The most common failing is that characters are made to say things that are out of character altogether or inconsistent. In *The Countess Cathleen,* Oona's lyricism, as in the closing lines of the play, is inconsistent with her down-to-earth distrust of Aleel's song. At the death of the Countess the Peasants are given some very unpeasant-like lines. In *The Land of Heart's Desire* too, Maurteen makes many unconvincing excursions in lyricism, which are not only out of character but, if retained (and it is fair to add that Yeats marked many of the passages as cuts), blur the contrast with Mary Bruin's appropriate lyricism. Bridget's outburst at Mary's death is surely out of character:

> Come from that image; body and soul are gone.
> You have thrown your arms about a drift of leaves,
> Or bole of an ash-tree changed into her image.
>
> [*CPl* 71]

On the other hand, Shawn's language in his love-dialogue with Mary [*CPl* 61-62] teeters on the edge of convincingness. There must be something in him that draws him to the half-mystical Mary, which makes him not only one of those who stand for the values of 'quiet hearths', but also aware of 'all that bewilderment of light and freedom' [*CPl* 62]. But it is difficult to see why Mary rejects him, who can speak so kindly and eloquently. Similarly the language of the Soldier in *The King's Threshold* is inconsistent. It is in character when he offers food to Seanchan:

> Here's meat for you.
> It has been carried from too good a table
> For men like you, and I am offering it
> Because these women have made a fool of me.
>
> *(A pause)*
>
> You mean to starve? You will have none of it?
> I'll leave it there, where you can sniff the savour.
> Snuff it, old hedgehog, and unroll yourself!
>
> [*CPl* 125]

But it is out of character when at the end of the play he blocks the way at the King's command before the Pupils:

> Here is no place for you,
> For he and his pretensions now are finished.
> Begone before the men-at-arms are bidden
> To beat you from the door.

[*CPl* 142]

I doubt if even an Irish private soldier would use the word 'pretensions'.

It is not difficult to find examples of the fault that Yeats himself diagnosed – the way in which dialogue is turned aside by the lure of metaphor, so that the resulting language becomes self-consciously poetic, in which the poetry, as it were, is stuck on as decoration instead of emerging inevitably from the interaction of situation, theme and character. Examples from *The Countess Cathleen* are:

> I have sworn,
> By her whose heart the seven sorrows have pierced,
> To pray before this altar until my heart
> Has grown to Heaven like a tree and there
> Rustled its leaves, till Heaven has saved my people.

[*CPl* 27]

And:

> If the old tales are true,
> Queens have wed shepherds and kings beggar-maids;
> God's procreant waters flowing about your mind
> Have made your more than kings or queens; and not you
> But I am the empty pitcher.

[*CPl* 27]

These poetic conceits are mere embroidery. But even Yeats, severe self-critic that he was, was not always consistent in this respect. Some of the passages in *The Land of Heart's Desire,* for example, which he advised amateurs to cut by printing them in brackets, are indeed excrementitious:

> Maureen [*to Father Hart*]:
> It is but right that youth should side with youth;
> She quarrels with my wife a bit at times,
> And is too deep just now in the old book!
> But do not blame her greatly; (she will grow
> As quiet as a puff-ball on a tree

> When but the moons of marriage dawn and die
> For half a score of times.)

[*CPl* 54]

but not all of them: for example the passage of dialogue between Bridget, Maurteen and Mary after Mary has taken milk and carried it to the door [*CPl* 58-9], which arises naturally from the situation and contains information which it is necessary for an audience unfamiliar with Irish folk-lore to know.

The King's Threshold reveals both weakness and growing strength. The opening speech of the King on words and music is almost pure decoration and tortuous at that. The parallel drawn between words and music and man and woman is not followed up, nor is the conceit about the angels driving the horse of Time. Indeed it is not clear whether it is an angel, or a horse or a chariot that is either golden or silver. The prologue is workaday stuff, and it is not until the introduction of the key images of dream and moon, and of the opposing concepts within the creative imagination, fragility and strength, joy and grief, that the language comes to dramatic life.

The descent into prose for the episode with the Mayor and the Cripples is basically appropriate, but the prose lacks bite and is totally inconsistent with the poetic chant sung by Brian, the Mayor and the Cripples.

Nevertheless, in spite of these failings, Yeats's growing strength as a poetic dramatist is demonstrated by the way in which metaphor and simile are made increasingly the vehicles not of poetic decoration but of dramatic meaning. Yeats's own estimate of *The King's Threshold,* already given, is on the whole justified. This play shows him moving out of tentative apprenticeship towards assured mastery.

The Countess Cathleen

This is the first play that Yeats allowed into the canon, though it took five major revisions – in 1895, 1899, 1901, 1907 and 1912 – from its genesis in 1895 before it reached its final form in 1919. However interesting the study of the play's development up to its first publication in 1892 (the date given in *CPl*) may be, it is with its final form that we have to come to terms.

It is not so much the construction and the dialogue that are at the root of the play's weaknesses, though it is not difficult to support Yeats's own criticism of the language for turning aside at the lure of word and metaphor, but the uncertainty of the dramatic aim. The original French story, which Yeats came across in a translation, tells a straightforward tale of the arrival in poverty-stricken Ireland of two demon-merchants who make great display of their wealth, buying the souls of the poor and the needy. The countess Ketty O'Connor, 'un ange de beauté', sells all her treasure, retaining only her castle and its surrounding pastures, in order to save the peasants. The Merchants, helped by a wicked valet (one of the characters who disappeared in the course of revision), rob her of her money. The peasants are left destitute, with no choice but to die of hunger or sell their own souls. Relief from the lands of the East is on its way but will take eight days to come. After a night of agony the Countess decides to sell her own soul for the highest price she can get – 150,000 *écus d'or*. Three days later she is found dead of grief. But the sale of her soul, entered into out of charity, is declared null and void by God. This simple story presented Yeats with clear dramatic opportunities: a straightforward external conflict between the Demons and a Countess already confirmed in her belief in charity and self-sacrifice, or a conflict between the Demons and a Countess whose character could be made more interesting by presenting her as someone whose moral convictions have to be developed and tested to the point of her final decision. But he complicated this clear outline by introducing other issues which are not dramatically sustained, and by the development of the role of Aleel (Kevin in the 1912 version). The hostility between Mary and her husband and son

introduces the theme of conflict between conventional Christian piety
and paganism, but this is only partially worked out in the play. The
Countess's soul is saved but Mary, in spite of her claim that 'God
. . . Will cater for us still' [*CPl* 5], is left to die. It is true that the
Angels' stern demeanour at the end of the play as they look down
in battle formation supplies a condemnation of the peasants'
behaviour, but the fate of Teigue and Shemus, whose blasphemy
and materialism invite the Demons into the house, is left unclear.
Are they damned? And if so, in what sense? Mary's claim that

> God will destroy you quickly.
> You shall at last dry like dry leaves and hang
> Nailed like dead vermin to the doors of God
>
> [*CPl* 15]

is not dramatically sustained. The Demons 'rush out' but they are
forgotten in the vision of Aleel and the Angel's forgiveness of
Cathleen.

Similarly, neither the personal relationship between Shemus and
Mary reflected in his bullying of her, nor the wider social situation
reflected in the discrepancy between the wealthy Countess and the
impoverished peasantry, however much they may reflect the 'customs
. . . of Christian Ireland' that Yeats referred to in his Preface to
The Countess Kathleen and Various Legends and Lyrics, 1892, are
adequately dramatized.

More important still is the fact that in spite of the progressive
enlargement of the role of Aleel to the point where he appears in
every scene, the relationship between him and the Countess is not
adequately developed, whether on the personal or symbolic level.
That we are invited to adopt a symbolic interpretation of the play
is indicated by the stage directions of scenes 1 and 2 as well as by
the contrast between Christian oratory and pagan wood of scene 3,
and also by Yeats's own letter to the editor of the *Morning Leader*:

The play is symbolic: the two demons who go hither and thither buying
souls are the world, and their gold is the pride of the eye. The Countess
herself is a soul which is always, in all laborious and self-denying persons,
selling itself into captivity and unrest that it may redeem 'God's children'
and finding the peace it has not sought because all high motives are of the
substance of peace. The symbols have other meanings, but they have this
principal meaning.

[*L* 319]

We see Aleel for the first time when he enters in scene 1 with

Cathleen and Oona, as they call at Shemus's cottage to enquire, somewhat incongruously, the way to her own castle. (Incidentally, the 1892 version, in which Shemus Rua's house is a hostelry known as 'The Lady's Head', provides a much more convincing reason for the demon-merchants to call at it than the final version.) This entry, even without the group of 'fantastically dressed musicians' of the 1895 version, serves to point up the contrast between the world of normal reality, with its poverty, hunger, suffering and death, the world known to the Countess's tenants, and the escape-world with which Mary identifies her castle:

> A place that's set among impassable walls
> As though world's trouble could not find it out.
>
> [*CPl* 6]

Cathleen's recognition of this as a dream world, although it prepares for her ultimate rejection of dreams in favour of responsibility, also weakens the force of her attraction for Aleel, which it is one of the functions of scene 3 (added in 1901) to present. For Aleel this dream world is not simply a negative escape from the world of reality but a positive assertion of a different order of reality altogether. This order is reflected in his music and his songs (lyrical as opposed to dramatic speech), his love, his appeal to a timeless pagan world, and in his vision. It is to the poet, the visionary, and to the suffering rejected lover that the ultimate fate of the Countess is revealed. This order is opposed both to Shemus's materialism and to what lies behind it, the sort of philistinism that Yeats was later to attack in such poems as 'At Galway Races' [*CP* 108], 'Pardon, Old Fathers . . .' [*CP* 113] and 'September 1913' [*CP* 120]. It is also opposed to the Countess's Christian charity and responsibility which leads to her self-sacrifice. Shemus's disapproval of Aleel is not developed beyond his muttered protest, the exchange of mutually hostile looks and his contemptuous reference to Aleel as a fool [*CPl* 9].

In the second scene, in which Aleel's part was added in the 1912 revision of the play, only the negative aspect of Aleel's world is presented – that which seems to be only an illusory escape from misfortune and 'the evil of the times' [*CPl* 19]. Cathleen is presented as drawn to this world and to Aleel. She is so absorbed in his story of Maeve that she does not notice her own castle. She prefers his arm to Oona's for support. But this illusory world in which she 'thought to have escaped misfortune' [*CPl* 20] is shattered dramatically, first by the entry of the steward telling of the robbery of Cathleen's garden by the starving poor and again immediately after by the arrival of Teigue and Shemus with the news of the peasants selling their souls. The Steward's tidings evoke her passionate assertion of God's infinite capacity to pardon any act, even robbery, if it be committed in unbroken faith:

> And if it be a sin, while faith's unbroken
> God cannot help but pardon.
>
> [*CPl* 21]

In effect she is prefiguring the forgiveness of her own 'sin' in selling her soul. Teigue and Shemus provoke her to the next stage of her development, the selling of her goods to save her tenants from starvation:

> Keeping this house alone, sell all I have,
> Go barter where you please, but come again
> With herds of cattle and with ships of meal
>
> [*CPl* 23]

In spite of her compassion for the wounded Aleel the stage is set for her rejection of all ties, whether they comprise the unimaginative practical piety of Oona or the unpractical imagination of Aleel, which will issue in her own self-sacrifice.

This obeisance to Christian self-abnegation is underpinned visually by the setting of the next scene, in which Cathleen kneels in front of the altar in the oratory within her house, while outside can be seen the trees of the garden, the symbolic landscape of Aleel's subjective paganism, but now 'dimly'. As far as the Countess is concerned this scene is her climax. In it she makes her choice between Christian responsibility and pagan self-absorption, between oratory and wood, between agape and eros. She is in effect already committed to her final gesture. But there is no dramatic tension created in the opposition of these forces. Her own imagination and heart are not shaken, in spite of what she says, nor does Aleel symbolize the passionate proud heart that derives its strength from Aengus, the god of love, youth and poetry. He gives up the struggle too easily. She moves towards the oratory door, he simply lets his clasped hands, which he holds out beseechingly to her, fall, and moves towards the door through which the wood can be seen. Yeats fails to work out adequately in dramatic terms the conflict within her own heart with all that Aleel represents. We are not convinced that she has ever loved him or that she realizes the power that makes poets 'more than kings or queens', in renouncing which she has made herself an 'empty pitcher' [*CPl* 27]. She pities him and she pities the peasants, though she is not the 'pity-crazed' Cathleen of 'The Circus Animals' Desertion'. In fact she is not crazed by anything. She lacks that kind of intensity. On the other hand Aleel is not given anything to say that would convince us of his authoritative consciousness of the world of poetry and passion. Nowhere is he given the opportunity to pit his personal passion in a blaze of eloquence against her generalized pity. Rejected by her he simply tires of life.

Similarly, Yeats has not adequately dramatized her opposition to the Demon-merchants. It is dramatically weak that after she has made her choice and rejected Aleel and gone into the oratory she should simply fall asleep while the Merchants ransack the treasury. It is even weaker that she should be so easily deceived by them and fail to identify them until after they have gone, in spite of the oddness of their dress as Eastern merchants in a setting that is predominantly that of the Irish countryside, and that the next stage of her development, the decision to redeem the souls of the peasants by the barter of her own, is taken without a direct confrontation with her enemies.

The next scene does not advance the central action concerning the Countess at all. Like the other Front Scene, scene 2, when played at the Abbey, it allows time for the following scene to be set up, and dramatically seems merely to stress the contrast between the materialism of the peasants and Aleel's absorption in the world of poetry, by the contrast between the peasants' blank verse and his somewhat cloudy lyricism.

The final scene opens with the apparent victory of the Demon-merchants. Mary, whose 'tongue grew rank/With all the lies that she had heard in chapel' [*CPl* 38], and who mocked at her husband's masters, lies dead. The peasants flock in to sell their corrupt little souls. Aleel, who has lost whatever energy his passionate and proud heart should have endowed him with, is led off-stage unaware of or unable to exercise the authority which even the Demons recognize. It is left to an ignorant peasant to awaken a challenge to their power, and to the Countess, now presumably acting on the 'strange thought' she comes to at the end of scene 3 [*CPl* 34], to redeem the souls of the peasantry in the same coinage with which they put them at risk. Aleel recovers his energy in his attempt to prevent the Countess from signing her soul away and in his vision of the evil spirits that emerge through the brazen door of Hell. But the scene is confused. First Aleel is dragged away by Shemus, Teigue and the peasants, then the Countess goes out to distribute the money, then the merchants rush out – we never know their ultimate fate – then Aleel recovers and gives his account of the legendary figures which Yeats himself came to recognize did not work in the theatre because audiences were ignorant of Irish mythology. Oona, who might have been expected to be with the Countess, comes in to pray for her safety. Aleel kneels beside her, but it is not clear to what extent he shares in this appeal to the Christian 'Maker of all' [*CPl* 46]. In the end he says his heart is 'smitten of God' [*CPl* 49] and he kneels again when the Angel tells of her pardon, but has nothing to say. It seems inappropriate that the final words – self-consciously poetic and out of key with her earlier blunt language – should be given to Oona. Back come the peasants with the dying Countess, to be lamented by them in language that is again inappropriate, and which Yeats removed from the shortened ending prepared for the 1911 performance at the Abbey. The episode is gratuitously theatrical and produces yet another poeticized outburst from the peasants:

> — She was the great white lily of the world.
> — She was more beautiful than the pale stars.
> — The little plant I loved is broken in two.
>
> [*CPl* 48]

It is a sign of Yeats's uncertainty of touch that he retained these lines even in the shortened 1911 ending, though he did remove references to Irish mythological figures, replacing them by Belial, in Aleel's vision of the victory of the angels. But this vision, which it proved impossible to mount on the shallow Abbey stage, is mixed up with Aleel's declaiming against 'Time and Fate and Change'. It is Aleel who dominates the stage from the point when the Demon merchants rush out, and it is significant that what remained in Yeats's memory after thirty-five years was Florence Farr's performance in the role. For all the uncertainty surrounding him – is he reconciled to the Countess's death? – he carries more conviction than the Countess.

The Land of Heart's Desire

It was Florence Farr's request for a one-act play in which her niece, a girl of eight or nine, might make her first stage appearance that prompted Yeats to write this, his next play. Although it is not founded upon any particular story, it is rooted in the Irish belief in the power of the faeries to invade the mortal world and carry away a human soul to their own kingdom. But, as Yeats explained in an article in *The United Irishman,* such a rape is effected only in response to the subjective will:

"The Land of Heart's Desire" was, in a sense, the call of the heart, the heart seeking its own dream.

[*Comm. Pl* 28]

Or, as Father Hart puts it in the play, Mary's departure is ultimately the Soul's choice. Her land of heart's desire is a reflection of her own longing for a society

> Where nobody gets old and godly and grave,
> Where nobody gets old and crafty and wise,
> Where nobody gets old and bitter of tongue

[*CPl* 55]

so that it is dramatically appropriate that the faery Child should tempt her thither with her own words, adding significantly the further temptation to annul the one force that could possibly keep her in the mortal realm, her husband's possessive love:

> . . . where kind tongues bring no captivity.

[*CPl* 70]

What she does not realize until she has made her decision is that such choices, such spiritual resolutions, exact their own price – in suffering, death, or the withering of the heart that is the burden of the pitiless comment made by the reed of Coolaney with which the play ends. Indeed the play in performance needs a kind of heartlessness if it is to be preserved from the pretty-pretty

16

mawkishness dangerously inherent in the choice of the Child as the embodiment of the supernatural world, and if it is to realize the ambiguities latent in its surface simplicity, even if these ambiguities fall short of profundity.

No doubt it is this simplicity that has helped the play to its popularity – simplicity of setting, of characterization, of language, and of theme. But Yeats's natural sense of complexities gives it depth, even if his grasp of social realities leaves something to be desired. When he revised the play for a performance at the Abbey Theatre on 22 February 1912, he cast it back in time 'because the metrical speech would have sounded unreal if spoken in a country cottage now that we have so many dialect comedies' (*Comm. Pl* 22), but it is still not easy to place the Bruin family socially – a hundred-acre farmer with a taste for Spanish wine matured in bottle, sufficient business sense, or craftiness, to amass an inheritance that will leave his son potentially the wealthiest man in the neighbourhood, enough sophistication of mind to talk of his approaching death as a goodbye to Fate and Time and Change; a literary grandfather with a taste in leather book-binding, a son and daughter-in-law of considerable refinement – these are not consistent with the picture of poor folk suggested by Bridget. Clearly this absence of historical particularity is intended to support the contrast, once again reinforced by the stage setting, as in *The Countess Cathleen,* between the enclosed world of human domesticity, moral orthodoxy and social conformism, and the vague mysterious world of frustrated aspiration lit by a moon or late sunset, all that 'bewilderment of light and freedom ' [*CPl* 62].

But however generalized the characters may be, they are all given individualizing touches, which, if they do not make enormous demands upon the actors, at least offer amateurs (to whom the play so often appeals) some scope. Bridget is more than the typical shrewish peasant-wife complaining of the laziness of the young generation: she shows a maternal tenderness towards the faery Child. In her and her husband Yeats captured that ambiguity of attitude so characteristic of Irish country-folk: acceptance both of the framework of orthodox piety and at the same time recognition of the power of the pagan faeries – particularly their power for evil – and with it the need to preserve practices which Christian faith would logically condemn as superstitious, even though Father Hart would keep old innocent customs up. Maurteen, though given to sententiousness and complacency, is perceptive, compassionate – he defends his daughter-in-law against his wife – and good-natured – he brings the Child in from the cold and offers it food and drink. He sees that the dreary restrictions of the hearth have driven Mary to lose herself in dreams:

I've little blame for her;
She's dull when my big son is in the fields,
And that and maybe this good woman's tongue
Have driven her to hide among her dreams
Like children from the dark under the bed-clothes.

[*CPl* 56]

Shawn is to some extent a victim of his position: the young son waiting for his parents to die so that he can exercise the authority he feels is his. As husband he defends his young wife against the mother; he recognizes the restrictiveness that can thwart and wither the life-seeking impulses:

Would that the world were mine to give it you,
And not its quiet hearths alone, but even
All that bewilderment of light and freedom,
If you would have it.

[*CPl* 62]

But he accepts also the overriding claims of the 'indissoluble sacrament' [*CPl* 62] by which society has disciplined passion to marriage. Caught between these conflicting impulses he is powerless to save Mary from her own decision.

But Mary herself is not without conflict: she is not merely the passive vehicle of opposing orthodoxies. She moves from one to the other. Yeats's growing grasp of the medium of drama is demonstrated by the way in which this vacillation is expressed not only in her language but in her movements. Stage space, and the movement of characters within it, becomes a contributory factor to dramatic meaning. Clearly she is naturally responsive to the call of the faery world – this is shown by the way Yeats places her standing by the door and able to look out into the symbolic wood, and reading in the book through which her husband's grandfather neglected his worldly fortunes. When Father Hart asks her what she is reading, she replies in the tone of one who is lost literally in a fairy-tale world

Where nobody gets old and godly and grave,
Where nobody gets old and crafty and wise,
Where nobody gets old and bitter of tongue.

[*CPl* 55]

Her tone of voice here should prefigure the trance into which she falls when she dies. When first the '*girl child strangely dressed* . . .

comes out of the wood' [*CPl* 57] and takes away the sacred quicken wood that she has hung up, and then when the mysterious arm *'comes round the door-post and knocks and beckons'* [*CPl* 58] while Maurteen and Bridget are busied in mundane domestic matters, and then when the queer old man makes her a sign to show that he wants fire to light his pipe, she is compelled to accept the reality of this world. Shawn makes little attempt to support her, and, driven to exasperation, for she is a young woman of character, she first explodes

> What do I care if I have given this house . . .
> Into the power of faeries!
>
> [*CPl* 61]

and then appeals to them to take her out of it and restore to her all the freedom she has lost. It is only at this point that she loses faith in Shawn and adds, sorrowfully, since he recognizes his responsibilities here, the fourth tongue that she is weary of:

> . . . a kind tongue too full of drowsy love,
> Of drowsy love and my captivity
>
> [*CPl* 61]

Shawn's lyrical avowal of his love restores her sense of duty – 'I have said wicked things tonight' [*CPl* 63] – and the Child's blasphemy towards the crucifix and her dancing cause her to feel that the powers that have entered the house are unholy, and that it needs the protection of the Queen of Angels and kind saints from them. But Shawn lacks heroic conviction, and Father Hart, because his own religious convictions are themselves flawed by his half-belief in the reality of the faery world, has rendered himself powerless to defend those who gather behind him by yielding to the Child's blandishments and, in a fine stroke of irony, removing the crucifix. Shawn has no independent defence to offer, so that the field is left open for a straight choice between the house and the duties it imposes on the one hand, sanctified by 'the dear Name of the One crucified' [*CPl* 70], and on the other youth, gaiety, joy, freedom, sanctified by the 'name of your own heart' [*CPl* 70]. Only after Mary has made her decision 'I will go with you' [*CPl* 70] does the Child declare that 'clinging mortal hope must fall' [*CPl* 71] from her. Mary displays momentary hesitations in response to Shawn's last desperate gesture, but it is too late.

The play is a little bit more subtle than it appears on the surface.

It is not about a simple opposition between the life-denying forces of moral orthodoxy and social conformism on the one hand and gaiety and aesthetic vitality on the other – the phrase is John Rees Moore's – and he is right in saying that it makes 'a familiar Yeatsian point: to deny, or accept, the heart's desire is no laughing matter' [*MLD* 65]. Indeed, as Mary ought to have known, the faeries are dangerous, even if they offer eternal beauty, joy and freedom.

To get that point over in performance is the problem, and the problem takes us back to the genesis of the play in Florence Farr's request for a role for her child niece. It is not easy, perhaps impossible, to convey through a child dancer the unearthliness, the Homeric indifference, the force, not only superhuman but inhuman, of the Faery world. This is the impression, however, that should be attempted in her actual dance, which ought to reflect that self-absorption, that retreat into an entirely personal subjective world to the exclusion of everything else which is a characteristic of some solo traditional Irish dances. The Faery Child is a kind of undeveloped Woman of the Sidhe, a potential Fand, whose childishness has nothing to do with age. Some of Yeats's revisions support this view, in that they remove associations with the behaviour and speech of childhood. For example, the neutral 'The wine is bitter' [*CPl* 64] replaces the naturalistically childish 'They are both nasty'. 'Have you no sweet food for me?' replaces 'Have you nothing nice for me?' [*CPl* 64]. 'Here is level ground for dancing' [*CPl* 66] replaces 'O, what a nice, smooth floor to dance upon!'. Maurteen's gift of 'ribbons that [he] bought in the town / For his son's wife' [*CPl* 67] replaces 'I will buy lots of toys'; and the invisible barrier that separates Shawn from her is more sinister than the earlier barrier of primroses that the Child takes and strews between herself and the priest and about Bridget Bruin. Something could be done with make-up and costume to suggest this unearthly and ageless quality which is essential to the figure of the Child, but we sense not only a discrepancy between symbol and the things symbolized but also an uncertainty of dramatic direction. The play hovers between naturalism and symbolism, and neither attains a satisfactory balance between these modes nor effectively explores the potentialities of either.

Cathleen ni Houlihan

This play shares with *The Land of Heart's Desire* a symbolic action involving the irruption into the mundane world of commonsense, domesticity, 'getting on' and materialism, of values totally alien to it, which, when followed, bring suffering: in the former case death and in this the desertion of a bride-to-be. In neither play does Yeats concern himself with exploring the consequence in the mundane world of this invasion from beyond it: he is content to state it. It also shares with *The Land of Heart's Desire* a setting in Ireland, though in this case it is precisely defined as 2 August 1798, the day on which a French force of a thousand republican soldiers under General Humbert landed at Killala in Co. Mayo on the west coast of Ireland [*Comm. Pl* 32]. It differs from *The Land of Heart's Desire* in its use of a prose which is a much more convincing representation of country speech, which, as Stephen Gwynn suggested, no doubt Lady Gregory had helped Yeats to perfect. Yeats himself linked the two plays when he said that *The Land of Heart's Desire* 'was, in a sense, the call of the heart, the heart seeking its own dream; this play is the call of country . . .' [*Comm. Pl* 28]. In both cases the call from beyond demands a total response, regardless of consequences:

If any one would give me help he must give me himself, he must give me all.

[*CPl* 84]

The stage presence of Maud Gonne, who played the Old Woman when the play was first produced on 2 April 1902 in Dublin, supported this generalized theme – 'her great height made Cathleen seem a divine being fallen into our mortal infirmity' [*Comm. Pl* 36], and to be fair to this aspect of Yeats's intentions in writing the play, an actress ought to try to convey this impression. But Yeats's denial that this was a political play of a propagandist kind [*Comm. Pl* 36] is a trifle disingenuous. It is difficult to believe that he was unaware then of the potentially explosive material that he saw the play to be

21

in his old age when he wrote:

> Did that play of mine send out
> Certain men the English shot?

[*CP* 393]

Certainly it was recognized by Stephen Gwynn, who wrote:

The effect of *Cathleen Ni Houlihan* on me was that I went home asking myself if such plays should be produced unless one was prepared for people to go out to shoot and be shot.

[*Comm. Pl* 30]

Jeffares is right when he says that even without a knowledge of the patriotic street ballad, the 'Shan Van Vocht', audiences have been moved by the beauty and dramatic skill of the play's conclusion, but the full impact of the play can only be felt if the audience is aware of the great weight of patriotic associations behind Yeats's references to the French landings at Killala, and its connections with Wolfe Tone, the implications of 'hurling', 'strangers', the 'four beautiful green fields' that have been taken from the Old Woman; the significance of 'the O'Donnells from the north', the 'O'Sullivans from the south' and 'O'Brien that lost his life at Clontarf'. Without this kind of knowledge it is difficult for an audience to understand the force of the appeal to Michael which leads to his abandoning poor Delia. This climactic moment is skilfully prepared by Michael's growing interest in the mysterious Old Woman, which is aroused after her first snatch of song [*CPl* 82], by his question, 'What is it that you are singing, ma'am?' [*CPl* 82], is then transferred from dialogue to movement during the conversation between Bridget and Peter, as *'Michael sits down beside her on the hearth'* [*CPl* 83] and revived in dialogue with greater intensity after she has rejected Peter's shilling. A long crescendo leads up to the moment of decision, worked out in skilfully varied levels of language: the plain naturalistic speech of Bridget, the unearthly song of the Old Woman and her heightened prose, and Michael's rapt response. This is skilful dramaturgy by any standards.

The moment of decision distinguishes those for whom patriotism is only something in a song or an empty gesture such as Peter makes when he takes his pipe out of his mouth and his hat off, and those for whom it is a call to action in which the consequences, spelled out, it is true, by Cathleen, and later to be explored by Yeats in *The Dreaming of the Bones,* are lost in the vision of her transformation:

Peter: Did you see an old woman going down the path?
Patrick: I did not, but I saw a young girl, and she had the walk of a queen.

[*CPl* 88]

As a curtain line, Patrick's still has a spine-chilling quality.

The Pot of Broth

If the full impact of *Cathleen Ni Houlihan* depends almost entirely upon the audience's background knowledge of Irish history, that of *The Pot of Broth,* which Yeats himself described as a 'trivial, unambitious retelling of an old folk-tale' [*Comm. Pl 37*], depends almost as much upon the actor playing the Tramp, though his insouciance and blarney must be complemented by the coarseness and peasant greed of Sibby. Trivial it is, in the sense that it lacks significance, but it can be appealing when deftly performed. It certainly seems to have given William Fay an opportunity to demonstrate his gifts for humour, delicacy and charm as a comedian, and also, to judge by Yeats's story, given in *Comm. Pl* 38, his ability to carry a play on his stage personality.

The only problem that has to be decided is whether John sees through the Tramp's tricks and is content to go along with him in order to repay his wife's spite, or not. The former seems the more attractive.

Yeats's comments are just:

I hardly know how much of the play is my work, for Lady Gregory helped me as she has helped in every play of mine where there is dialect, and sometimes where there is not. In those first years of the Theatre we all helped one another with plots, ideas, and dialogue, but certainly I was the most indebted as I had no mastery of speech that purported to be of real life. This play may be more Lady Gregory's than mine, for I remember once urging her to include it in her own work, and her refusing to do so. The dialect, unlike that of *Cathleen ni Houlihan,* which was written about the same date, has not, I think, the right temper, being gay, mercurial, and suggestive of rapid speech. . . The dialect of *Cathleen ni Houlihan* is, I think, true in temper but it has no richness, no abundance. The first use of Irish dialect, rich, abundant, and correct, for the purposes of creative art was in J. M. Synge's *Riders to the Sea,* and Lady Gregory's *Spreading the News.*
[*Comm. Pl* 38]

It is this gay, mercurial character that the Tramp embodies – a tramp out of folk-tale, and a long way from the romantic outsiders of Synge.

24

The King's Threshold

Writing to Frank Fay in August 1903, by which time the first version of the play had taken shape, Yeats referred to its construction as 'rather like a Greek play' [*L* 409], and though he changed much in his subsequent revisions, he kept its basic form. The play begins with a kind of Euripidean prologue, shared between the King and the Oldest Pupil, which establishes the situation and announces the major themes. This is followed by a number of episodes (*epeisodia*), in effect temptation scenes, which are linked together not by the choric passages (*stasima*) of the strict Greek tradition but by transitional passages of dialogue. After the climax of Seanchan's death, there is an episode equivalent to the song sung by a Greek Chorus as it moved off stage, the *exodos,* as the Pupils and Fedelm go off bearing the dead body of Seanchan to the sound of mournful music. As in *Prometheus Bound* and *Samson Agonistes* the action is unified in both place and time, the dramatic interest centring on the progressive hardening of Seanchan's attitude and the exploration of that attitude expressed in terms not only of his rejection of successive external temptations but also of the inner tensions which are at the root of it.

The action dramatizes the last hour – or however long it takes to act the play, since dramatic time and acting time are identical here– in the life of the poet Seanchan, and is confined to one place, the threshold of the King's palace, a physical representation of that realm where the action of so many of Yeats's plays occurs, the place where opposing visions and values meet, interact, and illuminate each other. It is doubtful whether much is gained by an audience, Irish or not, from Yeats's care in particularizing the scene by placing it in the recognizable district of Gort and its neighbourhood. He may even have reduced its universal appeal by trivializing it, since there is something slightly ridiculous in talking about the King and his elaborate structure of authority, which includes an ecclesiastical hierarchy, an army, a justiciary, a municipal structure, in terms of a small country town. But Yeats was always aware of the danger, inherent in symbolic drama, of the action disappearing into a mist

25

of abstraction, and attempted to counteract this by sharp localization.

The King's first speech announces the theme which in the end is developed most fully – the value of art:

> I welcome you that have the mastery
> Of the two kinds of Music: the one kind
> Being like a woman, the other like a man.
> Both you that understand stringed instruments,
> And how to mingle words and notes together
> So artfully that all the Art's but Speech
> Delighted with its own music; and you that carry
> The twisted horn, and understand the notes
> That lacking words escape Time's chariot; . . .
>
> [*CPl* 107]

His second speech stresses the choice that Seanchan has made, death. His third announces the theme that concerned Yeats so deeply, the relation of the poet to society. As he wrote in a note to *The King's Threshold*:

> It was written when our society was beginning its fight for the recognition of pure art in a community of which one half is buried in the practical affairs of life, and the other half in politics and a propagandist patriotism.
>
> [*Poems 1899-1905*, p.279 *VPl* 315]

This relation is seen as a mutual opposition: the King, the man of action, banishes Seanchan the poet, the man of words, from his court:

> Three days ago
> I yielded to the outcry of my courtiers –
> Bishops, Soldiers, and Makers of the Law –
> Who long had thought it against their dignity
> For a mere man of words to sit amongst them
> At the great council of the State and share
> In their authority. I bade him go . . .
>
> [*CPl* 108]

But the opposition is not altogether stark: on the one hand the King, for all his pragmatism, is conscious of the 'wild thought' [*CPl* 110] of the poet, and on the other the poet embodies somewhat uneasily the concept of the imagination as truth, but also as delirium, first brought on by his physical weakness and then as an inherent frenzy that 'overruns the measure' [*CPl* 110].

It is a weakness that we are not shown the poet retaliating with the only weapon he has, a weapon that is all the more potentially effective in that the King recognizes its power – the power of verbal invective – but with the physical gesture of a hunger-strike, which at the outset looks dangerously like a fit of the sulks. It may well be that Yeats's choice of a hunger-strike here anticipates the action of Terence MacSwiney, Lord Mayor of Cork, who died on hunger-strike in 1920, and would thus set up political reverberations in today's politically knowledgeable audience, but this is not the main point of the play, which is that poetry transcends politics.

The first episode, between Seanchan and his Pupils [*CPl* 110-114] expresses the latent contradictions within the imagination. On the one hand there is a subjective lunar fantasy (anticipating, incidentally, the image of the heron/crane in *Calvary*):

> . . . though I all but weep to think of it,
> The hunger of the crane, that starves himself
> At the full moon because he is afraid
> Of his own shadow and the glittering water,
> Seems to me little more fantastical
> Than this of yours.
>
> [*CPl* 111]

On the other there is an apocalyptic creative force defined in some of the most memorable lines of the play:

> And I would have all know that when all falls
> In ruin, poetry calls out in joy,
> Being the scattering hand, the bursting pod,
> The victim's joy among the holy flame,
> God's laughter at the shattering of the world.
> And now that joy laughs out, and weeps and burns
> On these bare steps.
>
> [*CPl* 114]

These conflicting qualities are acted out in the subsequent episodes (except the second, which is concerned largely with the poet/society theme) until they reach their logical and dramatic conclusion in Seanchan's last words, which are simultaneously an exultant cry of victory and a death-rattle. This first episode also establishes in the quasi-socratic dialogue between Seanchan and the Oldest Pupil, who is made to admit the power of poetry in powerful metaphorical language that is itself its own justification, the primacy of the creative imagination as the vehicle of truthful vision. This is truly dramatic verse which, in Eliot's words, justifies itself dramatically, does not interrupt, but intensifies the dramatic situation:

> *Seanchan:* At Candlemas I bid that pupil tell me
> Why poetry is honoured, wishing to know
> If he had any weighty argument
> For distant countries and strange, churlish kings.
> What did he answer?
> *Oldest Pupil:*   I said the poets hung
> Images of the life that was in Eden
> About the child-bed of the world, that it,
> Looking upon those images, might bear
> Triumphant children. But why must I stand here,
> Repeating an old lesson, while you starve?
> *Seanchan:* Tell on, for I begin to know the voice.
> What evil thing will come upon the world
> If the Arts perish?
> *Oldest Pupil:*   If the Arts should perish,
> The world that lacked them would be like a woman
> That, looking on the cloven lips of a hare,
> Brings forth a hare-lipped child.

[*CPl* 111-112]

The second episode, with the Mayor of Kinvara, the Cripples and Brian, is the weakest. The descent into prose is justifiable, in that the episode parallels the opposition between Seanchan and the King and his exalted Establishment on the lower level of petty authority and the common people, but at the same time it makes the rhythmic chants at the end of the episode unacceptable. The prosaic world is incapable of attaining to the level of the poetic imagination. But Yeats's satire directed against the Mayor, who is the symbol of all dolts, merchants and clerks, of the prudential, rational virtues that dry the marrow from the bone, is too obvious, almost puerile, to be effective. The Cripples are introduced partly to demonstrate that the uneducated recognize the authority of the poet and partly to make their second appearance in the fourth episode less of a shock. But their functions differ in the two scenes. Here, they fill in the theme of the poet in society; later they seem to be an externalization of Seanchan's now delirious imagination. It is not at all clear why they move off when the Chamberlain appears here but find no difficulty in remaining present when he appears for the second time. Brian, whose sincere concern for Seanchan is contrasted with the Mayor's hollow pomposity, serves to fill out the social theme – 'What do the great and powerful care for rights / That have no armies?' [*CPl* 122] – and at the same time provokes Seanchan to a hardening of his attitude, as he refuses to respond to either offers of friendship or family claims.

Indeed the entire theme of the relation of poet to society is

inadequately handled and is finally left behind as Seanchan grows
from individual to the symbol of poetry itself. If the Chamberlain,
who introduces the third episode [*CPl* 123], is right in saying to
Seanchan:

> your work
> Has roused the common sort against the King,
> And stolen his authority
>
> [*CPl* 123]

then this support, which is stressed again later when the Chamberlain
tells the Soldier 'The common sort would tear you into pieces / If
you but touched [Seanchan]' [*CPl* 126], could have been used to
help Seanchan to compel the King to change his attitude. But this
is not really Yeats's purpose. Seanchan has to die in order that he
may establish the supreme value of poetry and attain to a vision that
embraces and reaches out beyond death. But the effect of his death
on society is not worked out.

The exploration of Seanchan's attitude begins in the third episode
through his response to the Chamberlain himself and those he brings
with him, the Monk, the Soldier, the Girls. The Chamberlain in his
concern with authority and political manipulation is another Mayor,
but on a higher, more elegant plane. By his apparent recognition
of the value of poetry, Yeats uses him to widen the theme from the
personal to the general. In driving Seanchan from the Council, the
King has driven out the creative imagination:

> *Seanchan:* Somebody has deceived you . . .
> In making it appear that I was driven
> From the great council. You have driven away
> The images of them that weave a dance
> By the four rivers in the mountain garden
>
> [*CPl* 126-7]

an image that reappears in Seanchan's dialogue with Fedelm, who
however, is incapable of comprehending it. In making the
Chamberlain a poet of a sort, Yeats is able to heighten the contrast
between those who pay lip-service to poetry and those whose
dedication to it is uncompromising and total. The Chamberlain's
language here [*CPl* 127] is apt, especially the phrase 'in some
measure', which captures both the unctuous speech of the literary
civil servant and the aldermanic timidity that shies away from the
poet's wasteful, and dangerous, virtues.

The Soldier's initial blunt indifference to both sides is probably

nearer to the attitude of the 'common sort' than Yeats would have
us believe, and his subsequent anger at Seanchan's gibes in character.
But it is difficult to accept his yielding to the entreaties of the Girls,
even if he yields with something less than good grace. It is his blunt
language – 'Snuff it, old hedgehog, and unroll yourself! [*CPl* 125]
– that produces a key development in Seanchan. The poet's
imagination seizes upon the image and develops it in terms that
anticipate both the individual's absorption in his role and his
detachment not only from society but in the end from life itself:

> You have rightly named me
> I lie rolled up under the ragged thorns
> That are upon the edge of those great waters
> Where all things vanish away, and I have heard
> Murmurs that are the ending of all sound.
> I am out of life; I am rolled up, and yet,
> Hedgehog although I am, I'll not unroll
> For you, King's dog!

[*CPl* 125-6]

The Girls, with their love of play (dancing and hurling) and their
sensuality are linked both to the Monk, whose peculiarly Irish brand
of Roman Catholic puritanism condemns dancing and hurling as
products of the wanton imagination, and to Seanchan, whose
imaginative grasp embraces and extends such images of desire:

> Go to the hurley! Gather up your skirts. . . .
> Your feet delight in dancing, and your mouths
> In the slow smiling that awakens love . . . .
>   Go to the young men.
> Are not the ruddy flesh and the thin flanks
> And the broad shoulders worthy of desire?
> . . . it is I that am singing you away –
> Singing you to the young men.

[*CPl* 130]

Visually, too, they introduce in their sensuous stroking of the Soldier
the sequence of 'hand' images which extends into the language,
through the episodes with the Princesses and Fedelm right up to
Seanchan's dying speech.

The Monk calls out Seanchan's scorn for all those who in the name
of discipline and order emasculate spiritual commitment by making
it submit to the demands of temporal authority, but at the same time
there is a significant touch of hysteria both in his clinging to the
Monk's habit and in his mimed representation of a wild God reduced
to a tamed domesticated pet:

Seanchan: You did not think that hands so full of hunger
Could hold you tightly. They are not civil yet.
I'd know if you have taught him to eat bread
From the King's hand, and perch upon his finger.
I think he perches on the King's strong hand,
But it may be that he is still too wild.
You must not weary in your work, a king
Is often weary, and he needs a God
To be a comfort to him.
          (The Monk plucks his habit away and goes into the palace.
          Seanchan holds up his hand as if a bird perched upon
          it. He pretends to stroke the bird.)
                    A little God,
With comfortable feathers, and bright eyes.

                                        [*CPl* 129-30]

This moment makes the connection in the fourth episode between
Seanchan's progressive physical debilitation and the inner qualities
of the imagination clearer. His wild imagination supposes that a
leper's blessing has contaminated the mother of the Princesses and
that the contamination has been passed on to her daughters, so that
the hands of the Princesses who offer him food have become
contaminated too, and finally that the source of the contamination
is God himself. The Cripples return for a moment to beg for the
food that he will not accept and in their entry become an actualization
of Seanchan's distorting imagination, which in turn sees their physical
condition as the product of the influence of bad poets on their
mothers. But in his delirium, before the Mayor and Fedelm enter
for the fifth and final episode, he at least recognizes the abiding and
superior strength of God, holding up his hand in a leprous blessing
on all and sundry.

Again the hand image links the interior and exterior action as the
dying Seanchan takes Fedelm's hand when she comes to lead him
away from the threshold. Her mention of marriage in 'the wild
middle of the summer' [*CPl* 135] sets his imagination aflame in an
extravagant vision of the marriage of the stars and clouds out upon
the ploughlands, from which a race of supermen would emerge:

Seanchan: Who taught you that? For it's a certainty,
Although I never knew it till last night,
That marriage, because it is the height of life,
Can only be accomplished to the full
In the high days of the year. I lay awake:
There had come a frenzy into the light of the stars,
And they were coming nearer, and I knew

> All in a minute they were about to marry
> Clods out upon the ploughlands, to beget
> A mightier race than any that has been.
>
> [*CPl* 135]

In her human desire to nurture his ailing body and assuage his tortured spirit Fedelm offers him an escape to an earthly home:

> *Fedelm:* Come with me now. . . .
> For I have a great room that's full of beds
> I can make ready;
>
> [*CPl* 136]

But his imagination at once transforms this into an unearthly paradise. Her offer is not made in treachery, but from her inability to respond to the force of vision. The gap between the two is underlined by the way his language moves from shared blank verse to song. Her attempts to get him to eat bread dipped in wine are made in love, but even that, in fact all human relationships, must be sacrificed to the supreme value of art. She would dominate his imagination and therefore, even as her appeal ironically stimulates it, she has to be rejected. Like Hamlet casting off Ophelia Seanchan is perverse and ruthless in his rejection:

> I cast you from me like an old torn cap,
> A broken shoe, a glove without a finger,
> A crooked penny; whatever is most worthless.
>
> [*CPl* 138]

But he recognizes the frenzy in this outburst, reasserts his love but nevertheless subordinates it to the higher and dangerous demands of his art:

> I was about to curse you.
> It was a frenzy. I'll unsay it all.
> But you must go away.
>
> [*CPl* 139]

This is more than a reconciliation, since Fedelm has now adopted Seanchan's point of view. It is she who tells the King that he will not eat until the right of the poets has been restored, and it is with her hand that Seanchan pushes away the bread that the King himself offers. The final rejection is presented as a joint choice:

> We have refused it.
>
> [*CPl* 140]

The trouble is that the relationship between Fedelm and Seanchan is insufficiently developed. Fedelm is given little to say from the moment she bursts into tears at what seems to her his obduracy until she acquiesces in his decision. Somehow the actress playing her must indicate this development.

In the final episode the King plays his last card. Having brought in the Pupils under threat of death with halters round their necks, he calls on them to beg Seanchan to save their lives by getting him to change his mind. But the Pupils, in a passage that Yeats substituted in his 1922 revision for the ending of previous versions in which the poet's right was restored as the King knelt before him and accepted the crown from his hands, urge him to die. Seanchan, strengthened now by the joyful recognition that his spirit has been renewed in them, regains his physical strength as he walks down from the threshold to the point where the decisiveness of his gesture is completed in the awful joy of his death.

> King! King! Dead faces laugh.
>
> [*CPl* 141]

After this, the climax, in which the ambiguities in the power of the imagination, its capacity for truth and delusion, prophecy and imprecation, are given visual expression as the features of Seanchan stiffen into a grin — there should be no hint of serenity here — all is anti-climax. His heroic gesture, like a beacon, both illuminates the world that has rejected him and is a guiding light for those who survive it it:

> . . . we who gaze grow like him and abhor
> The moments that come between us and that death
> You promised us.
>
> [*CPl* 141-2]

Death is both a destruction and a renewal:

> The ancient right is gone, the new remains,
> And that is death.
>
> [*CPl* 142]

But the language of the scene, in which Seanchan's spiritual victory over physical death is celebrated, is strangely out of key with what has gone before. Rajan aptly calls it 'romantic heroics' [*YCI* 53]. Even the Soldier's tough matter-of-factness evaporates in incongruous abstraction:

> Here is no place for you,
> For he and his pretensions now are finished
>
> [*CPl* 142]

and the Pupils, in their vision of Seanchan's apotheosis, introduce
a set of nature-images which, unlike those in *Deirdre,* are unrelated
to the dramatic texture as a whole:

> He seeks high waters and the mountain birds
> To claim a portion of their solitude . . .
> . . . he claims
> The mountain for his mattress and his pillow.
>
> [*CPl* 142]

The musicians, who must have brought their instruments with them
in spite of the halters round their necks, are addressed in inflated,
quasi-biblical, rhetoric:

> O silver trumpets, be you lifted up
> And cry to the great race that is to come.
> Long-throated swans upon the waves of time,
> Sing loudly, for beyond the wall of the world
> That race may hear our music and awake.
>
> [*CPl* 143]

Indeed the quality of the Pupils' language carries no conviction that
poetry is reborn in them. Yeats, wishing to concentrate on the
splendour of the hero's gesture, made in defiance of society's claims,
makes no attempt to show the effect it may have on either society
or the individual. The representatives of society are not present, and
Fedelm is silent. Such considerations, it is hoped, are lost in the visual
tableau of the epilogue.

The Shadowy Waters (Acting Version)

It is difficult to resist the temptation to discuss this version of *The Shadowy Waters* except in terms of its genesis, its development in manuscript and in published versions, and the variations in them. There is a wealth of comment on these lines: by Sidnell, Mayhew and Clark in their masterly study of the manuscripts, *Druid Craft*; by Bushrui in *Yeats's Verse Plays;* by Parkinson in *W. B. Yeats: Self Critic.* With the exception of Moore's and Donoghue's there have been few attempts to look at the *Acting Version* itself. Nathan concerns himself primarily with the 1900 version, and Ellmann with charting and explaining the symbolic structure of the poetic version that Yeats retained in *Collected Poems,* most of which is removed from the Acting Version. It is equally difficult to resist the conclusions of Moore, Bushrui and Donoghue that in spite of the changes that Yeats made in his efforts to make it more viable on the stage — condensation, removal of secondary symbolism, tightening-up of language — the play remains what Yeats called 'more a ritual than a human story' [*L* 425]; 'deliberately without human characters' [*L* 425], an impression that is established at once for an audience by the non-representational setting and sustained subsequently by the non-naturalistic stillness of the stage figures. It is this quality that should be aimed at in performance and is best caught by marionettes, whose stylization of face and gesture helps to maintain that distance from life that Yeats was to come to require from drama. The marionette's physical limitations, its austerity of movement, allow us to concentrate all the more readily on the play's essential sensuality, which resides in the language. This ritualistic, stylized element, to be strengthened later by Yeats's contact both with the conventions of Noh drama and with Gordon Craig's theories, finds expression in the dance plays, especially in *At The Hawk's Well,* in which he actually instructs his actors to move like marionettes. It is possible that a reason for Yeats's continuous involvement with this play over nearly a quarter of a century is that not only in the manner of its presentation but also in its matter, he was tentatively, subconsciously, groping towards the kind of drama that he was later to write, in, for example, *A Full Moon in March,*

35

where 'character' is reduced to pure essence, setting becomes visually emblematic of meaning and events are shown, not told. In respect of its matter, the play is seminal in its handling of the theme of the hero's passionate quest for something beyond human experience.

The function of the first scene is to establish one of the two poles on which the play turns – the tension between our knowledge of, and in, the habitable world of time and place as we know it, of love as we know it, in the ageing flesh and the obstinate virginity of the soul, and our vision of an ideal, supernatural world of permanence which transcends time and finds its place in

> . . . a country at the end of the world
> Where no child's born but to outlive the moon
>
> [*CPl* 165]

where love is a consummation in which individuality is both destroyed and fulfilled, and is also the resolution of all antinomies. These two orders of experience Yeats was to call the terrestrial condition and the condition of fire [*M* 356].

The Sailors are part of the former world, the terrestrial condition, and Yeats, in introducing the contrast between prose and poetry, is trying to express the tension between this condition and the condition of fire both verbally and by contrast of mood. But with what degree of success is doubtful. Yeats never really mastered the speech of the native Irish countryman, and the brand of Kiltartanese, which is presumably intended to fix the Sailors in the harsh reality of a real pirate ship at sea, and to establish their total concern with material wealth and the pleasures of the senses (money, drink and sex), and their absolute lack of response to Forgael's vision of spiritual wealth, also has to be used for a totally different purpose, to introduce their involvement in and recognition of Forgael's quest for 'Happiness beyond measure, happiness where the sun dies' [*CPl* 148] under the pilotage of the mysterious man-headed birds. This mixture of coarseness and vision goes better in the poetic version, where there is no attempt to reproduce natural speech. As it is, the conversation between the first and second Sailor in which they testify to the reality of Forgael's vision, is extraordinarily unconvincing:

First Sailor: I was sleeping up there by the bulwark, and when I woke in the sound of the harp a change came over my eyes, and I could see very strange things. The dead were floating upon the sea yet, and it seemed as if the life that went out of every one of them had turned to the shape of a man-headed bird – grey they were, and they rose up of a sudden and called out with voices like our own, and flew away singing to the west. Words like this they were singing: 'Happiness beyond measure, happiness where the sun dies'.

Second Sailor: I understand well what they were doing. My mother used to be talking of birds of the sort. They are sent by the lasting watchers to lead men away from this world and its women to some place of shining women that cast no shadow, having lived before the making of the earth.

[*CPl* 148-9]

The gap between this kind of eloquence and the Sailors' brutal plan to murder Forgael is far too great.

If the gap is bridged at all it is by Aibric, who for the time being rejects their plan to murder Forgael and set their course back to the natural world, but at the same time makes some kind of contact with him. The dialogue in which each defines his own values and draws a distinction between them is the most eloquent in the play. That it is conducted in verse shows that Aibric can at least partially enter into Forgael's vision, though he dismisses it as a mere dream. He becomes, in his down-to-earth humanity, a kind of Enobarbus to Forgael's Antony:

> *Aibric:* I know their promises. You have told me all.
> They are to bring you to unheard-of passion,
> To some strange love the world knows nothing of,
> Some Ever-living woman as you think,
> One that can cast no shadow, being unearthly.
> But that's all folly. Turn the ship about,
> Sail home again, be some fair woman's friend;
> Be satisfied to live like other men,
> And drive impossible dreams away. The world
> Has beautiful women to please every man.
> *Forgael:* But he that gets their love after the fashion
> Loves in brief longing and deceiving hope
> And bodily tenderness, and finds that even
> The bed of love, that in the imagination
> Had seemed to be the giver of all peace,
> Is no more than a wine-cup in the tasting,
> And as soon finished.
> *Aibric:*   All that ever loved
> Have loved that way – there is no other way.
> *Forgael:* Yet never have two lovers kissed but they
> Believed there was some other near at hand,
> And almost wept because they could not find it.
> *Aibric:* When they have twenty years; in middle life
> They take a kiss for what a kiss is worth,

And let the dream go by.
Forgael: It's not a dream,
But the reality that makes our passion
As a lamp shadow – no – no lamp, the sun.
What the world's million lips are thirsting for
Must be substantial somewhere.

[*CPl* 150-1]

The problem for Forgael is not the question whether he will choose
the one world or the other, but how to define the nature of the mystic
joy he is haunted by (ultimately to be embodied in his fusion with
Dectora) and how to be certain that that joy, when defined, *is* reality:

I can see nothing plain; all's mystery.
Yet sometimes there's a torch inside my head
That makes all clear, but when the light is gone
I have but images, analogies,
The mystic bread, the sacramental wine,
The red rose where the two shafts of the cross,
Body and soul, waking and sleep, death, life,
Whatever meaning ancient allegorists
Have settled on, are mixed into one joy.
For what's the rose but that? miraculous cries,
Old stories about mystic marriages,
Impossible truths? But when the torch is lit
All that is impossible is certain,
I plunge in the abyss.

[*CPl* 152]

But beneath the ebb and flow of certainty and uncertainty there is
an undertow and a momentum of inevitability which culminates in
the ecstatic union of Dectora and Forgael. When the Sailors sight
the ship that brings both types of riches, material treasure and
spiritual wealth, Forgael is convinced that the truth that each is led
to, he on one level, Aibric and the Sailors on another, has in fact
been brought by his pilots, the man-headed birds that have access
to a transcendent reality. He is convinced that the vision by which
he is haunted, of the 'hair that is the colour of burning' [*CPl* 148]
is true, and that he will find its owner. He has set out on his
metaphysical voyage of discovery and becomes increasingly certain
that he will reach his destination. He and Dectora are literally
destined for each other.

Both you and I are taken in the net.
It was their hands that plucked the winds awake

And blew you hither; and their mouths have promised
I shall have love in their immortal fashion.
They gave me that old harp of the nine spells
That is more mighty than the sun and moon,
Or than the shivering casting-net of the stars,
That none might take you from me.

[*CPl* 156]

What the plot has to do is to present that destiny as a choice: Forgael must recognize that Dectora, who at first sight casts a shadow and therefore seems not to be the world's core, is the reality that makes natural passion as a lamp shadow, and Dectora must recognize in Forgael her predestined lover of a thousand years. Forgael must recognize too that the power vested in the magic harp is greater than he is; that the poet is the servant of his images, and that the images he creates are not a trick, a deceit, an illusion, but a reality; that Dectora has become the substance of what his lips had thirsted for, and that their joint commitment to it is total. That is why there is no sense of conflict or sacrifice in Forgael. He is no Antony, pulled as in Dryden's *All for Love* by conflicting claims of Rome and Cleopatra. His decision, 'I am going on to the end' [*CPl* 165], is accompanied by no agonized awareness of what he is giving up by so doing, it is simply the affirmation of his original intention and the fulfilment of his destiny. It is not, therefore, a tragic decision. He is the epic hero who achieves his quest. The quest is for that revelation of truth that can only be achieved by union with Dectora. Before that can be achieved, Dectora herself must establish herself as a participant in that quest.

What agonies Forgael does experience are derived first from the frustration he feels at the beginning of the play when he is both convinced of the reality of this transcendent love yet unable for the time being to achieve it; then his momentary disappointment at Dectora's first appearance – he had expected a 'shadowless unearthly woman' [*CPl* 154] whereas she casts a shadow – then his guilt at having deceitfully, as he thinks, cast a spell on her by his harp playing, so compelling her to love him. Finally, even when she dismisses that as of no importance in comparison with her exclusive love for him, he continues to weep. He weeps because he now understands that the vision he offers contains not only fulfilment but its opposite, 'desolate waters and a battered ship' [*CPl* 164], not a 'roof of ivory and gold' but 'bare night' [*CPl* 164]. The verbal image is actualized in the stage setting: '*The sea or sky is represented by a semi-circular cloth of which nothing can be seen except*

a dark abyss.' [*CPl* 147]. It is Dectora's adoption of the role his
imagination has created for her, her willing acceptance of the
obliteration of everything that is not themselves, that confirms him
in his desire to go on to the end and to make that desire a necessity
– 'We have to follow' [*CPl* 165] – a decision that is paralleled by
the behaviour of his pilots, the birds, which now 'have taken to the
road' [*CPl* 165], have found their direction.

Before this, in Forgael's speech before the first appearance of
Dectora [*CPl* 153], the birds hover over the masthead. Like the wild
swans at Coole they point to an immortality of love but as yet they
do not set out on the road to it – 'Why are they still waiting?' [*CPl*
154]. They speak to Forgael of things that seem to be irreconcilable,
of the reality of the 'shadowless unearthly woman / At the world's
end' [*CPl* 154] and at the same time of powerlessness to attain her
– 'What can we do, being shadows?' [*CPl* 154]; of love and hate,
sleep and waking. But all, for the time being, is mystery, nothing
is resolved.

His questions are answered dramatically by Dectora's arrival. This
begins the process of resolution, though it is not completed until after
her opposition has been first asserted, then overcome and finally
turned into free co-operation. At first Dectora reflects what Yeats
called a vivid force; she is a force seeking life in the natural world
and love in a mortal fashion; she casts a shadow. She demands to
be treated as a queen. She demands punishment for those who killed
her husband. In reply Forgael asserts that the agents of supernatural
order have destined them to meet. Even if he were to put her back
into her ship with Sailors to obey her commands, they would still
meet:

> Both you and I are taken in the net.
> It was their hands that plucked the winds awake
> And blew you hither; and their mouths have promised
> I shall have love in their immortal fashion.
>
> > [*CPl* 156]

The instrument that will ensure that he will achieve this kind of love
is the harp. The power of the harp is both the power of imagination
which can create reality and also the means by which the knowledge
of that reality is completed. Dectora responds immediately but
subconsciously to the power of the harp:

> For a moment
> Your raving of a message and a harp
> More mighty than the stars half troubled me.
>
> > [*CPl* 156-7]

She tries to suppress this instinctive recognition, calling his harp music a 'Druid craft of wicked music' with which he will force her to accept his will. First she threatens suicide in order to escape him. But the Sailors deflect her from this by promising to take her home on her own ship. Then she tries to bribe the Sailors to kill Forgael, and when he prevents that by casting them under a spell, she tries to kill herself. But under the influence of the harp music her plans fail.

The function of the harp-music scene is first of all to get rid of Aibric and the Sailors, so that Forgael can cast his spell over Dectora. This is done easily – too easily. Again the gap between the naturalistic and the symbolic is too wide, the poetic version providing a better framework for this incident. More importantly the function of the scene is that it shifts the action from the natural to the supernatural world, where the movement of time is indeed shaken. It is at this point that Dectora begins to demonstrate that what the harp has created is not an illusion but a timeless truth, that Forgael is Iollan, that she loves him of her own will. Memory of the dead Iollan is obliterated, and with it, grief. She is consumed by joy in her love for Forgael. She has loved Forgael for a thousand years. In other words she moves from the natural world towards his supernatural one. The birds cry out, at first, as he thinks, for what he takes to be the wrong of his deceit. But when her laughter corroborates his view that in playing the harp he is merely fulfilling the instructions of the Ever-living, he makes a complementary move in her direction, from the supernatural world to the natural one, when he admits that the immortal love towards which the birds have pointed him contains elements derived from natural humanity:

> There is not one among you that made love
> By any other means. You call it passion,
> Consideration, generosity;
> But it was all deceit, and flattery
> To win a woman in her own despite,
> For love is war, and there is hatred in it.

> [*CPl* 162]

Now, as Dectora asserts her love for him, a love that has been created by his own imagination, symbolized by the harp, he has to accept the defeat of his view that human love is *only* a brief longing and a deception, 'no more than a wine-cup in the tasting / And as soon finished' [*CPl* 151]. He has to accept the wider knowledge which imagination has created: that love is war, and that there is hatred in it, that images of fulfilment are complemented by images of desolation and emptiness, that the road to the spirit is paved with the flesh. Only when she has rejected everything that is not him is he convinced that he must follow the birds to an unimaginable happiness:

> We have to follow, for they are our pilots;
> They're crying out. Can you not hear their cry? –
> 'There is a country at the end of the world
> Where no child's born but to outlive the moon.'
>
> [*CPl* 165]

In this mood it is inevitable that Forgael should reject the final appeal of Aibric and the Sailors – prosaic in content but upgraded in expression to the poetic in order to reflect their excitement – to return to the natural world and enjoy the material riches that they have found in Dectora's ship. What is still not clear is where this unimaginable happiness is to be found – in death, as Aibric had suggested earlier [*CPl* 151], or in life. Nor is it clear, as yet, whether Dectora will finally accompany him:

> *Forgael:*   I am going on to the end.
> As for this woman, I think she is coming with me.
>
> [*CPl* 165]

Dectora, like Fedelm, would momentarily prefer 'some sure country, some familiar place' [*CPl* 166], but Forgael cannot resist the appeal of the birds. Dectora's reply, 'I am a woman, I die at every breath' [*CPl* 166], is obscure. It seems to lead to her throwing in her lot with him. Aibric sees there is no point in arguing with Forgael any longer and leaves with the Sailors. Forgael gives Dectora one more chance to alter her decision:

> Go with him
> For he will shelter you and bring you home
>
> [*CPl* 166]

but instead she reaffirms it, orders Aibric to cut the rope that binds them to the natural world, and triumphantly sails on with Forgael to their ultimate destination.

Dectora's last speech contains the only fossils of the system of symbols embedded in the earlier poetic version, but they are dramatically acceptable in that they contribute to the sense of ecstasy that this final episode should create, culminating in the picture of

Forgael enmeshing himself in the net of Dectora's hair in the light of the burning harp. Even though Yeats's stage carpenter was unable to produce a harp whose strings actually flamed, the idea is right, because the burning harp is part of the image-pattern of the play as a whole. Dectora and Forgael enmesh themselves in each other in a decision which is a free choice of the net of necessity, against a background of the burning harp, symbolic of the creative imagination, which is also the torch in the light of which mysteries become certainties, dreams become truths, and which becomes one with the hair which is the colour of burning. The burning harp becomes the symbol of that condition of fire into which entry is gained by the ecstasy of their union.

PLAYS OF TRANSITION

The Unicorn from the Stars, The Green Helmet, The Player Queen, The Hour Glass, On Baile's Strand, Deirdre.

These plays have been grouped together because all of them in some way, either in respect of form or content, look forward to Yeats's central achievement. Two of them, *The Green Helmet* and *The Player Queen,* with their tone of mockery, anticipate the much bitterer tone of the three last plays, *The Herne's Egg, Purgatory, The Death of Cuchulain.* Even the weakest of them, *The Unicorn from the Stars,* which in one way looks back to the early work, in that Yeats reverts to the practice of setting the action precisely in time and place, looks forward to the later and much more successful attempts to express timeless vision in dramatic terms. *The Hour Glass* and *The Player Queen* are not set in identifiable time; *On Baile's Strand* and *Deirdre* are built on material taken from the heroic period, while *The Green Helmet* is set in the heroic period but laced with contemporary applications. In form they exhibit features, as yet still deployed experimentally, which will later become the hallmark of Yeats's assured manner: dance, chorus, mask. The dance is first used in *The Player Queen*; the chorus is first used in *Deirdre,* and the mask makes its appearance in the 1911 revival of *On Baile's Strand. The Unicorn from the Stars* excepted, they move in the direction of non-naturalistic drama of mythic or psychological types, though in the case of *Deirdre* and *On Baile's Strand* the types have a firm base in psychological naturalism. Yeats's letter about Cuchulain to Frank Fay, who created the part, shows that he clearly thought of him in terms of naturalistic character as well as of timeless myth:

About Cuchullain. You have Lady Gregory's work I know. Remember however that epic and folk literature can ignore time as drama cannot — Helen never ages, Cuchullain never ages. I have to recognise that he does, for he has a son who is old enough to fight him. I have also to make the refusal of the son's affection tragic by suggesting in Cuchullain's character a shadow of something a little proud, barren and restless, as if out of sheer strength of heart or from accident he had put affection away. He lives among young men but has himself outlived the illusions of youth. He is probably about 40, not less than 35 or 36 and not more than 45 or 46, certainly not an old man, and one understands from his talk about women that he does not love like a young man. Probably his very strength of character made him put off illusions and dreams (that make young men a woman's servant) and made him become quite early in life a deliberate lover, a man of pleasure who can never really surrender himself. He is a little hard, and leaves the people about him a little repelled – perhaps this young man's affection is what he had most need of. Without this thought the play had not had any deep tragedy. I write of him with difficulty, for when one creates a character one does it out of instinct and may be wrong when one analyses the instinct afterwards. It is as though the character embodied itself. The less one reasons the more living the character. I felt for instance that his boasting was necessary, and yet I did not reason it out. The touch of something hard, repellent yet alluring, self assertive yet self immolating, is not all but it must be there. He is the fool – wandering passive, houseless and almost loveless. Conchobhar is reason that is blind because it can only reason because it is cold. Are they not the cold moon and the hot sun?

[*L* 424-5]

On Baile's Strand also shares Yeats's realization that myth, and especially heroic myth, must be grounded in actual life if it is to inspire and illuminate it, hence the counterpointing of the 'heroic' story with that of the Fool and Blind Man. *Deirdre* is less successful in this respect since the chorus of naturalistic minstrels, who are also required to complete the mythic function of Deirdre herself, are not entirely convincing. They are made to play the dual and incompatible roles of participants in the action and yet detached commentators on it. Yeats's later handling of the chorus as commentators totally divorced from the exterior action but fundamental to the interior action by their dramatic poetry, is much more successful.

All these plays, with the exception of *The Player Queen,* which is disproportionate in its parts and diffuse in the whole, show a marked advance in construction. Even *The Unicorn from the Stars* is a competent piece of dramatic carpentry. The others in some degree move towards the realization of Yeats's ideal as formulated in *Samhain, 1904*:

A farce and a tragedy are alike in this, that they are a moment of intense life. An action is taken out of all other actions; it is reduced to its simplest form, or at any rate to as simple a form as it can be brought to without our losing the sense of its place in the world. The characters that are involved in it are freed from everything that is not a part of that action; and whether it is, as in the less important kinds of drama, a mere bodily activity, a hairbreadth escape or the like, or as it is in the more important kinds, an activity of the souls of the characters, it is an energy, an eddy of life purified from everything but itself.

[*E* 153-4]

This simplicity is reflected in the plays' construction, their tighter cohesion of action, visual effects and language. All lead to a climactic gesture. In *The Green Helmet* this is in the end a comic one – the only completely comic gesture in the whole of Yeats's dramatic *œuvre*. Its nearest parallel, *The Cat and the Moon,* is partially comic: the Blind Man is granted sight, but the Lame Man remains lame. In the other plays the gesture is tragic. But it is not negative. In *The Unicorn from the Stars* Martin is shot by accident – he does not choose his destiny – but he has had his mystic vision. Deirdre, the Wise Man and Cuchulain all master their destiny by freely choosing it. They embody dramatically what in the poetry is called tragic joy, when the individual's temporal gesture of completion coincides with the timeless perfection of death.

Yeats's contact with Gordon Craig and his ideas bore fruit in his increased awareness of the dramatic possibilities of scene design. The 1911 revival of *The Hour Glass,* using Craig's scene design, his screens and the superb mask of the Fool, must have added theatrical substance to the somewhat thin contrast between reason and faith embodied in the Pupils and the Wise Man. It was Craig's masterly masks, used for the first time for the Fool and Blind Man in *On Baile's Strand,* that opened Yeats's eyes to the dramatic possibilities of masks which were to find further expression in the dance plays. In *Deirdre* too, décor and stage space become an integral part of the dramatic meaning. In *The Green Helmet* the grotesque and garish colour-scheme that Yeats wanted does seem to be the only way in which the extravagance of the piece could be effectively mounted.

The rollicking ballad metre that Yeats chose for the play is also appropriate and is one of the signs of Yeats's breaking out of the strait-jacket of Elizabethan blank verse. Even though the other verse plays in this group are written for the most part in this metre, Yeats varies it by the use of prose and by other metres. In *On Baile's Strand* the prose, which is interspersed with the Fool's snatches of Shakespearean song, is dramatically appropriate for the 'low' characters of the Fool and Blind Man, and much better in itself than the Kiltartanese of the Sailors in *The Shadowy Waters.* The same effect is achieved in *The Hour Glass.* Here Yeats came to see the necessity of conveying the richness of the Wise Man's consciousness compared with that of the other characters by using prose for them but raising his speech to the level of poetry – some of it, especially his last speech, Marlovian in its rhythmical freedom. In *Deirdre,* the only play of this group completely in verse, the staple blank verse is varied by the Musicians' lyrics, the difference pointing to the different plane that they for the most part occupy compared with the characters in the main action. Both *On Baile's Strand* and *Deirdre* continue the advance in the handling of dramatic poetry already noted in *The King's Threshold,* which Yeats recognized as containing his best dramatic verse to date (1903). Language, still referring inwards, as it were, to its source in character, also refers outwards by metaphor, simile and image-clusters, to theme. With the achievement of *Deirdre* and *On Baile's Strand* Yeats had made himself into a dramatic poet.

The Unicorn from the Stars

As is so often the case, Yeats is his own most searching critic:

I wrote in 1902, with the help of Lady Gregory and another friend, a play called *Where There is Nothing,* but had to write at great speed to meet a sudden emergency. Five acts had to be finished in, I think, a fortnight, instead of the five years that would have been somewhat nearer my natural pace. It became hateful to me because, in desperation, I had caught up from a near table a pamphlet of Tolstoy's on the Sermon on the Mount, and made out of it a satirical scene that became the pivot of the play. The scene seemed amusing on the stage, but its crude speculative commonplaces filled me with shame and I withdrew the play from circulation. That I might free myself from what seemed a contamination, I asked Lady Gregory to help me turn my old plot into *The Unicorn from the Stars.* I began to dictate, but since I had last worked with her, her mastery of the stage and her knowledge of dialect had so increased that my imagination could not go neck and neck with hers. I found myself, too, stopped by an old difficulty, that my words never flow freely but when people speak in verse. and so after an attempt to work alone I gave up my scheme to her. The result is a play almost wholly hers in handiwork, which is so much mine in thought that she does not wish to include it in her own works. I can indeed read it after the stories in *The Secret Rose* and recognize thoughts, points of view, and artistic aims which seem a part of my world. Her greatest difficulty was that I had given her in my re-shaping of the plot – swept as I hoped of dogmatism and arrogance – for chief character, a man so plunged in trance that he could not be otherwise than all but still and silent, though perhaps with the stillness and silence of a lamp; and the movement of the play as whole, if we were to listen, if we were to understand what he said, had to be without hurry or violence. The strange characters, her handiwork, on whom he sheds his light, delight me. She has enabled me to carry out an old thought for which my own knowledge is insufficient, and to commingle the ancient phantasies of poetry with the rough, vivid, ever-contemporaneous tumult of the roadside; to share in the creation of a form that otherwise I could but dream of, though I do that always, an art that murmured, though with worn and failing voice, of the day when Quixote and Sancho Panza, long estranged, may once again go out gaily into the bleak air. Ever since I began to write I have awaited with impatience a linking all Europe over of the hereditary knowledge of the countryside, now becoming known to us through the work of wanderers and men of learning, with our old lyricism so full of ancient frenzies and hereditary wisdom; a yoking of antiquities; a Marriage of Heaven and Hell.

[*VPl* 713-4]

The friend was Douglas Hyde and the emergency was 'to keep George Moore from stealing the plot' [*L* 503]. Tolstoy's pamphlet is the basis of much of Act 3 in *Where There is Nothing,* and it is arguable that there is nothing in *The Unicorn from the Stars* that compares with it for theatrical effectiveness. Paul Ruttledge, the earlier play's equivalent of Martin Hearne, is a much more effective counterpart to the rejects, misfits, outcasts and visionaries who people the stories of *The Secret Rose* and *The Tables of the Law.* He really does throw in his lot with the Tinkers, even 'marrying' one, whereas Martin remains aloof or merely their gullible dupe. Martin's fundamental weakness is his uncertainty, both as to what he has seen and what he has to do, however much it may be the psychological justification for his *volte-face* from revolution to revelation. Worse still, the play's fundamental weakness lies in the vagueness of his vision. Instead of being the initiator and director of the action he becomes the victim of the others' not unreasonable misunderstandings. He lacks that spiritual intoxication which alone could carry conviction. As Ellis-Fermor says [*IDM* 105], 'we are never quite sure whether Martin is an inspired visionary or a bewildered dreamer.' Even the tinkers, though they are an improvement on their counterparts in *Where There is Nothing,* lack the bite, the the tough condensed language of Synge's, and become at one point in their scene of tedious bickering [*CPl* 352-6], almost irrelevant.

The rehandling of the material in *The Unicorn from the Stars* brings a greater cohesiveness, both of story and symbolism, compared with the anarchic, fitful energy of *Where There is Nothing.* By setting the entire action back into the 18th century and by linking Martin's vision with the destruction of the golden state-coach that he is building, with its emblem of Lion and Unicorn, the misunderstanding of his vision in terms of politics is made more plausible. The action is centred in fewer characters who, though lacking in depth, are adequately defined. The first act is a competent piece of craftsmanship in that it establishes the polarities within which the action proceeds to its tragic conclusion, material practicality and vision. Thomas stands for the ethos of work, Martin for vision. For Martin the unicorn seems to be a symbol of a divine force working within the soul and manifested in a moment of joyous vision that will bring destruction and renewal. In between these two are those characters who operate in a kind of spiritual no-man's-land: Andrew, who does not entirely accept the ethos of work, can understand spiritual intoxication, but only in terms of hedonism and drunkenness; the tinkers, who can only interpret the unicorn in terms of a romantic politico-social revolution to be effected by violence;

and Father John, the only complex figure in the play, who recognizes the disturbing force of Martin's vision and has already paid the penalty for his unorthodoxy at the hands of the Establishment. The ignition point that lights the touchpaper leading to the final combustion is neatly effected in the misunderstanding, by Martin this time, of Johnny's cry 'Destruction on us all!' [*CPl* 345].

The second act begins with Father John's giving support to the force of Martin's vision, though this still remains ill-defined. It continues with Andrew's misunderstanding of it, and is interrupted by the largely irrelevant altercation among the tinkers, before they add their interpretation in terms of social revolution. The first part of Martin's vision now takes shape in the form of the destruction of the Law and the Church, institutions which have smothered the 'exaltation of the heart' [*CPl* 359]. Thomas arrives with the news of the effect of Andrew's misinterpretation of the vintage of the Lord as the mundane juice of the barley. Martin's reaction to this news borders on the ludicrous:

I wonder how that has happened? Can it have anything to do with Andrew's plan?

[*CPl* 361]

One wonders what sort of leader this is. Martin, now as spiritually intoxicated as the townspeople are literally drunk, adopts the role of a metaphysical drop-out from the rat-race of routine labour. He determines to raise the banner of the army of the Unicorn, and finally translates the symbolic into the actual by setting fire to his own golden coach.

The third act presents the aftermath of the 'revolution': two big houses burned and looted, Martin himself apparently dead, the tinkers, one of whom has brought candles in preparation for Martin's funeral, disorganized, directionless and leaderless; Andrew with a hangover, but just enough wit to send for the priest. When Father John does come, he is now just as anxious not to waken Martin as he was to arouse him in the first act: he must be left to penetrate to the heart of his vision by himself. For a moment there is some dramatic tension as Father John argues with the tinkers and Andrew, which is resolved by Martin's awakening. The first part of what is his second vision, once again to be misunderstood, takes shape.

His second vision, no less ill-defined than the first, takes the form of the music of Paradise, the continual clashing of swords, and is now reformulated:

It is only now I have the whole vision plain. As I lay there I saw through everything, I know all. It was but a frenzy, that going out to burn and to destroy. What have I to do with the foreign army? What I have to pierce is the wild heart of time. My business is not reformation but revelation . . . I was mistaken when I set out to destroy Church and Law. The battle we have to fight is fought out in our own mind. There is a fiery moment, perhaps once in a lifetime, and in that moment we see the only thing that matters. It is in that moment the great battles are lost and won, for in that moment we are a part of the host of Heaven.

[*CPl* 377-8]

Not unnaturally the tinkers see this as a flat betrayal. Rapt in his vision of a thousand white unicorns trampling, a thousand riders with their swords drawn and clashing, for a brief moment he does pierce the wild heart of time. But the logic of events takes over. Abandoned by Father John to the mercy of God and attacked now by his former supporters, the populace, and by the Constables, the representatives of law and orthodoxy, his death is inevitable. And it comes in the one theatrically effective scene of the play when he extinguishes one by one the candles that had been lit for him as he gives eloquent expression to his final vision of mystical annihilation:

I thought the battle was here, and that the joy was to be found here on earth, that all one had to do was to bring again the old wild earth of the stories – but no, it is not here; we shall not come to that joy, that battle, till we have put out the senses, everything that can be seen and handled as I put out this candle. (*He puts out candle.*) We must put out the whole world as I put out this candle (*puts out another candle*). We must put out the light of the stars and the light of the sun and the light of the moon (*puts out the rest of the candles*), till we have brought everything to nothing once again. I saw in a broken vision, but now all is clear to me. Where there is nothing, where there is nothing – there is God!

[*CPl* 381-2]

Even this passage, the only one in the play in which aural and visual qualities combine to produce a powerful theatrical impact, is more effective as part of Paul Ruttledge's sermon on primitive Christianity in Act 3 of *Where There is Nothing*. This attempt to embody a mystical experience in dramatic terms must be accounted a failure.

Postscript on *Where There is Nothing*

In spite of the fact that Yeats suppressed the earlier version of this play, *Where There is Nothing,* and excluded it from the *Collected Plays,* it is not entirely without interest for its general qualities and its effectiveness in the theatre. The enthusiasm shown for it by such theatre people as William Fay, Edith Craig and the Shaws, which led eventually to performances by the Stage Society in June 1904, is not surprising.

Its most interesting aspect, from the point of view of Yeats's development as a dramatist, is the element of fantasy in it. This is embodied not only in the general treatment of plot and character, but in the staging, the décor and stage movement. This element in Yeats's work, excised in the revised version, *Unicorn from the Stars,* was to emerge to some extent in *The Player Queen* and *The Herne's Egg. Where There is Nothing* is a tentative forerunner of these. Yeats's sudden perception, which he wrote about in a letter to Lady Gregory after having examined stage designs by Pamela Smith and Edith Craig, that Act 1

. . . could all be made fantastic by there being a number of bushes shaped Dutch fashion into cocks and hens, ducks, peacocks etc

[*L* 386]

is penetrating. It pierces to a fundamental quality in the play. Stage décor becomes an integral part of the play's theme as well as an externalization of the workings of Paul Ruttledge's mind. 'It can be supposed', Yeats continued in the letter

that these fowl have been the occupation of Paul Ruttledge's ironical leisure for years past. I never did know before what he had been doing all that time.

[*L* 386]

For the 1903 version of the play, replacing the Dublin and New York editions of 1902, the text was amended in such a way as to establish the symbolic equation of these fowl with the figures of the

52

establishment. The poached animal that the anti-establishment outsider, Charlie Ward, brings with him, in the early versions a duck, which would have confused the symbolism, becomes a rabbit, and the dialogue is changed accordingly.

Similarly, as another letter, to A. B. Walkley, shows, Yeats was consciously experimenting in this play – 'I am trying to learn my business', he wrote – in the technique of showing meaning in terms of visual effects. The stage picture confirms, heightens and drives home the intellectual content of dialogue to our imaginations. He was well aware that the play was loosely constructed, but he pointed out that it is not so ramshackle as it appears:

Those children [at the end of Act 1] were not Paul's but his brother's, in fact the fools that he got. If you look again . . . you will find that the children are a part of the situation. I have tried to suggest, without saying it straight out, that Paul finds himself unnecessary in his own house, and therefore the more inclined to take to the roads. I think too that I could arrange the acting so that the end of Act 1 would not be an anti-climax. I see the perambulator on the middle of the stage, or rather I cannot see it, for everyone is standing round it, stooping over it with their backs to me. Is it not the conqueror of all idealists? And are not all these magistrates but its courtiers and its servants?

[*L* 405]

In the event, however, these insights remain fitful. They do not inform the mode of the play as a whole, which is grounded in social and psychological realism.

Fantastic, too, is the scene in the Monastery, Act IV, scene 2, with the Friars dancing round the figure of Paul Ruttledge as he lies on the altar steps in a trance. Again, the scene is a tentative precursor of Yeats's later dramaturgy, in this case the exploration of dance for dramatic effect. In itself it could be theatrically very effective, but Yeats was right when he wrote that this scene 'was in a different key from the others' [*L* 384].

Bordering on the fantastic, and equally effective theatrically, is the Trial scene – removed from *The Unicorn from the Stars* – in which the Establishment figures who profess Christianity are all found guilty of breaking the Law of Christ. Indeed the spring-board of Paul's spiritual revolution, a mixture of Tolstoyan primitive Christianity and Nietzschean ecstasy, is a much more consistent jumping-off point for his spiritual development than Martin's somewhat vague and generalized anarchism in *The Unicorn from the Stars*. Paul's nihilism shares with Martin's the overthrow of Law, the Church, the structures of society and the ethos of work, but it continues in the direction of mystical negativism in its demand for the obliteration of Hope, Memory and Thought. This extension, though inappropriate to a hero who initiates dramatic action, is, however, appropriate to one who merely contemplates reality in what is left after everything that is not God has been destroyed, and who realizes that that destruction must be effected 'inside our minds [*VPl* 1158]. The inclusion of this aspect of Paul's vision makes his entire sermon and the candle episode, which is a kind of link between the fantastic and the naturalistic modes, much more effective. In *The Unicorn from the Stars,* the scene has lost much of its eloquence.

Had Yeats re-shaped his material in terms of what is its imaginative core, the elements of fantasy and heightened naturalism, we might have had a compelling and original play. It would almost certainly have broken the mould of Ibsenite social drama, and A. H. Bullen may well have been right when he suggested that *Where There is Nothing* should have been written in verse. But even so, Yeats would still have had to solve the problem of how to define and express in terms of dramatic form and action a mystical vision whose essence lies in the quietude of meditation. As they stand, neither play solves the problem.

The Green Helmet

This is the first of the plays in which the note of mockery and satire, which will sound more stridently in *The Player Queen* and *The Herne's Egg,* can be heard. The play is a reworking in verse of the earlier prose version, *The Golden Helmet,* which he had had performed at the Abbey Theatre two years previously, in March 1908. When he reshaped it, Yeats strengthened the identification of the setting with Ireland while at the same time heightening the satire. It is clearly intended to satirize the petty divisive squabblings, the ignorant herd-mentality and aldermanic small-mindedness that he had encountered in his dealings with officialdom and the mob between 1906 and 1910, when this version was performed. At the same time the play's visual fantasy helps to keep it fixed in the generalized world of heroic legend, where he found its source, 'The Feast of Bricriu', in Lady Gregory's *Cuchulain of Muirthemne.* Yeats's own note makes this point:

We staged the play with a very pronounced colour-scheme, and I have noticed that the more obviously decorative is the scene and costuming of any play, the more it is lifted out of time and place, and the nearer to faeryland do we carry it.

[*VPl* 454]

The pronounced colour-scheme should set the tone of any performance – Conal's house orange-red, the furniture and props black, the rocks black and touched with green, the sea green and luminous and all the characters except the Red Man and the Black Men dressed in various shades of green. The Red Man himself, crowned by his enormous green helmet is larger than life and the Black Men with their eared caps and their eyes catching the light reflected from the green sea should suggest cats – the one dominant image of the play. In fact the play's most impressive feature is its visual impact. The climax, when the Red Man with his ominous black cat-headed followers come in, makes its effect by visual means. Even if the Abbey stage did not have the resources with which these could be

55

fully realized, it is easy to imagine the picture described in the stage
directions:

The Stable Boys and Scullions blow their horns or fight among themselves.
There is a deafening noise and a confused fight. Suddenly three black hands
come through the windows and put out the torches. It is now pitch-dark,
but for a faint light outside the house which merely shows that there are
moving forms, but not who or what they are, and in the darkness one can
hear low terrified voices . . .
A light gradually comes into the house from the sea, on which the moon
begins to show once more. There is no light within the house, and the great
beams of the walls are dark and full of shadows, and the persons of the
play dark too against the light. The Red Man is seen standing in the midst
of the house. The black cat-headed men crouch and stand about the door.
One carries the Helmet, one the great sword.

[*CPl* 241]

The exaggeration of all this suggests a sending-up of the whole
mythological setting. But although everything is blown-up out of
proportion by comically inflated fantasy, including the Red Man and
Cuchulain himself, the satire on Ireland is not blown to smithereens
in the process.

If the visual impact of the play is its strongest feature, the language,
alas, is its weakness. Reacting away from the blank verse which he
had used hitherto, he followed Wilfrid Scawen Blunt's experimental
use of the alexandrine in his play *Fand* and hit on the rhymed ballad
metre. The lilt and the rhymes at times move in the direction of
comedy:

Conall: He promised to show us a game, the best that ever had been;
And when we had asked what game, he answered, 'Why, whip off my head!
Then one of you two stoop down, and I'll whip off his,' he said.
'A head for a head', he said, 'that is the game that I play'.
Cuchulain: How could he whip off a head when his own had been whipped
   away?
Conall: We told him it over and over, and that ale had fuddled his wit,
But he stood and laughed at us there, as though his sides would split,
Till I could stand it no longer, and whipped off his head at a blow,
Being mad that he did not answer, and more at his laughing so,
And there on the ground where it fell it went on laughing at me.
Laegaire: Till he took it up in his hands –
Conall: And splashed himself into the sea.

[*CPl* 229]

At other times the rhythm loses its lilt in its effort to avoid the tendency to doggerel yet does not keeep the movement of colloquial speech:

Conall: A law has been made that none, shall sleep in this house tonight.
Young Man: Who made that law?
Conall: We made it, and who has so good a right?
Who else has to keep the house from the Shape-Changers till day?
Young Man: Then I will unmake the law, so get you out of the way.
                (*He pushes past Conall and goes into the house*)
Conall: I thought no living man could have pushed me from the door,
Nor could any living man do it but for the dip in the floor;
And had I been rightly ready there's no man living could do it,
Dip or no dip.

[CPl 226]

On other occasions, rhyme and the conflicting demands of both colloquial and heightened language are hopelessly at odds with each other:

Conall: Go into Scotland again, or where you will, but begone
From this unlucky country that was made when the Devil spat.
Cuchulain: If I lived here a hundred years, could a worse thing come than that
Laegaire and Conall should know me and bid me begone to my face?
Conall: We bid you begone from a house that has fallen on shame and
    disgrace.
Cuchulain: I am losing patience, Conall – I find you stuffed with pride,
The flagon full to the brim, the front door standing wide;
You'd put me off with words, but the whole thing's plain enough,
You are waiting for some message to bring you to war or love
In that old secret country beyond the wool-white waves,
Or it may be down beneath them in foam-bewildered caves
Where nine forsaken sea-queens fling shuttles to and fro;
But beyond them, or beneath them, whether you will or no,
I am going too.

[CPl 227-8]

Nevertheless, if the lines are spoken with appropriate emphasis and if the movements of the actors are treated in a somewhat balletic and stylized way, the generally inflated tone can be maintained.

Once again, as in other plays, the setting preserves the contrast between the expansive heroic world of the sea, the home of the larger-than-life, if somewhat absurd Red Man, and the all too human restrictiveness of a fool-driven land in which Conall's house – Ireland – is inhabited by dolts and knaves. Its disgrace and threatened destruction can only be staved off by a human gesture comparable in scope with that of the superhuman Red Man. Cuchulain alone

is capable of such a gesture. He has all the attributes of the Yeatsian
hero, even if they are enlarged to the point of parody. First there
is luck:

Conall: . . . he has all that he could need
In that high windy Scotland – good luck in all that he does.
                                                                [*CPl* 224]

Laegaire and Conall stress this over and over again.

Laegaire: He was born to luck in the cradle, his good luck may amend
The bad luck we were born to.
Conall: I'll lay the whole thing bare.
You saw the luck that he had when he pushed past me there.
                                                                [*CPl* 228]

He has the self-confidence and the authority to impose his
individualistic ethos on others, which comprises courage, passion,
contempt for mediocrity. These are all qualities that are discernible
in the Cuchulain of *On Baile's Strand, At the Hawk's Well* and *The
Only Jealousy of Emer.* They are opposed to Laegaire's and Conall's
cowardice and aldermanic concern with protocol:

Laegaire: I would he'd come for all that, and make his young wife know
That though she may be his wife, she has no right to go
Before your wife and my wife, as she would have done last night
Had they not caught at her dress, and pulled her as was right;
                                                                [*CPl* 225]

But whereas in those plays these qualities are set in opposition to
a social ethos, in this play Cuchulain is not only involved in his society
but assumes a social responsibility. He perceives that the challenge
thrown down by the Red Man is in itself extraordinary and requires
an extraordinary response. It is not only a challenge to personal
bravery but to Ireland itself. Conall and Laegaire treat the helmet
as an excuse for petty personal rivalry. Cuchulain on the contrary
would turn it into a loving-cup:

Cuchulain (filling Helmet with ale): I did not take it to keep it – the Red
   Man gave it for one,
But I shall give it to all – to all of us three or to none;
That is as you look upon it – we will pass it to and fro,
And time and time about, drink out of it and so
Stroke into peace this cat that has come to take our lives.
                                                                [*CPl* 233]

(In performance nothing would be lost by having him fill the helmet with Guinness.) But his first efforts in that direction are thwarted dramatically by the entry of the noisy mob of charioteers, kitchen and stable boys, carrying horns and ladles, wearing, one could imagine, saucepans on their heads for helmets. Laeg the charioteer stokes up the fires of political jealousy, but Cuchulain, who receives some support from the crowd, makes some headway with them:

Cuchulain: It [the helmet] has been given to none: that our rivalry might
    cease,
We have turned that murderous cat into a cup of peace.
I drank the first; and then Conall; give it to Laegaire now
(*Conall gives Helmet to Laegaire*)
That it may purr in his hand and all of our servants know
That, since the ale went in, its claws went out of sight.

                    [*CPl* 236]

But this attempt is again thwarted, this time by the squabbling of the wives. Cuchulain's effort to put an end to their silly rivalry over who should enter the house first by breaking down the painted walls and letting them all come in together is again thwarted by their mutual jealousies, though in the process Emer establishes herself in her song as a fit mate for him. She is moon to his sun, steel to his fire. This time Cuchulain, justly exasperated, in effect tries to evade the issue by throwing the helmet out to sea. But this is no solution. The challenge must be met. The Red Man returns to face him with it again. Cuchulain meets the challenge with a gesture that derives its sanction ultimately from a superhuman world. He resists the tug of his wife's domestic passion in lines that link him to the source of the heroic, the sea:

Cuchulain: Would you stay the great barnacle-goose
When its eyes are turned to the sea and its beak to the salt of the air?
                    [*CPl* 242]

Cuchulain here embodies the aristocratic virtues of pride, independence, courtesy, the recklessness, the *sprezzatura* that Castiglione thought necessary in good manners – to which can be added the ability to laugh in the teeth of frustration – virtues that enlarge his human dimension. In choosing the man who hits his fancy the Red Man acknowledges light-heartedly the qualities that Yeats celebrated in verse:

              And I choose the laughing lip

That shall not turn from laughing, whatever rise or fall;
The heart that grows no bitterer although betrayed by all;
The hand that loved to scatter; the life like a gambler's throw
                                                    [*CPl* 243]

and in prose:

The heroic act, as it descends through tradition, is an act done because a man is himself, because, being himself, he can ask nothing of other men but room amid remembered tragedies; a sacrifice of himself to himself.
                                                    [*WB* 75, *VPl.* 569]

Such a gesture is also made by the Cuchulain of *On Baile's Strand,* by Deirdre and by Emer, but in this case there is no tragic sacrifice. In fact Cuchulain does not have to sacrifice himself, he makes an offer and the offer is accepted. He becomes not the tragic hero who in losing his life paradoxically finds his own soul, but a triumphant comic hero who is neither defeated nor mocked.

The play is therefore very different from *The Player Queen* and *The Herne's Egg,* with which it has been compared. What is mocked here is not the heroic ethos, which in the two later plays is itself called into question, but unheroic Ireland. The message of *The Green Helmet* anticipates the implications of *The Dreaming of the Bones,* namely that peace in Ireland – the achievement of which is the explicit motive in offering his head in the earlier version, *The Golden Helmet* – can only come about by the kind of imaginative gesture that none but the heroic are capable of, and Ireland is running out of heroism – 'Romantic Ireland's dead and gone' [*CP* 121]. Failure to face up to that inescapable challenge – the helmet will always come back – will lead to disaster. Behind the gaiety and kindliness of the Shape-Changer lurks his power. The cat, even when tamed, still has his claws.

The Player Queen

In spite of all the exegetical attempts of the commentators, readers and audiences alike are still likely to react to this play in the same way that its first audience did in 1919, as described by Kavanagh: 'after the performance everyone was asking one another in the foyer what it was all about. No one knew, and everyone assumed it to be high art' (quoted by Moore, *MLD* 190), though nowadays there would be plenty to challenge the idolatrous assessment of its artistic value. For instance Henn finds it 'difficult to read and more difficult to act' [*HT* 208-9]; Ure 'an imperfect achievement' and 'a poor choice for an audience that expects meanings to be conveyed through the dramatic context' [*YTP* 145]; Taylor finds that the ending 'suggests that action and symbolic design are not perfectly integrated' [*DWPY* 150]; Vendler declares it 'is not really stage-worthy' [*YV* 124] even after allowing for the 'responsible and informed directing' [*YV* 272] of William Becker, the critic who finds the most coherence in the play, though Bloom [*Y* 328] denies it this quality. On the other hand critics have responded to its flashes of dramatic energy, even though these vary in intensity and nature, from grotesque fantasy to almost naturalistic high comedy. It does contain a number of magnets which are bound to attract anyone interested in Yeats's symbols and ideas: the image and significance of the unicorn, the doctrine of the Mask, the cyclical view of history that envisages an apocalyptic moment when one era, disintegrating in anarchy and violence, collapses into a new and antithetical dispensation. But the very existence of these concerns in the play creates the danger of interpretations which rely on material taken from outside it and then imported into it. Thus Wilson [*YT*] and Melchiori [*WMA*] relate it to the early story 'The Adoration of the Magi' (1897) [*M* 308], in the 1925 version of which a Parisian prostitute gives birth to a 'cold, hard, and virginal unicorn', the emblem of a new anti-Christian era. Wilson claims that 'it is certainly suggested that the harlot Decima is to copulate with the unicorn and so, a new cycle arriving, propagate a new race' [*Y&T* 182]. But this is not in the play. As Peter Ure pointed out, the new dispensation is the result of a comic intrigue in which Decima marries the Prime Minister. Vendler, who also accepts the putative coupling of Decima and unicorn, sees it not in terms of historical, but aesthetic revolution, and in her interpretation of Decima as tyrannical Muse goes against the run of her characterization by calling her 'metallic'. She is too humanly complex to be simply that. Similarly she treats Septimus's drunkenness as pure symbol for poetic inspiration: she has no time for the comic effect of his tipsy rhapsodic extravagance. The play's very variety is both a temptation to the critic to rewrite it in terms of his own interests, and at the same time a justification of the liberty of interpretation that it has attracted. And not only literary interpretation: it is one of the few plays by Yeats of which one feels that there is scope for the *actor's* interpretation. In the obviously symbolic and stylized plays the actor has little or no room for manœuvre: facial expression is concealed by the mask; gesture, physical movement and even tonal and rhythmical variations of speech are not projections from the 'character's' subconscious, but are determined by the dramatic 'score'. Here, however, in spite of their symbolic suggestiveness, some of the characters, and especially Septimus and Decima, have enough depth to make a variety of different interpretations plausible. The same is true of the play as a whole: one can imagine performances which would bring out different emphases, and one can also imagine emphases emerging from the actors trying out various approaches in order to discover what would 'go' on the stage. For all its unconventional exterior there is a strong element of traditional theatricality about it. In this respect it is quite different from the Noh-like plays, and for it, as for the later *The Herne's Egg,* with which it has much in common, Yeats abandons his theatrical austerity and demands elaborate, almost prohibitively expensive mounting.

No matter to what unfavourable verdicts on its worth as drama the procedure may lead – and the consensus of critical opinion, anyhow of that opinion that sees it as something more than a repository of Yeatsian ideas, is unfavourable – it is best to try to take the play as it is. One can accept Becker's analysis (*Sewanee Review* 61,1953) of its narrative structure in terms of the two linked stories of which it is constituted: one about the impending revolution, the New Dispensation, in which Decima, the Queen and the Prime Minister and the common people are involved, and the other concerning the relationships between Septimus, Decima and Nona, though one may doubt that the linking idea between them is the doctrine of the Mask. The two stories are not in fact very well linked. The threat of the impending revolution is announced clearly enough in scene 1, but for the whole of the central episode from Decima's entry to the dance of the Players as animals, and then again for the crucial episode between Septimus, Decima and Nona until Septimus's exit, Yeats forgets it, only returning to it with the arrival of the Old Beggar. The working-out of the human relationships between Septimus, Decima and Nona, and also the presentation of two of them considered separately, Decima and Septimus, *can* be thought of in terms of the achievement of wholeness by the recognition and assumption of a true mask – Decima's becoming the Queen; or of the rejection of a false mask – the Queen's not becoming a martyr; or in terms of the equilibrium of opposites – Septimus as both inspired Poet and dissolute husband; or indeed of the mockery or frustration of these concepts – Septimus drunk, Decima having to marry the third-rate blustering Prime Minister, divine Unicorn becoming a donkey. But it is difficult to relate these concepts either to Nona, who is incapable of aspiring to anything, or to the New Dispensation idea, except in so far as it is true to say that the New Dispensation we get is not a new dispensation at all – things go on as before and the revolution that brings it about is a very far cry from the expected apocalyptic cataclysm. Nevertheless it is helpful to use as guide-lines what E. M. Forster called the finer growths that the narrative structure supports in the form of three themes: poetry and its relation to society, the New Dispensation theme, and the doctrine of the Mask.

The play opens in a setting which Yeats was at pains to neutralize by the use of Gordon Craig's screens. When he published it in *PPV* he wrote:

It is the only play of mine which has not its scene laid in Ireland . . . My *dramatis personae* have no nationality because Mr. Craig's screens, where every line must suggest some mathematical proportion, where all is phantastic, incredible, and luminous, have no nationality.

[*VPl* 761]

But in spite of this disclaimer, small details which may be linked to Yeats's life and to events in Ireland nag at the mind, even though they are not significant in themselves as factors in our understanding of the play. Examples are the hints, in Septimus's worship of the image, and beyond that of his worship of Decima, of Yeats's own worship of Maud Gonne as an image of the unattainable to which he longed to be united. There is the conflict between Septimus and the 'bad, popular poets' [*CPl* 391] and the Prime Minister's choice of a play that everyone can understand and that no-one is offended by as opposed to 'some dull poetical thing', which reflect the tensions within the Irish dramatic movement, and Yeats's desire for a culturally elitist audience as opposed to a popular one. The 'Castle's' rewarding the Players seems to suggest an inversion of the antagonisms between the directors of the Abbey Theatre and Dublin Castle in the early stages of its growth. Yeats was working on the tragic version of the play as far back as 1909, at the time of the fight with the Castle over Shaw's *The Shewing-up of Blanco Posnet,* chronicled in Lady Gregory's *Our Irish Theatre.* But whether these links are intentional or not, they are left hanging in the air.

In an inordinately long build-up Yeats paints a picture of a society, seen first from below in the Citizens and the Countrymen, whose fabric is moth-eaten with inadequacies: with pretence and self-regarding timidity (the Old Men); with hypocrisy (the two poets anxious to conceal from their wives that they are returning from a brothel); with philistinism and brutality (the Big Countryman); with fickleness (the Citizens switch from violent opposition to authority at the beginning to toadying acceptance at the end); with a religion that simply provides an excuse for barbarism. Although there are glimmerings of decency and restraint in the 1st and 2nd Countryman, this society's claim to abide by reason is undercut by its irrational acceptance of the Tapster's fantastic story. When the picture is completed in scene 2 by the people at the top, they are seen to be no better: a neurotic Queen, a time-serving Bishop and a blustering, ineffectual, crafty Prime Minister. It is a society whose degradation suggests that it is ripe for change, for a New Dispensation. The dawn symbolism of the first scene is obvious, though it is not carried over into the second. But at the same time this society is dominated by fear (the Citizens and Countrymen are terrified of the Old Beggar) and it lacks the courage to carry out its revolutionary aspirations. This cowardice is applicable in varying degrees to other characters as well: to the Queen, who cannot face martyrdom; to Nona, who runs away; to the Players, who are intent on saving their own skins; even to Septimus, who is afraid of Decima; and to Decima herself, who cannot screw herself up to the heroic gesture of suicide, though these last two display a compensatory courage. Its aspirations are not really revolutionary at all. The Citizens do not want to change society; they are more interested in security. All they want is the comfort of a familiar, visible and tangible authority, a social pacifier that will soothe their toothless discontents, and they are quite happy with the one they get in the end. The Queen's social irresponsibility in refusing to play the role that is expected of her is paralleled by the passivity of the man in the 3rd Countryman's story who found life a vale of tears and responded to it by returning to bed for forty-four years until he died [*CPl* 395]. She finds life a perpetual invitation to penance, but her psychological inadequacies distort this impulse into a neurotic desire for a martyrdom for which she is totally unfitted by nature. Being the most self-centred of creatures, and cowardly to boot, she is quite incapable of dying 'for God's glory' [*CPl* 425]. All she can do is run away into the shelter of a fugitive and cloistered chastity, which is not an active enemy to sin, but a totally passive denial of life itself. As the Prime Minister points out, 'Is there sin in an egg that has never been hatched?' [*CPl* 405]. After Decima has taken over her role, she just 'loses her name' and disappears into a convent [*CPl* 427].

At the beginning of the play her disappearance from the purview of the Citizens, obscurely paralleled by the disappearance of Decima, threatens the structure and stability of society. The mob fills the gap created by her absence with fantasies masquerading as reality and which, if left uncontrolled, would lead to revolution. This is the political problem that the Prime Minister has to solve. (It is solved in the end, but not by him.) These fantasies – the Prime Minister makes the point in an exclamation deleted from *CPl*: 'Give the people some plain image or they will invent one' [*VPl* 733] – cluster round the image of the Unicorn. Peter Ure was right to question the kind of interpretation of the Unicorn that relies on external aid, such as Wilson's 'form in which divinity is to descend to Decima' [*Y&T* 182], or Melchiori's 'scourge from above which will bring renewal, through ruin' [*WMA* 53], pointing out that

throughout the play the unicorn in its aspect of immanent beast-deity is the property of Septimus's imagination and has, as it were, gone off with him when he withdrew from the story.

[*YTP* 144]

Like Ibsen's wild duck the Unicorn has several aspects, which relate it to other characters, though it never materializes as an actual beast in the play, remaining for each of them a projection of their subjective attitudes. For the Tapster and the mob, incapable of abstract vision, it is a real animal, and the story of its coupling with the Queen, which they accept as gospel, is a projection of their suppressed sexuality. To the Queen it is an image of her own self-mortification, prudery and perverse masochism. To Septimus it has multiple significance. In its chastity and purity it seems to represent the purity of art, the ideal Image, inhabiting its own inaccessible dimension, 'the high table lands of Africa' [*'CPl* 397], aloof yet tyrannous in its claim upon the spirit, the master to whom all artists, creative or executant, poets or players, must give allegiance. It is divine inspiration, the matrix from which new images, new works of art, are born. But the act of begetting fresh images, of shaping abstract vision into concrete form, requires the energy that is generated by the interpenetration of ideal and real, eternal and temporal. Until that is achieved they remain unborn children: 'His [the Unicorn's] unborn children are but images' [*CPl* 417]. The divine Unicorn must be made to invade the human, and conversely the human must be fertilized by Godhead. Such an act is both fiercely destructive and creative, so that the Unicorn also stands not only for the opposing forces in the creative life but also for the contradictions present in love – beauty, cruelty and power. Thus Decima in her beauty and her cruelty, her *terribilitá,* is a reflection of the virginal Unicorn. Finally the Unicorn is related to Septimus himself, in as far as he achieves the strength of artistic integrity: 'Because I am an unforsworn man I am strong: a violent virginal creature' [*CPl* 423].

Septimus's courageous defence of the Unicorn as an ideal, for all that it is based on Dutch courage, for which he is brutally assaulted by the Big Countryman, highlights the theme of the poet and his relation to society. Septimus himself is a complex figure. One aspect of him is tinged with the reductive mockery with which Yeats has coloured the play. At one point he literally has a bucket of cold water poured over him [*CPl* 390]. Divine inspiration is reduced to commonplace intoxication, the proud self-sufficiency of the artist to maudlin dependence on his wife Decima. Conversely he has no compunction whatsoever in treating Nona egoistically as a sexual convenience. Peter Ure pointed out that his drunkenness is 'a literalized and comical version of the spiritual intoxication of Paul Ruttledge and Martin Hearne, drunk with the grapes of wrath' [*YTP* 137]. The characteristic tone of his speech is a mixture of romantic self-pity and grandiose rhetoric, absurdly inflated. He identifies himself with Christ:

Carry me, support me, drag me, roll me, pull me, or sidle me along, but bring me where I may sleep in comfort. Bring me to a stable – my Saviour was content with a stable.

[*CPl* 391]

He claims divine status:

Go away, did you say, and my breast-feathers thrust out and my white wings buoyed up with divinity?

[*CPl* 397-8]

He is a parody of the romantic poet *par excellence,* as Becker points out, but it is not quite right to dismiss him as Bloom does as 'only parody' [*Y* 333], 'a pistolian rhetorician and not a poet' [*Y* 330]. The samples we are given of his work are not at all bad (one of them, anyway, good enough to find a place in his creator's *Collected Poems*). More important than that, he does stick to his guns: he alone does not go over to the mob [*CPl* 419]. He alone preserves with a kind of dignity the properties of art, and with a kind of integrity that is aware of its own shortcomings, his independence of both Decima and Nona, and furthermore continues to assert at the risk of punishment not so much the truth *of* the Mask as the truth *behind* it, the reality behind the appearance, when he keeps on telling the Prime Minister that it is Decima who is pretending to be the Queen. For all this he suffers the fate of artist who (as Yeats regarded himself), 'out of phase' with his time, proclaims values that his philistine, materialistic and mediocre society rejects. He recognizes his kinship with the Old Beggar – 'Then we are indeed brothers' [*CPl* 401]. Both are mouthpieces of the Oracle, though there is a difference between the poet's inspiration and the medium's trance. The poet can have a vision of the New Dispensation, can articulate that vision in artistic form, can even will it ('I will bid him trample mankind to death and beget a new race' [*CPl* 417], whereas the medium is merely the ignorant channel for the annunciation of the destined event. The first scene ends in the growing light of a symbolic dawn with the two, Poet and Old Beggar, going off together to greet with characteristic overstatement a New Dispensation in which the poet, as if in a new Byzantium, will be integrated in society, will 'sleep in the Castle of the Queen' [*CPl* 401]. But such optimism is impressionistically dispelled by the return of the timid, tired Old Men with their commonplace talk of the Tapster's old dog coming down from Cooper Malachi's ash-pit, a bleak bone in its mouth.

The second scene begins with a development of the two themes already announced in the first: the poet/society theme and the New Dispensation theme, and maintains the tone of mockery already established by a combination of sardonic reduction and comic inflation. The picture of society is completed in the form of the Prime Minister dictating not only artistic but social policy in an attempt to control the anger of the mob that is being directed at the Queen and to prevent her martydom at their hands. His plan is to marry the Queen himself and have the play, 'The Tragical History of Noah's Deluge' performed by the Players. In the event the play is not performed nor does he marry the Queen. A larger, more powerful force is in control of events, and his ineffectuality is comically rendered both by his bluster, his lack of understanding of Decima, whom he quite wrongly dismisses as 'a bladder full of dried peas for a brain, a brazen, bragging baggage' [*CPl* 404], and, to a lesser extent, the irony of Decima's appearance to the audience from under the throne when everyone thinks she is lost, and finally by his somewhat irritating habit of trivilizing things, by calling, for example, God, Old Man in the Sky – not unlike Shaw's *penchant* for nicknames.

With the entry of the Queen the mask theme now emerges. She is clearly the reverse of the image of queenliness, totally lacking in the qualities that the Prime Minister expects in a Queen: 'charm, dignity, royal manner' [*CPl* 405], quite incapable of an 'eagle look, a vulture look' [*CPl* 406]. She is also the opposite of the mob's vision of her as a sexual pervert. It can be argued that the role of queen is her False Mask in that she cannot wear it, but on the other hand the idea of fulfilment by uniting with a True Mask is irrelevant to her because she simply has not got a True Mask with which to unite.

The play continues on its abstract, semi-symbolic level with the pantomine of Nona enticing Decima back into the role that she has refused to play, Noah's wife, or into adopting a Mask contrary to her nature, with the lure of 'a bottle of wine and a boiled lobster' [*CPl* 406]. It is not clear whether this is intended to be the food of the queen, denied to Decima here but eventually obtained later: for when Decima has seized the role of Queen, she eats from a plate and drinks from a bottle of wine but there is no mention of the lobster [*CPl* 428]. (Another loose end lies in the uncertainty of Septimus's position among the Players. He is certainly a 'player, a playwright' and at least in his own opinion 'the most famous poet in the world' [*CPl* 391], but according to Nona [*CPl* 408] he must also be the manager of the company, whom the Prime Minister threatens with a gaol sentence. The irony of making Septimus, whose sphere is vision not action, a theatrical manager, if intended, is not explored.)

At the same time as the Mask theme emerges with the entry of Decima, the New Dispensation theme disappears, and, to the detriment of the play's cohesiveness, the level moves fitfully in the direction of naturalistic and bitchy comedy. Decima's song establishes her contrast with the Queen and anticipates her instinctive grasp of her proper role, the adoption of her True Mask:

'He went away', my mother sang,
'When I was brought to bed.'
And all the while her needle pulled
The gold and silver thread.

> She pulled the thread and bit the thread
> And made a golden gown,
> She wept because she had dreamt that I
> Was born to wear a crown.
>
> [*CPl* 406-7]

She is born to royalty and in the final scene does in fact wear the golden gown, her role of state. At this point she rejects the role of Noah's wife:

> an old peaky-chinned, drop-nosed harridan that a foul husband beats with a stick because she won't clamber among the other brutes into his cattleboat.
>
> [*CPl* 408]

In the dialogue that follows, up to the entrance of the Stage Manager, which is full of spitefully comic ironies, she is clearly contrasted with Nona. They are two different kinds of women. At this level Decima in her cold, self-centred beauty is a *femme fatale,* Nona an easy-going, practical, down-to-earth creature whose emblems are appropriately domestic: they are the scissors, needle and thread with which she can snip at a dress for Noah's wife – she will never make a golden gown for a queen. Decima is narcissistically proud of her position as inspirer of Septimus's poetry; Nona is completely unresponsive to it. She may have had a poem tapped out on her shoulder-blade and spine, but she has never read a word of it. When Septimus is completely absorbed in the problem of preserving the implements of art and indeed of the function of art:

> We must carry into safety the cloak of Noah, the high-crowned hat of Noah, and the mask of the sister of Noah

her only reaction is

> Thank God you can still stand upright on your legs.
>
> [*CPl* 420]

She is a kind of Emer but without any of the qualities that enlarge a person to superhuman dimensions. She is a pragmatist who regards oaths as mere expedients which no sober man would hesitate to break if it served his practical advantage to do so, and in the end runs off

to her own safety when she realizes that Septimus will not play her
game. Intoxication or inspiration mean nothing to her. Decima is
a woman of a different sort. When she realizes that Nona has become
Septimus's mistress, she falls momentarily into a kind of trance:
'Why are you standing there as if in a trance', the Stage Manager
asks when he comes in at the moment [*CPl* 413]. This trance may
be intended as a contrast with the trance of the Old Beggar into which
he falls just before the new dispensation is announced. For the Old
Beggar, trance brings neither knowledge nor power, for Decima it
brings power, expressed dramatically in that from this moment on
she dominates the action more and more. But her cry:

. . . thank God! she has got him and I am free. I threw away a part and
I threw away a man – she has picked both up.

[*CPl* 414]

is not to be taken at a symbolic level, because she later tries
desperately to get Septimus back. It is an expression of jealous
hysteria that is obviously human. She is caught up in contradictions.
She wants to maintain her position of aloof beauty from which she
can extract a sadistic pleasure in Septimus's sufferings, but she cannot
bear it when her cruelty drives him to assert his freedom from her
and seek comfort elsewhere. Her very human anger is directed at
him, not at Nona, but it is expressed symbolically as she tries to cut
through the breast-feathers of the player/swan – though an audience
would have to remember Septimus's earlier identification of himself
with the swan of divine inspiration. This castration-image links the
human Decima with the symbolic Decima, though it is less a link
than a means of yoking together by force of contradictory aspects.
Yeats moves too violently from a naturalistic to a non-naturalistic
mode of drama, and in the movement we lose our bearings. Her
second song, sung while the actor/brutes dance round her, suggests
the contradictory forces inherent in human sexuality in general as
well as those inherent in her relationship with Septimus – cruelty and
possessive love. Decima the inspirer of Septimus's poetry becomes
also the symbolic Muse exacting an endlessly repeated sacrifice from
her worshipper. But this role simply does not fit in with her attempts
to get him back. The dance-song 'Shall I fancy beast or fowl' [*CPl*
416] shifts the dramatic level onto the symbolic. This is maintained
when Septimus enters immediately afterwards, but is dropped again
when the Players begin squabbling naturalistically among themselves.
The song itself does suggest the concept of the Harlot-beast,

human-divine conjunction, though there is nothing else in the play
to support the view that Decima is a harlot. In point of fact Septimus
is more promiscuous than she. Nor does the song say anything about
a New Dispensation emerging from such a conjunction. It is Septimus
who, by announcing the end of the Christian era and the coming
of a New Dispensation, raises the expectation that it is the Unicorn
that will be its progenitor. But three points must be borne in mind:
one, that even for Septimus the Unicorn remains obstinately chaste
– there is no conjunction; two, that it has a special and limited
significance for him; and three, that the play does not fulfil the
expectation – it is the Prime Minister who goes off with Decima and
there is nothing to suggest that he will be ultimately cuckolded by
the Unicorn. For the romantic poet the Unicorn exists at the level
of aesthetic, not historical allegory, in the world of the mind, not
in the world of action. It is divine inspiration. Service to the Unicorn
involves the risk of death – 'let us prepare to die', says Septimus
[*CPl* 417] – on two levels, literal and figurative. In a society hostile
to art, the artist risks being beaten up, rejected, banished or killed
– 'We will hang him in the morning', says the Prime Minister [*CPl*
429]. Figuratively the death involves that immolation of personal
experience on the altar of form which is endlessly renewed in the
creative act. There is no limit to the sacrifices demanded by the Muse
of the artist who serves her. From this immolation will emerge new
creations and it is this process that Septimus bids the Unicorn to
inaugurate by trampling mankind to death and begetting a new race
[*CPl* 417]. For the time being he rails upon the Unicorn for not
initiating it. He has not yet had the flash of inspiration in which
he perceives the function of art and the artist.

But the death that is figurative to him is terrifyingly literal to the
Players, and their way of saving the images and implements of art,
since as living symbols of art in their beast-costumes they are servants
of art too, is the very human one of saving their own skins by hiding
'in some cleft in the rocks' [*CPl* 419]. From that sanctuary,
traditionally associated with prophetic utterance, like Delphi or the
'cleft that's christened Alt' [*CP* 393], and in the impersonality of
their symbolic guise as beast-images, they can bear witness to the
conviction that divine reality can be apprehended through art. But
art requires artists and artists are only human, even if they can create
super-human images, and their jealousies, their self-centred
bickerings, remind us of this.

Seeing their departure as cowardice Septimus for a moment
luxuriates in the vision of himself as the sole custodian of art,
sustained by his own subjective emotions, as he imagines the Unicorn

to be intoxicated by the water he has bathed in:

When my master the Unicorn bathes by the light of the Great Bear, and
to the sound of tabors, even the sweet river-water makes him drunk; but
it is cold, it is cold, alas! it is cold.

[*CPl* 419]

Nona, the voice of commonsense, calls him to his social function.
The poet must accept the responsibility of preserving his art,
symbolized by the properties of Noah, including the mask of Noah's
sister who was drowned in fact because she refused to accept the
validity of prophetic utterance, but who survives in art:

Septimus: You are right. I accept the reproach. It is necessary that we who
are the last artists – all the rest have gone over to the mob – shall save the
images and implements of our art. We must carry into safety the cloak of
Noah, the high-crowned hat of Noah, and the mask of the sister of Noah.
She was drowned because she thought her brother was telling lies; certainly
we must save her rosy cheeks and rosy mouth, that drowned, wicked mouth.

[*CPl* 419-20]

Art, Septimus realizes in a flash of inspiration, that is, a second swig
at the bottle, must do two things: it must hold the mirror up to nature
even though what is reflected in it is an image of human weakness
and folly, and it must create for man an image of what he might
be in order that he may become it:

Man is nothing until he is united to an image.

[*CPl* 420]

When body and image are united, there is a kind of rebirth and the
occasion will deserve a marriage-song:

Now the unicorn is both an image and beast; that is why he alone can be
the new Adam. When we have put all in safety we will go to the high
tablelands of Africa and find where the Unicorn is stabled and sing a
marriage song. I will stand before the terrible blue eye.

[*CPl* 420]

But, just as in all his human fallibility he is preparing to depart
on his symbolic journey to the high tablelands of Africa where he
will be granted his vision of the Unicorn as a symbol of unity, no
longer to be railed upon for its chastity, but to be celebrated for
its defloration by experience, he is interrupted by Decima in all her
beauty, as in her brittle fierceness she prepares to do battle with Nona

for him. All three are literally and figuratively locked within the gates of their situation, and the upshot of the battle is that all three make their way out of it by different routes. Nona the pragmatist seizes her opportunity and runs off to her own safety, leaving the field to the other two. Septimus defeats Decima, or at least rises above her, in that he remains faithful to his principles such as they are. Refreshed by his bottle, he remains true to his inspiration, true to his intoxication, true to his essential nature as a poet. Decima at one level is a manifestation of the Unicorn, aloof and fierce, in so far as she too is an inspirational source of the poet's creative powers, but she compromises this position by descending to the human level in refusing to allow Septimus the right to remain true to her in his own way. She tries to compel his loyalty, to fetter his imagination.

Decima: I will unlock this gate when you have taken an oath to drive her from the company, an oath never to speak with her or look at her again, a terrible oath.

[*CPl* 421-2]

But she fails. Septimus remains unforsworn, true to his inspiration, of which Decima has now become the tarnished image, but one which still exerts a fascination for him. He picks up, with difficulty, the hat of poetry, leaving the mask of Noah's wife behind. He goes out courageously, with dignity, though somewhat unsteadily, defiantly asserting in song the freedom of the artist, a kind of '*non serviam*' that includes a rejection of all those ties, human and social, that will hold him to the ground and prevent him from taking the swan's flight into the divine, and the right to turn his divine discontent with the tyrannical demands of the Unicorn itself into art. One authority, however, he will not question: the cold, rocky voice of Delphi.

Bloom declares that 'there is certainly no divinity in *The Player Queen*' [*Y* 330], but surely the Oracle, whose mouthpiece is the Old Beggar, is that divinity, what Moore describes as

whatever we want to call that tendency in the universe to impose a meaning on the shape of things.

[*MLD* 172]

Ultimately the Oracle is the power behind the throne, whoever sits on it. The Christian era may have come to an end, but destruction has not brought the New Dispensation – the machinations of Delphi have seen to that [*CPl* 423]. It is the Oracle that determines the outcome of events. It is the Oracle that decrees that in spite of his plans the Prime Minister shall have Decima, not the Queen, for wife:

Prime Minister: The crown has changed and there is no help for it. Sleep of Adam, I must have that woman [Decima] for wife. The Oracle has settled that.

[*CPl* 429]

The power of the Oracle in overriding human decision is demonstrated dramatically by the providential arrival first of the Old Beggar and then of the Queen.

Rejected by Septimus, Decima is left in a state of furious despair, melodramatically determined on suicide. But she is prevented by the Old Beggar. The dramatic purpose of his arrival at this moment, which postpones Decima's decision, is to suggest that events wait in the hands of destiny and that fulfilment is close at hand. At the same time, true to the reductive tone of the play, the Old Beggar mocks at some of Yeats's most deeply-held beliefs: in reincarnation,

You don't know what you will be put to when you are dead, into whose gullet you will be put to sing or to bray

and in the union of spirits after death:

Decima: Do those who are dead, old man, make love and do they find good lovers?
Old Beggar: I will whisper you another secret. People talk, but I have never known anything to come from there but an old jackass. Maybe there is nothing else. Who knows but he has the whole place to himself?

[*CPl* 425]

But the Old Beggar is also the evangelist of her transformation, since immediately destiny presents her with her moment of choice. The Queen arrives. Decima turns chance into choice and with a swiftness of decision that dramatizes the overwhelming power of revelation, she grasps her Mask, accepts the role of Queen, and dons the golden robe her mother had predicted for her. The New Dispensation has come for her, sardonically corroborated by the donkey's bray. She rises magnificently to the demands of her new role. She accepts the political advantages of the Bishop's ignorance of who the Queen is. She masters the flabbergasted Prime Minister, who recovers from the shock in time to confirm and exercise his position of power. And she masters the fickle mob. But she does not master Septimus. There is a price to pay for this mastery. She must accept the contradictions in her own nature and the ambiguities of her choice. As woman she

loses love, and the commanding gesture of choosing the role of Queen
involves her in ignoble and reductive compromises. She must ally
herself with the third-rate representatives of religious and secular
authority, and she must descend to the mediocrity of marriage with
the Prime Minister, and finally she must abandon her role and the
art that could sustain her in it. For these devaluations the apt symbol
is the foolish smiling face of Noah's sister. But she retains a degree
of queenly courage in the very act of depriving herself of the
independence by which she has acquired her role of Queen: she
herself *chooses* her new Mask, the Mask of all the things that as
queen she was not. She has gone over to the Establishment, but she
knows she has.

This last gesture of hers is perhaps the final irony in a play full
of ironies – 'perhaps' because motives and meanings are left obscure.
Yeats wrote in *Mythologies* that

active virtue, as distinguished from the passive acceptance of a code, is
therefore theatrical, consciously dramatic, the wearing of a mask . . .
$\qquad\qquad\qquad\qquad\qquad\qquad\qquad$ [*A* 469, *M* 334]

Here is the theatrical gesture, but can it be virtue actively to accept
a code that your inner nature rejects? If the gesture is an
acknowledgement of her betrayal of herself as artist, and also of
her fellow-artists, then the money she flings at the Players can be
seen as conscience-money. But are they worth it – the gesture implies
contempt too – since they have betrayed themselves already? They
have gone over to the mob in their own way, dumbly acquiescing
in their own banishment, dancing their own defeat, tongue-tied by
authority.

It is impossible to conclude that all the factors in the play add
up to a whole number. Structurally its parts are disproportionate.
The first scene is both too long as an introduction, raises issues that
are not satisfactorily developed and fails to introduce others that
are. The major concerns of the play are not integrated. There is a
good case for saying that none of the characters have the dramatic
substance to inhabit the same play as Decima and Septimus. The
Old Men, the two poets, the Stage Manager, the Citizens, the
Countrymen are all mere puppets. This is one weakness of the play:
both Decima and Septimus are too big for their setting. Decima in
all her complexity, a part written with the multi-faceted personality
of Mrs Patrick Campbell in mind, like Shylock in *The Merchant of
Venice,* shatters the comic framework of the play. The treatment
of the episodes varies wildly. Yeats has failed to give it that

consistency of tone that makes its descendant, *The Herne's Egg,* much more effective. But at the same time one is left with the impression of a fitful, uncoordinated dramatic vitality, sometimes traditional, as in the scenes between Septimus, Decima and Nona, sometimes bizarre and unconventional, as in the beast/dance, and, lurking behind the action with his secrets like some metaphysical Ben Gunn, the figure of the Old Beggar and his donkey-bray. Indeed its hee-haw seems to voice the whole tone of mockery in the play, as if Yeats were blowing a raspberry at his own thought (though why he should want to is another matter); to concentrate in its cacophany the mood of deflation, the denial of expectations raised, the reduction to the absurd and the trivial. For in the end what does the New Dispensation bring? For Nona nothing; for the Queen disappearance, this time for good; for the Players the bleak rewards of their retreat; for the Prime Minister a life not with the servile Queen but the dominant Decima; for the Citizens and Countrymen life as before; for Septimus the frustration of his vision – there is no cataclysm – and continued alienation from his audience, continued service to his inspiration, the search for rhymes, the tapping out of rhythms, on a new shoulderblade perhaps, but still the same old grind; for Decima alliance with the second rate, the betrayal of spiritual majesty – a bleak revelation indeed.

The Hour Glass

It is inevitable that a play whose composition and revision were spread over twenty years should reflect widely differing attitudes and techniques. Its thematic base – the conflict between opposing orders of experience, reason and faith, intellect and intuition – looks back to *The Shadowy Waters,* with its conflict between a transcendental and natural love. Just as in the *Acting Version* of that play Yeats paralleled that conflict by contrasting prose and verse, so in this play, which was originally written in prose, he came to realize the necessity of raising the level by the introduction of verse. The element of conversion in *The Shadowy Waters* – for Forgael and Dectora are each to some extent converted to the other's attitude – is made a structural principle in *The Hour Glass,* which in essence turns on the conversion of the Wise Man from one kind of wisdom based on the view that there is 'nothing but what men can see when they are awake. Nothing, nothing' [*CPl* 306] to another, based on the view that

> We perish into God and sink away
> Into reality – the rest's a dream.
>
> [*CPl* 322]

This is a movement from prosaic appearance to poetic reality, from reflection to illumination. The idea is a little more complicated than that stark opposition would seem to indicate, since the play also turns to some extent upon the ironic ambiguities implied in the 'dream'. Is this an illusion or a vision of the truth?

The original version, printed in the *North American Review* in September 1903, was subtitled 'A Morality', and the play adopts the morality-play convention by which characters stand for ideas or attitudes. There is no point in looking for 'character-development' in Bridget, the Pupils, or the Fool, but there is in the case of the Wise Man, whose conversion is rooted in his own spiritual resources. The mood in which such a conversion can and does fructify, 'a crisis of the spirit' [*CPl* 308] 'spiritual terror', reflects not only the early

77

The Unicorn from the Stars (1907) but also the later poetry of 'The Supernatural Songs' [*CP* 327] and 'A Prayer for my Daughter' [*CP* 211]. In terms of dramatic convention the externalization of the morality-play tradition is married with the interiorization suggested by the Faust-like agony of the Wise Man who also 'has but one bare hour to live', and by his Lear-like spiritual odyssey.

Bridget and the Pupils have the simplicity of caricature, a simplicity which Wilfrid Scawen Blunt put his critical finger on after the first performance of the original version, which he castigated as 'a stupid imitation of that dull old morality "Everyman", which bored me so much last year. What Yeats can mean by putting such thin stuff on the stage I can't imagine' – (quoted by Bushrui, *YCE* 34). Bridget and the Pupils are indeed 'thin stuff'. It is a fundamental weakness of the play that Yeats should have made his representatives of reason so unreasonable and uninteresting and thus failed to explore his central conflict. The Pupils simply repeat parrot-wise the Lockean assertions of their master, and Bridget has ceased to think of anything at all except housework. The interest of the piece lies in the Wise Man and in Teigue the Fool.

Teigue is a Yeatsian invention. The story on which the play is based, 'The Priest's Soul', which Yeats read in Lady Wilde's collection *Ancient Legends of Ireland,* 1887, (reprinted in *VPl*), has no Fool: the Priest's soul is saved by a little child. Frank Fay's performance elicited Yeats's admiration: he called it 'beautiful, wise and subtle' [*L* 409]. Although Yeats is clearly right in implying, in the same letter, that the Fool remains within the morality-play tradition of characterization in that 'it has to be created more or less from without', the subtlety of the role has not always been perceived. Clearly he represents a kind of vision – he *sees* things – and in the end the Wise Man accepts vision as superior to reason, but it is not at all certain that the Wise Man's vision and the Fool's are the same, or that the play shows 'the wisdom of the fool putting down that of the wise man' [Ellis-Fermor, *IDM* 108], or that it is the Fool who saves the Wise Man [Nathan,*TD* 89], or, as Orwell said [*PCA* 192], that the Fool, 'God's Fool', 'the natural born innocent . . . is always wiser than the wise man.' Orwell also said: 'If it is really true that a village idiot, as such, is wiser than a philosopher, then it would be better if the alphabet had never been invented' [*PCA* 192]. The play does not suggest this.

The first thing that strikes one about the Fool is the banality of his language, the poverty, the meanness, of his imagination. His account of 'the invisible' country [*CPl* 301] is merely an extension of what the First Pupil has already said; and his account of what he has heard and seen [*CPl* 304] is a description of appearances, not an interpretation of them, and even the explanation he gives of them is second-hand. His highest flight of imagination is his account of how men try to snare angels in nets, and how he cuts the nets with his shears and releases them. It is not fair to blame Yeats for not being Shakespeare, but nowhere does Yeats's Fool approach the inspired reason-in-madness of *King Lear*'s Fool. But then he is not meant to.

His words at his first appearance (incidentally he should be carrying a pair of shears with him when he comes in) strike a note that echoes throughout the play: a calculated materialism, a peasant cunning based on money. He can do nothing, say nothing, except for money. Even food is less important to him than money – 'Give me a penny'; the phrase become his *leitmotiv*. Both just before and immediately after the Wise Man dies he will only tell what he knows for money. There is nothing here of the Shakespearean Fool's pathetic affection for King Lear, only a crafty calculation – at one stage he ups the stakes to fourpence – and an ignorance that looks like superior wisdom but isn't. The subtlety in the treatment of the Fool lies not in the suggestion that he knows more than he says, but that he does not understand what he intuitively knows. This is what he should try to convey, for he combines the blessed simpleness of the seer and the shallowness of the simpleton – qualities that are caught in the superb mask that Gordon Craig designed for the part.

The second important thing about the Fool is that he is incapable of interpreting his vision. He has the innocence of the child but also his lack of understanding. This is part of the point of the scene which begins when some Pupils enter with him and dance about him [*CPl* 310]. Visually – the visual effects in Yeats's drama should never be underestimated – the Pupils sit like children round their master, but the irony of the scene is that they are wiser than he, and even he, and even they, in the context of the play as a whole, are not wise. Conversely it suggests the childishness of the Pupils' 'reason': they are still children in that their reason lacks intelligence. All that the Fool can answer to their snatches of song (which develop his references to the roles of wild creatures and the angels) is 'give me a penny', and to the disputation that follows between the Wise Man and the Pupils he has nothing to contribute, not even when the Wise Man offers him proof 'that an Angel / An instant ago was standing on that spot' [*CPl* 314], nor when the 3rd Pupil says that 'Teigue sees angels' [*CPl* 314], nor does he reply to the Second Pupil's question, 'What sort are the angels, Teigue?' [*CPl* 315]. He remains on stage, silent and unhelpful in the face of the Wise Man's growing perturbation. The first version's stage-direction suggests what Teigue is doing: *'sitting on a stool by the door, reckoning on his fingers what he will buy with his money'* [*VPl* 618]. His mind cannot detach itself from that level. At the final crisis, when the Wise Man has only the Fool left to answer his question, he will not answer, except to explain how in reply to the bodach on the road he clings tighter to his money. He goes off-stage, leaving the Wise Man to discover his truth alone.

It is true the Fool has vision, but it is an inarticulate vision, one that he is unable either to interpret or to carry over into his mind so that subsequent understanding can affect action. He says nothing; he remains the Fool fixed in his folly. His identification at the end of the play of himself and the now dead Wise Man – 'We are the two fools, we know everything but we will not speak' [*CPl* 323] – is patently foolish, for the simple reason that the Wise Man has indeed seen, conceptualized what he has seen, spoken and acted. The Fool remains passive, unthinking, although witness to the reality of vision. He begins the play as Fool and ends it as Fool. He has learned nothing.

This view is corroborated by the way Yeats uses his stage space. The action begins on the forestage and it ends there, with the Fool standing outside the stage curtains. The central action of the play, the Wise Man's discovery of non-rational reality and its consequences takes place on what may be called the inner stage, behind the stage curtain, from which everyone else, all the representatives of reason, are excluded. The Wise Man dies alone in his vision and in his belief. The Fool is there but is unable to share either and ultimately excludes himself from it.

The way in which the action turns on itself gives it coherence. The reality of dream, in the sense of non-rational truth, which the Wise Man comes to accept, is announced by the Fourth Pupil at the very opening of the play, though he treats the dream as something nonsensical:

Last night I dreamt that some one came and told me to question him. I was to say to him 'You were wrong to say there is no God and no soul – maybe, if there is not much of either, there is yet some tatters, some tag on the wind – so to speak – some rag upon a bush, some bob-tail of a god.' I will argue with him – nonsense though it be – according to my dream, and you will see how well I can argue, and what thoughts I have.

[*CPl* 299–300]

This is followed by a scene of visual irony in which Teigue is made to crouch down in the shape of an eagle-shaped lectern in a church, from which, it is implied, God's truth can be read out. But what issues from this lectern is certainly not the right cry of an eagle-cock, as the Third Pupil comments, but only the Fool's 'Give me a penny'. Visually the point can be made when the Wise Man's study is revealed as the stage curtains are opened to show him sitting at his desk. That desk should be shaped like a lectern, and on it the Pupils place a book from which the First Pupil reads out the 'text' whose truth the play's action confirms:

'There are two living countries, one visible and one invisible, and when it is summer there, it is winter here, and when it is November with us, it is lambing-time there'.

[*CPl 301*]

The first Latin sentence – 'I argue day and night, but those whom I have chosen, whom I have loved, are being brought to trial' confirms the visual irony of the Wise Man's appearing as the teacher who himself is to become the pupil. Again the Fourth Pupil is used ironically to foreshadow the conclusion as the Wise Man pursues in his own mind the implications of his premonition that the 'text' may be true. But only he has the intellectual courage and moral integrity to follow this line of speculation through. The others cannot. Theatrically this is established by the way in which the language moves into the intensified verse of what is in essence the Wise Man's soliloquy. There is no communication between the two worlds, so that dialogue becomes impossible. The Pupils, representatives of reason, go off stage, leaving the Wise Man alone with the Fool:

> *Wise Man:* Were it but true, 'twould alter everything
> Until the stream of the world had changed its course,
> And that and all our thoughts had run
> Into some cloudy thunderous spring
> They dream to be its source –
> Aye, to some frenzy of the mind;
> And all that we have done would be undone,
> Our speculation but as the wind.
> I have dreamed it twice. . . .
>
> *(Pupils go out)*
>
> Twice have I dreamed it in a morning dream,
> Now nothing serves my pupils but to come
> With a like thought. Reason is growing dim;
> A moment more and Frenzy will beat his drum
> And laugh aloud and scream;
> And I must dance in the dream.
>
> [*CPl 302–3*]

The scene that follows, between the Wise Man and the Fool, establishes the similarity as well as the difference between them. The Wise Man remains the teacher, the Fool, having taken his pennies, the unthinking, obedient pupil:

Wise Man: Well, there are your four pennies − Fool you are called, And all day long they cry, 'Come hither, Fool'.

> *(The Fool goes close to him.)*

Or else it's, 'Fool be gone'.

> *(The Fool goes further off.)*

Or, 'Fool, stand there'.

> *(The Fool straightens himself up.)*

Or, 'Fool, go sit in the corner'.

> *(The Fool sits in the corner.)*
> [*CPl* 307]

Once again the Wise Man's isolation is established by the way in which his speech shifts into soliloquy as the Fool goes off stage, leaving him to confront the Angel whom his own dreams have called up. True to the morality tradition in which the play is written, the Angel externalizes an aspect of the Wise Man's own mind.

Structurally the next scene parallels the first, in which we saw the Pupils first grouped round Teigue, then around the master. The same thing happens again, only with a difference. Intelligence dances like a child around the master who must now try to unteach all that he has taught in the past. All his efforts to do so seem like play-acting to them, but they admire the qualities that he shows, which prefigure the courage, intellectual and moral, that he demonstrates at his death:

> *First Pupil (to other pupils):* You'd think, the way he says it, that he felt it.
> There's not a mummer to compare with him.
> He's something like a man.
>
> [*CPl* 314]

But by arguing with the Pupils and still looking for a proof, the Wise Man is, as the First Pupil says, merely reasoning with himself − a profitless exercise, since what he has experienced is beyond reason. Yeats twists the action back on itself by once again using the Fourth Pupil, who had originally announced the 'text' of the play, this time to deny its truth:

> *Fourth Pupil:* Cease mocking at me, Master,
> For I am certain there is no God
> Nor immortality, and they that said it

> Made a fantastic tale from a starved dream
> To plague our hearts.
>
> [*CPl* 316]

Driven frantic by his situation — he has to find proof for something that cannot be proved — he falls back on Bridget in the male-chauvinistic hope that as a woman she may have some residue of inherited faith in her that has not responded to his arguments. But that fails, since her mind hardly operates at all except to do what her husband tells her and to get on with the household chores. Now totally isolated from her, but prevented from going out in search of a believer himself, the Wise Man retreats into the crumbling shell of his own mind as he perceives the truth that comes to us in intensity, illumination, or death:

> Go call my pupils — I can explain all now.
> Only when our hold on life is troubled,
> Only in spiritual terror can the Truth
> Come through the broken mind.
>
> [*CPl* 318]

When Bridget returns with the Fool in answer to his desperate plan to find someone who has not accepted his rationalistic teaching, it seems that the Fool is that person. But once again his words and his actions belie this. He is only capable of asking for money 'to buy bacon in the shops and nuts in the market, and strong drink for the time when the sun is weak' [*CPl* 319]. His mind simply turns round on itself, since these are precisely the words he had used in his first conversation with the Wise Man [*CPl* 304]. When Bridget goes back to her world, the kitchen, he follows.

Nevertheless it may be suggested that the Fool is the catalyst by which the Wise Man learns, comes to accept vision and is changed by it, becomes the instrument of salvation. But is this true?

Right from the start the Wise Man demonstrates the qualities that take him to the level of heroic dignity. These qualities, intelligence, imagination and an almost heroic integrity that impels him to what Jaspers called boundary-situations, Yeats very soon saw needed verse for their expression since they lift him far above the level of moral platitude. First, his intelligence interprets the passage chosen for the lesson, whereas the Fool can only embroider it:

The beggar who wrote that on Babylon wall meant that there is a spiritual kingdom that cannot be seen or known till the faculties, whereby we master the kingdom of this world, wither away like green things in winter.

> [*CPl* 302]

For the moment his intelligence rejects this view. Then his imagination seizes on its consequence if it were true (the shift from prose to verse is significant):

> Were it but true, 'twould alter everything
> Until the stream of the world had changed its course,
> And that and all our thoughts had run
> Into some cloudy thunderous spring
> They dream to be its source –
> Aye, to some frenzy of the mind;
> And all that we have done would be undone,
> Our speculation but as the wind.
>
> [*CPl 302–3*]

But truth to his own experience – his twice-repeated dream – compels him to face this possibility, which soon, through the symbol of the hawk, conveys by its swiftness, accuracy and power, a sense of supernatural conviction. But at the end of his conversation with Teigue, sceptical intelligence has dismissed it:

> There's nothing but what men can see when they are awake. Nothing nothing.
>
> [*CPl 306*]

Then like a Lear or Macbeth whose language asserts the reality of what he is denying, his dismissal of the spiritual world of superstition ('ghosts') or piety ('angels') creates the very thing he would destroy: the Angel. The Angel, who testifies to the truth of the world of imagination and spirit, should in performance speak in a voice that is different from that of the world of ordinary mortality, as Yeats himself directed:

> . . . when one wishes to make the voice immortal and passionless, as in the Angel's part in my *Hour-Glass,* one finds it desirable for the player to speak always upon pure musical notes, written out beforehand and carefully rehearsed. On the one occasion when I heard the Angel's part spoken in this way with entire success, the contrast between the crystalline quality of the pure notes and the more confused and passionate speaking of the Wise Man was a new dramatic effect of great value.
>
> [*Samhain, 1904, E* 174]

It is not clear from the 1922 version whether Yeats intended that the Fool should see the Angel, though this is probable since the Fool sees Angels even though he does not understand them, but it is absolutely clear that it is not the Fool who points out the Angel to the Wise Man. The Angel corroborates the dream. The Angel's line:

> I am the crafty one that you have called
> [*CPl* 308]

suggests that it was the dream that summoned the Angel, just as Faustus summoned Mephistopheles. In the only passage in the play in which reason operates through argument and not through blind assertion, the Wise Man is hoist by his own petard:

> *Wise Man:* And whither shall I go when I am dead?
> *Angel:* You have denied there is a Purgatory,
> Therefore that gate is closed; you have denied
> There is a Heaven, and so that gate is closed.
> *Wise Man:* Where then? For I have said there is no Hell.
> *Angel:* Hell is the place of those who have denied.
> [*CPl* 308–9]

The Wise Man has the humility to ask pardon, but this humility is no longer presented as it was in the 1903 version as a debasement – the Wise Man does not kneel here, but retains the self-sufficiency that is his strength and which even the Angel recognizes as the supreme moral quality:

> *Angel:* What's dearth and death and sickness to the soul
> That knows no virtue but itself?
> [*CPl* 309]

The disputation with the Pupils only confirms by the reference to Nebuchadnezzar's vision and a repetition of the hawk image the reality of vision:

> *Wise Man:* What proof have I to give, but that an angel
> An instant ago was standing on that spot?
> [*CPl* 314]

Now the ambiguity latent in the word 'dream' becomes apparent: what to one is illusion to another becomes reality seen as a waking dream.

In spite of his new-found recognition of spiritual reality and the place of faith, the Wise Man cannot undo what he has done. He must face, with the same kind of growing spiritual terror that humanizes Faustus, the threat of damnation. But his Devil is his own creation. It is he who imagines upon his own face the 'notch of the

Fiend's nail' [*CPl* 320], he who faces himself with the sound of his coming. True, he takes over the image of the blades of grass as the figure of God's certainty from the Fool's earlier speech, but with this significant difference: that he must speak it out. When Teigue enters blowing the dandelion − a visual parallel to the striking of the clock that punctuates Faustus's last speech in Marlowe's play − he remains inarticulate. In effect the Fool is like the blades of grass that can 'but make their sign into the air' [*CPl* 320].

Bushrui has shown that the moment and manner of the Wise Man's death represent a major alteration. In the 1911 version the Wise Man receives salvation from the Fool *before* he dies, when the Fool confesses to his belief in Angels, and *after* the Wise Man has actually knelt before him and begged for pity. In the 1913 version, the Wise Man still kneels before the Fool, but the Fool says nothing about his belief until after the Wise Man's death. The Wise Man dies in resignation to the will of God. Resignation comes close to the heroic dignity that J. B. Yeats saw as proceeding from the inner mind of the solitary soul by Yeats's addition in the 1914 version of the lines:

> Be silent. May God's will prevail on the instant,
> Although His will be my eternal pain.
> I have no question.
>
> [*CPl* 323]

The Wise Man has found his own salvation. That which he once dismissed as dream has now become the reality into which he perishes; that which he accepted as reality has become a mere dream. What his imagination had earlier seized upon, if the Beggar's inspired *graffiti* on the walls of reason were true, has now become true. The stream of the world *has* changed its course − but with this difference, that the frenzy of the mind which he once saw as the harbinger of irrational chaos he now sees as the spiritual terror which is the matrix of Truth; and that the windy speculation, once referred to the spiritual kingdom, is now applied to the world that the imagination transcends. Truth has come through the broken mind, 'as the pease burst / Out of a broken pease-cod' [*CPl* 318]. The broken mind, the Fool, remains to the end of the play, a witness to the truth of a vision he cannot comprehend.

On Baile's Strand

In this play Yeats achieved his finest success to date in dramatizing
the complex relationship of those forces in whose tensions he found
dramatic conflict and in the resolution of which he saw the essence
of tragedy. The relationship between, on the one hand, man's
limitations, expressed in the characteristically Yeatsian themes of the
process of growing old and the claims of love, friendship, family
affections and social responsibility, and on the other the desire to
achieve a superhuman transcendence of these limitations, expressed
as a gesture which is an assertion and a justification of heroic,
passionate individuality, and also as a kind of cosmic selfishness,
an anarchic delirium of the brave, is worked out in the interplay of
the characters with each other and within themselves, as well as in
the relation of the main plot concerning Conchubar, Cuchulain and
his son to the sub-plot concerning the Fool and the Blind Man.

The handling of this sub-plot, which is one of Yeats's additions
to the source of the play – Lady Gregory's version of the story 'The
Only Son of Aoife' in her *Cuchulain of Muirthemne* – demonstrates
his growing mastery of construction. It also reflects his perception
of the importance of getting his vision across to a theatre audience
by forging a link between the circumstantial world and the eternal.
In the connection between the main plot, grounded in the dignified
emotion of noble humanity, and the sub-plot, grounded in the
reductive meanness of peasant life, he caught that 'emotion of
multitude', that almost limitless reflection of the greater in the lesser
which he was seeking in drama and which he found in Shakespeare's
sub-plots:

We think of *King Lear* less as the history of one man and his sorrows than
as the history of a whole evil time. Lear's shadow is in Gloucester, who
also has ungrateful children, and the mind goes on imagining other shadows,
shadow beyond shadow. . . It is so in all the plays, or in all but all, working
itself out in more ordinary men and women, and so doubly calling up before
us the image of multitude.

[*E&I* 215–6]

(Incidentally the play has more allusions to Shakespeare than any other.) The play, ostensibly set in a past in which superhuman figures and emotions find their natural habitat, even though that habitat and those figures are not immutably fixed in time, is nevertheless rooted in naturalistic psychology, and through its variations of language, ranging from high blank verse to the rhythms of living speech, sends out shoots into the contemporary world of Yeats's own concerns. Yeats himself must have thought of Cuchulain in terms of 'character', as his letter to Frank Fay, who was preparing the role for the first performance, already quoted (p.44), indicates.

The play consists of five episodes, in which the central action of Conchubar, Cuchulain and his son is framed by the first and last. As in so many plays the setting is no mere backcloth: it emblematizes the critical ground on which the inner action is played out – the no-man's-land 'between the door and the sea' [*CPl* 277], between limitation and transcendence, temporality and eternity, the paradoxical 'concordance of achievement and death' [*L* 917].

The first appearance of the Fool and the Blind Man in their 'grotesque and extravagant' masks [*CPl* 247] should strike the keynote of this aspect of the play's meaning. To whatever extent they parallel Conchubar and Cuchulain in their actions and in their attitudes, they are degraded parodies of both – a quality admirably caught by Gordon Craig's masks. Moore is surely right when he describes the Blind Man as a 'degraded Tiresias [who] exemplifies the sinister small-minded prudence and greed forever gnawing at heroic pretension' [*MLD* 108], whose cleverness is suspect. Right, too, is Parkinson [*YSC* 83], who contrasts 'heroes [who] die in magnificent insane rage' with 'peasants [who] conspire to perform an act without the boldness of theft or the intelligence of swindle'. The Fool, for all his contact with the mysterious world of the witches, the air demons Banachas and Bonachas and the evil Fomor, for all the appeal that the vision of heroic action has for him – he can hardly tear himself away from the sight of Cuchulain fighting the waves at the end of the play – like the Fool in *The Hour Glass* remains locked in his uncomprehending childishness. The dependence of the Fool and the Blind Man upon each other and their mutual opposition may indeed parallel the relationship between Cuchulain and Conchubar, but it is a squalid parallel and it contains very different elements. They really are grotesquely, pathetically, and at times comically dependent upon each other, whereas Conchubar and Cuchulain inhabit mutually opposed worlds whose interdependence can only occur at a focus of tragedy. Their driving forces are greed, deception, cowardice and dishonesty. Their superiors evince none of these qualities. They have a dramatic life of their own which makes

them more than expositors of the situation − though they are that
as well − more than projections of the inner qualities of Conchubar
and Cuchulain. Like Falstaff, and even more appropriately, like
Thersites and Pandarus in *Troilus and Cressida*, they become not
only a contrast to the heroic world of Cuchulain and to the socially
responsible and stable world of Conchubar, but a destructive
commentary on them. They are squalid and puerile in themselves
and their function is continually reductive. The great woman-fighter
that Cuchulain got the mastery over in the North becomes merely
'one of those cross queens that live in hungry Scotland' [*CPl* 252];
Aoife, the malignant spirit of hatred and destructiveness, who
presides, though unseen, over the play, becomes in the Fool's
imagination a mere cap thrown in the air; Cuchulain's rage becomes
a petty squabble; hawk's feathers, the symbol of heroic birth as in
the story 'The Wisdom of the King', become the feathers of a
domesticated barnyard fowl, stolen at that; Cuchulain's anarchic
individualism degenerates into parasitism. These qualities should,
in performance, be reflected in their voices, their intonation, their
gestures and clothing. They are representative of a degenerating
contemporary world, hostile to heroism.

The parody element as well as the Shakespearean parallelism
becomes immediately apparent when the Blind Man plays Conchubar
to the Fool's Cuchulain, as the Prince plays his own father to
Falstaff's Hal in the tavern at Eastcheap, and introduces both the
oath-taking scene and the theme of fatherhood:

Blind Man: He will sit up in this chair and he'll say: 'Take the oath,
Cuchulain. I bid you take the oath. Do as I tell you. What are your wits
compared with mine, and what are your riches compared with mine? And
what sons have you to pay your debts and to put a stone over you when
you die?

[*CPl* 249]

But the Fool's response, '*crumpling himself up and whining*. . . ''I
want my dinner'' ' [*CPl* 249], is in his own character, not
Cuchulain's. The *Lear*-like snatches of song are indeed proleptic,
in that they foreshadow Cuchulain's fight with the non-human
element of the sea, and pick up the theme of witchcraft which has
already been established in the Fool's first two speeches, but there
is little of the *Lear* Fool's perception of the truth in Yeats's figure,
except in the way he sees through the Blind Man's lies. The last of
the Shakespearean echoes in this first episode is of another Fool −
Lancelot Gobbo in a state of conflict between his conscience and

his evil spirit over the question of leaving Shylock's service. Here, the Fool fails out of cowardice to ask Cuchulain who the young man's father is, and slips away fearfully, while repeating his snatch of song celebrating Cuchulain's bravery and exploits, which in the context of his death by water has an ironic effect. This hero is doomed.

The specific age that Yeats assigns to Cuchulain, 40, is a departure from the tradition in which he is generally described as dying young, and also a change introduced into this revised version. In the earlier version Cuchulain, though a good deal older than the young Kings who are his companions, is described as 'still young' [*VPl* 472]. The detail, together with verbal echoes in Cuchulain's description of Aoife of passages in the poems that relate to Maud Gonne and himself (*Comm. Pl* 103] is a clue to the autobiographical element in the play. Critics have noted that Cuchulain ages with the poet, but, more importantly, his ageing is part of the process by which Yeats complicates the oversimple youth/age contrast of the earlier version. His ageing is necessary in order to give a convincing naturalistic basis for Cuchulain's desire for fatherhood, the product of his inevitable bondage to time and ordinary human feeling. He knows he is no longer young, but is unwilling to recognize that the change in himself demands a readjustment of attitudes:

> I understand it all.
> It's you that have changed. You've wives and children now,
> And for that reason cannot follow one
> That lives like a bird's flight from tree to tree. –
> It's time the years put water in my blood
> And drowned the wildness of it, for all's changed,
> But that unchanged.
>
> [*CPl* 261]

In a gesture that is reminiscent of the recklessness of an Antony, or the stubborn rigidity of a Coriolanus who thinks his own passionate nature can bind human affection to his own will, he traps himself in swearing to be obedient to Conchubar and to uphold his children. Then, when the arrival of the Young Man awakens in him not only the memory of Aoife but all his suppressed instincts for human relationships, which are inevitably destructive of his anarchic individualism, he thinks he can abjure the oath. He is trapped within the jaws of his own divided nature, just as Conchubar is wholly confined by the demands of his social role as High King. What else can they do? Conchubar must assert his social authority, Cuchulain must assert his individualistic ethos.

That there is an essential opposition between them is the theme
of the second episode, which is externalized in the argument between
the two men, an argument in which Conchubar has a very strong
case:

> *Cuchulain:*   I'll not be bound.
> I'll dance or hunt, or quarrel or make love,
> Wherever and whenever I've a mind to. . . .
> *Conchubar:*   I would leave
> A strong and settled country to my children.
>
> [*CPl* 255]

But it is an argument that is subtilized by the complexities of both
men. Conchubar's anger and scorn at Cuchulain's anarchic and
individualistic behaviour is a reflection of his subconscious envy of
Cuchulain, which breaks out finally in his assertion of authority:

> No more of this. I will not have this friendship.
> Cuchulain is my man, and I forbid it.
>
> [*CPl* 270]

In the same way Cuchulain's totally unreasonable contempt for
something that Conchubar cannot help – after all, we all have to
get older – is a reflection of Cuchulain's subconscious recognition
that he cannot escape his human condition either. It is significant,
too, that at the very point and on the very issue on which he seems
most opposed to Conchubar, love, when Cuchulain rejects the sort
of emasculating domestic affection that is associated with
Conchubar's defence of 'threshold and hearthstone', and when he
opposes to it his own rapt vision of love as a passionate momentary
'forgiveness between opposites' [*CPl* 259], his reminiscence of Aoife
should reach its climax in the very image of family and social
responsibilities that he is ostensibly rejecting:

> Ah, Conchubar, had you seen her
> With that high, laughing, turbulent head of hers
> Thrown backward, and the bowstring at her ear,
> Or sitting at the fire with those grave eyes
> Full of good counsel as it were with wine,
> Or when love ran through all the lineaments
> Of her wild body – although she had no child,
> None other had all beauty, queen or lover,
> Or was so fitted to give birth to kings.
>
> [*CPl* 258–9]

It is from these fancies that Conchubar calls Cuchulain down to earth again. This call is reinforced by that of the Kings, not only the old, who may be expected to support Conchubar anyway, but also the young. There is nothing to suggest that Conchubar has rigged their support, so that Cuchulain's opposition begins to look like childish obstinacy. His behaviour reminds us of the 'boy' in Coriolanus. In spite of Yeats's own explanation that Cuchulain is 'the fool – wandering passive, houseless and almost loveless. Concobhar is reason that is blind because it can only reason because it is cold. Are they not the cold moon and the hot sun?' [L 425], it is a mistake to see Conchubar as an imperceptive ('blind') upholder of the rational, prudential, domestic and social virtues as if these were inherently inferior to the passion and imagination of Cuchulain. Conchubar is perceptive, and, if wisdom involves the ability to hold opposing qualities in solution, then he justifies his claim to it. He perceives the truth about Aoife, that she is possessed by hatred and will stop at nothing to destroy Cuchulain, and he perceives the truth about Cuchulain – 'I know you to the bone' [CPl 257] – that he is caught up in conflicting claims. Like 'ancient Ireland' of 'Under Ben Bulben' he 'knew it all'.

> Many times man loves and dies
> Between his two extremities
> That of race and that of soul
>
> [CP 398]

Cuchulain's fate is that he must act out this dilemma in a way which to the rest of the world seems, even if it holds a bewildering fascination for its recklessness, actually mad.

The third episode, the oath-taking ritual, also an innovation in this revised version, is something of a puzzle. Yeats's stage directions to the Chorus of Women and to Cuchulain [CPl 262–3] indicate that it hardly matters whether the audience hears what the Women have to say after the first few words. If these instructions are followed then it would seem that the general effect of the scene is, as Moore puts it [MLD 115], 'to suggest the barbaric solemnity of an occasion when the "evil" spirits may be hovering very close to those engaged in exorcising them'. On the other hand, what they say is extremely relevant and therefore ought to be heard. The chant of the women is an exorcism – ineffectual in the event – of the Shape-Changers, who are, as Nathan explains [TD 134], 'witches, actually Celtic goddesses . . . representing the super-natural forces, the mysterious, attractive powers that enter the life of the hero and inspire him both to greatness and ruin'. They are also destructive forces that externalize Cuchulain's own rejection of threshold and hearthstone. Like the Weird Sisters in *Macbeth* they destroy those who collaborate with them:

> But the man is thrice forlorn,
> Emptied, ruined, wracked, and lost,
> That they follow, for at most
> They will give him kiss for kiss
> While they murmur, 'After this
> Hatred may be sweet to the taste'.
> Those wild hands that have embraced
> All his body can but shove
> At the burning wheel of love
> Till the side of hate comes up.
>
> [*CPl* 262–3]

The rhythmical and verbal parallel is clear:

> He shall live a man forbid;
> Weary sev'nights, nine times nine,
> Shall he dwindle, peak and pine.
> Though his bark cannot be lost,
> Yet it shall be tempest-tost.
>
> [*Macbeth* I, iii, 21–5]

The lines are proleptic; that is why they should be heard. The Shape-Changers are clearly intended to be the same as the witches mentioned at the beginning of the play by the Fool, one of whom is thought to have maddened Cuchulain enough to attack the High King and to kill the Young Man whom he comes to see as their agent. To the Fool, who leaves the door of the Assembly hall open for them to enter by, they are not hostile, because he has nothing in him of the heroic quality that can lead to heroic transcendence. The chant of the three Women − again the three Weird Sisters of *Macbeth* come to mind, as well as the Fates of Greek mythology − brings us into the presence of the supernatural. The change from blank verse to rhymed tetrameters marks the shift.

But the chant fails to exorcize them. The entry of the Young Man, educated by Aoife to be the cause of his father's death, immediately after it indicates that a supernatural force centred in Aoife and the Shape-Changers presides over the action. Cuchulain too is subject to their power. Their power is felt in the sub-plot as well, since the Blind Man's blindness is a punishment from the Shape-Changers for his cursing them. The action may not be conditioned by this supernatural force – like the action of *Oedipus Rex* it is perfectly intelligible on the human plane, since Cuchulain and Conchubar do what they do because they are what they are – but the human action is given significance by being seen as part of a greater reality which includes the interpenetration of human and supernatural. For those reasons Cuchulain's speech from 'I'll take and keep this oath' to 'Should that be in the oath' [*CPl* 263] should not be spoken *against* the chant of the Women but inserted in it, after their line 'Of the ungoverned unicorn' [*CPl* 262]. After they have ended their song, the stage action should continue with two of the Women crouching in front of Cuchulain, holding the bowl above their heads while he spreads his hands over the flame as in the stage direction in *CPl* 262. He can then speak the last two lines of his speech. The song in the stage direction *'The song grows louder . . .'* [*CPl* 264] should be omitted and Cuchulain's prayer 'O pure, glittering ones . . .' should be answered dramatically by the knocking – one is tempted to write at the gate – which heralds, however, not as in *Macbeth*, the entry of the forces of good, Lennox and Macduff, but the agent of death. Further, if the chant of the Women is accompanied in performance by some kind of music, this should be repeated both when Cuchulain comes under the influence of witchcraft [*CPl* 268] and again, more insistently, when somewhat unconvincingly he acknowledges this influence [*CPl* 270].

Everything possible should be done in performance to make the entry of the Young Man effective. Two things must be established: first, that the Young Man is of heroic mould: he must be, in physique, appearance, gesture and voice, as impressive, as glittering and as golden as Cuchulain. Something of this effect must have been achieved by lighting in the 1904 production at the Abbey theatre, which Willie Fay described:

When the doors opened to Aoife's son, he stood silhouetted against a background of topaz blue, giving an effect of sea and sky, with an atmosphere that could never be obtained by paint.

[*IT* 253]

Secondly, Cuchulain's throwing himself between the Young Man and the rushing Kings must come across as a gesture that has behind it all the force of his suppressed desire to acknowledge fatherhood. Cuchulain's words:

> Put up your swords,
> He is but one
>
> [*CPl* 264]

may echo Othello's 'Keep up your bright swords, for the dew will rust them', but there is nothing here of Othello's deliberation, his dignified self-control. The gesture is an embodiment of that irrepressible, undeniable, and essentially human instinct for kinship and society that is one of the poles on which this fourth episode turns. This now *enacts* the emotions that had been expressed in the second episode as subconscious forces. The other pole, of course, is its opposite: the assertion of individuality. The dramatic strength of this scene lies in their ironic connection: it is only by his assertion of individuality that Cuchulain can achieve community. Or, to put the situation in another way, the community that he wants to establish is one that he claims the right to choose for himself and that has meaning only for himself, blind to the realization that in doing so he is repudiating the larger community to which by his oath of loyalty to the High King he has already committed himself, and that, so long as he persists in this attitude, he is alienating himself from it. In a real sense alienation, madness, is the only possible outcome, and it is not surprising that Conchubar, amazed at the lengths to which Cuchulain will go to assert his individuality, can only attribute his behaviour to the influence of witchcraft. It is beyond the range of ordinary human behaviour:

> O! tell her
> I was afraid, or tell her what you will.
> No; tell her that I heard a raven croak
> On the north side of the house, and was afraid.
>
> [*CPl* 268]

There must be a stunned silence after these words before Conchubar speaks, and Cuchulain should move and speak now as if in a trance, from which he only emerges when he claims the right to fight his son. He relapses when he seizes Conchubar and goes out to fight the Young Man. The Women's prediction of the outcome of the fight – it would have been better if Yeats had reverted to the metrical pattern of their earlier chant – is both true and false. It is true that Cuchulain's household will be destroyed by the killing of the Young Man, and in this respect the passage prepares for the revelation that the Young Man is his son, and it is true that Cuchulain has gone out to die [*CPl* 271], but it is not true that Cuchulain will 'meet his end at this unnoted sword' [*CPl* 271]. The Shape-Changers, the Everliving, are capable of deception. Man must find his own truth.

That truth can exist on many levels, which run parallel and intersect. Both conditions are exemplified in the fifth and final episode, in which the two actions are both linked and yet remain curiously distinct. Against the background of clashing swords and the distraught cries of the Women, the Fool and the Blind Man enter, squabbling over their stolen chicken in a quarrel which, even if it is a petty parallel to Cuchulain's rage, is nevertheless as real to them as his is to him. They are only interested in Cuchulain so long as they can involve him in their situation. They ignore his. Their actual dependence on each other does reflect in a general way the interdependence of Conchubar and Cuchulain, but it does not disguise either the difference between them or the separation of the two worlds they inhabit. The Blind Man is just as incapable of entering into the vision of the Fool as Cuchulain is of entering into Conchubar's world of threshold and hearthstone, but, unlike Conchubar's, the Blind Man's world knows nothing of family ties or social responsibility. It knows only physical needs and shabby ways of satisfying them. And the Fool's vision is merely moon-struck, abject and submissive, knowing nothing of Cuchulain's solar vitality. The Fool's snatch of song:

> When you were an acorn on the tree-top,
>   Then was I an eagle-cock;
> Now that you are a withered old block,
>   Still am I an eagle-cock
>
> [*CPl* 274]

seems to hint obliquely at a quality he shares with Cuchulain – his inability to accept the changes imposed by the time-bound process of ageing – while the picture of the hero wiping his sword on the Fool's chicken-feathers more than forges a parallel link between them, it brings Cuchulain into the only world left to him, a sordid, stupid and cowardly world, but the only world in which truth can be known. There is no High King to strike out against now, only an empty chair, a Blind Man crafty and dishonest enough to be concerned solely with his own survival, and a Fool ingenuous and mindless enough to blurt out what he knows without thinking of the consequences.

There are four stages to these consequences in so far as they affect

Cuchulain. His first reaction is to blame 'the pale windy people' [*CPl* 276], and like Congal in *The Herne's Egg,* to pit his manhood against their power ('My sword against the thunder'[*CPl* 276]). But then he realizes that it is not they who are his enemies. They are the forces that have always inspired him, are almost a part of himself, the 'daemons' who bring heroic man again and again to 'the place of choice' [*M* 361]. But if it is not the Shape-Changers who are his enemies, then possibly it is people like Dubthach the Chafer or Laegaire, the servants of the King. But they are too petty; it must have been Conchubar the High King himself. But the world he finds himself in, inhabited by a Fool and a Blind Man, a world of social conformity and mediocrity, is no place for a Cuchulain. He must seek his enemy elsewhere. But the only place where he can find him is the ambiguous no-man's-land between conflicting claims, the threshold and the sea. He goes out at first to find Conchubar, but in his final act of choice realizes that his enemy is not Conchubar, but something bigger than him, the sea, and in his madness, for heroic action in the eyes of the world is always tinged with madness, goes out to fight that which in its infinite complexity, inscrutability, and even hostility, turns love into hatred, self-achievement into self-destruction, and by its very vastness and indestructability is the only thing that there is left for the hero, always striving after that which lies beyond the constricting limitations of the human condition, to fight.

The play ends on a bitter note: the eyes of the world through which this last heroic gesture is seen, however fascinated by it they may be, belong to a Fool whose will is mastered by a Blind Man who sees in that gesture only another opportunity for a display of degeneracy. Together they embody a disease of the spirit which mocks at, and by its mockery, devalues heroic dignity. They shuffle off together, appropriately by the side door, leaving us with – what? The empty stage, with its chairs and throne and great threshold symbolic of domesticity and order, and beyond that the suggestion of the mysterious appeal of the sea, and the enigmatic juxtaposition of a heap of chicken-feathers and a hero's cloak.

Deirdre

> One woman and two men; that is the quarrel
> That knows no mending.
>
> [*CPl* 194]

In these words Conchubar points to the naturalistic foundations, commonplace enough, of the play. The interest for audience and reader lies in the superstructure that Yeats erected on them. For Yeats, the excitement ('I do believe I have made a great play . . . most powerful and even sensational' [*L* 482]) lay, one suspects, not so much in his sense of achievement, whether objectively assessed or coloured by the impressive effect of Mrs Pat Campbell's playing of Deirdre, which would, he was to think more than thirty years later, haunt him upon his deathbed, but rather in the way the selection and compression of his source material, the use of choric musicians, the intricacy of the play's verbal and visual imagery, the drawing of the action into one climactic gesture, all these factors were leading him in the direction of his most distinctive contribution to drama, the dance plays.

The stage setting, *'A guest house in a wood',* is a visualization of the central images in the play, which are expressed both in language and in action: the place is a trap. But beyond it *'the great spaces of the wood, the sky dimming, night closing in'* [*CPl* 171], suggest, as Clark rightly says 'a liberty to be achieved only in a love-death' [*YTDR* 33]. The brazier symbolizes the passion of love from which the torches are lit. These, together with those brought in by Fergus and his followers, both illuminate the lovers in death, and are a symbol of their union — a prefiguring of that radiance from beyond the tombs of Baile and Ailinn that will later illuminate Ribh's holy book. Symbolism is carried over from décor into movement, as Clark points out:

On the opposite side of the stage is the chess table suggesting that the action has many qualities of a game played according to the rules. Although . . . the men usually stand near the chess table and the women near the brazier, Deirdre moves back and forth as she fluctuates between passion and craft, fear and honour.

> [*YTDR* 35]

98

The realization of the symbolic qualities of the setting seemed within reach by the use of Gordon Craig's scene:

The barbarous dark-faced men, who have not hitherto been all I imagined (perhaps because our stage is shallow), will not show themselves directly to the eyes when they pass the door, nor will the dark-faced messenger when he comes and says that supper's ready, nor it may be Conchubar when he comes to spy and not to fight. I will see passing shadows and standing shadows only. Perhaps the light that casts them may grow blood-red as the sun sets, but of that I am not sure. I have tried these shadows upon the stage and thought them impressive, but as I have not tried them before an audience I leave the old directions for the present.

[*PAIT, VPl* 396]

Suggestiveness would help lessen the impact of a too-insistent psychological naturalism which makes Fergus and Naoise at times obtuse.

The Musicians do not create a complete framework for the play's action. They introduce it but do not complete it. They begin the play outside the action, which then takes over from them (much as the action of Shakespeare's *Pericles* takes over from the chorus figure of Gower) and in which they participate and on which they comment. Life, in the form of actions that are the product of various human emotions acted out in the temporal world, love, trust, jealousy, betrayal, overwhelms the impulse to shape it into a tidy structure. The Musicians' 'tale' is completed not by them but by Naoise, Conchubar and Deirdre, whose interaction creates the situation which brings about the end of the story. Not until it is ended can art – the completed play – embody it in a structure that lifts it out of time. The raw material of legend, temporal actions, becomes timeless when woven into the fabric of art. This is the inmost theme of the play. It bears witness to the power of art to create a deathless image.

The opening dialogue of the Musicians not only gives us the beginning of the story but also establishes them as artists, and finally introduces one of the image-clusters that occur throughout the play, the prefiguring of Deirdre's and Naoise's apotheosis 'Somewhere beyond the edges of the world' [*CPl* 172], in terms of hills, mountains, woods, later to be strengthened by the contrast between eagles and valley-keeping birds.

Fergus recognises the Musicians' praise of love but ironically thinks it is a matter of luck [*CPl* 173] that they – who have already said that they have come by chance to Conchubar's guest-house [*CPl* 171] – will have Deirdre and her man to celebrate in their story. Neither he nor they can know at this stage that the story cannot be

completed until Deirdre and Naoise have by their own wills turned
chance into choice and so fulfilled their tragic destiny which it is
the play's concern to celebrate. Yeats must manipulate his fable in
such a way that what appears to be necessity is in fact freedom; that
the trap is not a trap but a means of escape into another order of
reality.

Fergus's role is the least satisfactory in the play, in that his
symbolic and naturalistic functions are hard, if not impossible, to
reconcile. Symbolically he stands for belief in a code of honourable
conduct, which is going to be betrayed by Conchubar, for belief in
the value of political expediency – 'it was policy to pardon them'
[*CPl* 174] – which is going to be subordinated to the urgencies of
personal passion, and for disbelief in the value of art, which for him
is a mere 'dazzle of old fabulous tales' [*CPl* 176] that bear no
relation to reality as he sees it, tales that are created by artists who
are no more than 'wanderers . . . [who] would have weighed / Some
crazy fantasy of their own brain / Or gossip of the road with
Conchubar's word '[*CPl* 181], but who are useful not as seers of
the truth, but as mere entertainers, good for

> a verse
> Of some time not worth remembering,
> And all the lovelier because a bubble.
>
> [*CPl* 176]

Ultimately he sees them as 'cockscombs' [*CPl* 177]. In so far as
he represents a level of comprehension that is blind to the insights
of the imagination, it seems incongruous that he should speak in
verse. Naturalistically he is implausible on three counts: in his
complacent belief in Conchubar's promise of forgiveness for the
lovers, in his refusal to entertain seriously the possibility of the old
king's jealousy, in his obtuseness in failing to recognize the purpose
behind the presence of Conchubar's henchmen, whose strange non-
Irish appearance should be enough to put anyone on his guard.

The commonsense suggestion of the Musicians that the truth of
the matter is that Conchubar is simply jealous, that political
calculations are of less weight than irrational feelings, their suspicions
of Conchubar's 'murderous purpose' [*CPl* 175] and now Fergus's
own ironic reference to the story of Lugaidh Redstripe, later
expanded by Naoise [*CPl* 179], all help to build up an atmosphere
of inevitable doom. This is established by the song the Musicians
sing [*CPl* 177]. The first stanza picks up the apotheosis image-
cluster:

> 'Why is it', Queen Edain said,
>   'If I do but climb the stair
> To the tower overhead,
>   When the winds are calling there,
> Or the gannets calling out
>   In waste places of the sky,
> There's so much to think about
>   That I cry, that I cry?'

The second establishes that the motive-force pushing the lovers to their choice is their internal passion born out of 'immoderate thought' that rejects half-measures and in the end will not bargain:

> But her goodman answered her:
>   'Love would be a thing of naught
> Had not all his limbs a stir
>   Born out of immoderate thought;
> Were he anything by half,
>   Were his measure running dry.
> Lovers, if they may not laugh,
>   Have to cry, have to cry.'

Finally the third stanza repeats the hunting/trap image-cluster in the traditional image of lovers united in the symbolic conjunction of the apple and the yew after death, which prefigures their end:

> But is Edain worth a song
>   Now the hunt begins anew?
> Praise the beautiful and strong;
>   Praise the redness of the yew;
> Praise the blossoming apple-stem.
>   But our silence had been wise.
> What is all our praise to them
>   That have one another's eyes?

The positioning of Deirdre and Naoise on stage after their entry [*CPl* 178] is a visual reinforcement of their attitudes. Deirdre, responsive to the Song and its implications — Naoise at this point ignores the Musicians — and naturalistically concerned with how she looks, moves symbolically over to the Musicians at the brazier, uneasily afraid that in obeying Naoise she is being false to her own nature, which, nurtured in the woods and on the hills, is opposed to social codes:

> It is my husband's will
> I show my trust in one that may be here
> Before the mind can call the colour up.
> My husband took these rubies from a king
> Of Surracha that was so murderous
> He seemed all glittering dragon. Now wearing them
> Myself wars on myself, for I myself —
> That do my husband's will, yet fear to do it —
> Grow dragonish to myself.
>
> [*CPl* 178]

Naoise at this point shares Fergus's trust in the King's word, though not his complacency nor his readiness to ignore the possibility that trust may turn out to be treachery. Naoise has to be *led* to the chess-board. If it is treachery, then true to his code of honour he should meet it with an 'equal mind' [*CPl* 180], just as Lugaidh Redstripe and his wife met theirs. Deirdre's comment

> An empty house upon the journey's end!
> Is that the way a king that means no mischief
> Honours a guest?
>
> [*CPl* 180]

already suggests that she is a very different kettle of fish from

> that woman
> That had but the cold blood of the sea in her veins.
>
> [*CPl* 192]

Left alone with the Musicians, Deirdre faces the possibility, corroborated by them, that they have been trapped, that Conchubar will murder Naoise and keep her as bride. For all her perceptiveness and strength she appeals to Naoise for a second time. That he should respond now as he did when Conchubar first chose her for wife and they began their seven years' wandering upon 'the windy summits' [*CPl* 186], prefigures their final union, even though for a time a gap seems to be opening up between them. Fergus, trapped in his own illusions, dismisses her fears as a mere story:

> You have been listening
> To singers of the roads that gather up
> The stories of the world.
>
> [*CPl* 184]

Deirdre replies that she has a story that beats all others, a story whose ending she sees in Naoise's death and her forced marriage. Her problem is how to avoid that ending with Naoise, how to avoid 'The net of the fowler or the wicker cage' [*CPl* 184]. Now begins the process of her role-playing, her adoption of a series of masks that is not completed until, assured of Naoise's recovered values, she fuses herself and her true mask. Destiny is not merely accepted but chosen, and in the act of choice she achieves tragic stature. But first she must restore Naoise to a belief in personal passion which has been temporarily overlaid by his acceptance of a code of social honour. This she does by provoking not only his jealousy but his anger. Her first impulse is that they should run away together:

> Were we not born to wander?
> These jewels have been reaped by the innocent sword
> Upon a mountain, and a mountain bred me;
> But who can tell what change can come to love
> Among the valleys? I speak no falsehood now.
> Away to windy summits, and there mock
> The night-jar and the valley-keeping bird!
>
> [*CPl* 186]

But Fergus, in an access of common sense, points out the impossibility of this course of action. Deirdre's reply is to suggest a way out of their situation by means of a violent personal gesture that would nevertheless leave her essential being untouched:

> I'll spoil this beauty that brought misery
> And houseless wandering on the man I loved.
>
> [*CPl* 186]

Naoise's fatalism is momentarily strengthened by the arrival of the Messenger, but in the event the message itself convinces him of Conchubar's treachery. Now he sees that the trap has been sprung, the crib has fallen. But there is no point in the captured bird fluttering this way and that in an attempt to escape from the inescapable. Better to act out an aristocratic derision of death in the self-absorption of their high game of chess. It is important that the actor playing Naoise should make the audience see that beneath his assumption of Stoic contempt of fate there is the pressure of an heroic, passionate self-assertion that will eventually propel him beyond the world of political bargaining, clear of the nets of a social code, onto the eternal summits where eagle calls to eagle:

> What need have I, that gave up all for love,
> To die like an old king out of a fable,
> Fighting and passionate? What need is there
> For all that ostentation at my setting? '
> I have loved truly and betrayed no man.
> I need no lightning at the end, no beating
> In a vain fury at the cage's door.
>
> [*CPl* 190]

But their self-absorption is not a solitude. There has been a shift in Naoise's stance. From having first ignored the presence of the Musicians and then dismissed them as mere purveyors of 'gossip of the roads' [*CPl* 184], he recognizes that they are his only friends, that the deaths of Lugaidh Redstripe and his wife and ultimately his own and Deirdre's passion will only achieve a timeless validity when transmuted into song, that Art shapes transient reality into timeless permanence. He gives the order for the torches to be lit.

Deirdre falls in with his mood, but not for long. The external pressure of the Musician's lyric, 'Love is an immoderate thing . . .' [*CPl* 191], which asserts passion as the vehicle of the longing to escape the limits of the natural world, together with the internal pressures of her own being against her adopted role, soon break through the calm of their chess-playing tableau. At root this is artificial for both of them. The intellectual game of chess soon turns into love-play:

> I cannot go on playing like that woman
> That had but the cold blood of the sea in her veins.
> *Naoise:* It is your move. Take up your man again.
> *Deirdre:* Do you remember that first night in the woods
> We lay all night on leaves, and looking up,
> When the first grey of the dawn awoke the birds,
> Saw leaves above us? You thought that I still slept,
> And bending down to kiss me on the eyes,
> Found they were open. Bend and kiss me now,
> For it may be the last before our death.
> And when that's over, we'll be different;
> Imperishable things, a cloud or a fire.
> And I know nothing but this body, nothing
> But that old vehement, bewildering kiss.
>
> [*CPl* 191–2]

In fact each absorbs elements of the other: he her passion, she his control. This interpenetration is the ground of their apotheosis.

Deirdre's reassertion of physical passion shatters the 'steady thinking that the hard game needs' [*CPl* 191], and Naoise's anger at Conchubar's arrival breaks through his surface calm as he rushes out after him, only to be caught in a 'blind-beast rage' [*CPl* 194] that he thought he had suppressed. Deirdre, left alone with the Musicians, breaks out of the world of conditioned fable in which they would have cast her as passionate victim, and in seizing a knife from one of them, begins to direct her own fate, though she recognizes that only when the heroic gesture has been memorialized in art can it be taken out of time and illuminate the temporal world:

> Women, if I die,
> If Naoise die this night, how will you praise?
> What words seek out? for that will stand to you;
> For being but dead we shall have many friends.
> All through your wanderings, the doors of kings
> Shall be thrown wider open, the poor man's hearth
> Heaped with new turf, because you are wearing this
> > (*Gives Musician a bracelet*)
> To show that you have Deirdre's story right.
>
> > > [*CPl* 193–4]

But before the Musicians can do this, they have to get the story right, and they cannot do that until after Deirdre herself has found the right ending for it. As yet she does not know what ending it will have. She first tries building on Conchubar's appearance of mercy:

> He never doubted you until I made him,
> And therefore all the blame for what he says
> Should fall on me.
>
> > > [*CPl* 194]

But when it becomes clear that he intends to keep her alive as a forced bride, her whole being rebels, and as if unable to face the truth of her own earlier premonition, frantically pleads with Conchubar to assert his goodness by pardoning them both. When his implacability proves that hope to be illusory she makes one more attempt to save Naoise at the cost of her own integrity, though it is a cost that she insists has to be underwritten by Naoise himself:

> *Deirdre:* [*to Naoise*]   It's better to go with him
> Why should you die when one can bear it all?
> My life is over; it's better to obey.
> Why should you die? I will not live long, Naoise.

> I'd not have you believe I'd long stay living;
> O no, no, no! You will go far away.
> You will forget me. Speak, speak, Naoise, speak,
> And say that it is better that I go.
> I will not ask it.
>
> [*CPl* 196]

At this point, before the death of Naoise, her femininity still asserts itself in her dependence upon him for strength and her hoping that there is after all some other way out of the trap, that Conchubar will be merciful, that life and death can be bargained for. But she begins to move away from it towards the final role of superhuman heroine, a steel will forged out of the heat of passion, as Yeats's comment, quoted by Ure, implies: 'red-heat up to Naoise's death, white heat after he is dead' [*YTP* 55]. Whereas up to this point she is either playing a part against her own nature − coming to the guest-house in the first place against her own judgement, uneasily accepting the social code, playing the part of a queen playing chess to please her husband, or casting about in a desperate attempt to avoid the necessities of her own being − now she *knows* she has to play a part in order to fuse her inmost being to the image of herself that she has finally chosen and so end the story in the way that she has decided. The theatricality of this ending presents a formidable challenge to the actress, who has to make it clear to the theatre-audience that she *is* playing a part here, indeed a number of parts as she assumes different attitudes, yet must also convince her stage-audience, Conchubar, that she isn't − and all this without drawing attention to her own virtuosity or to her own personality as an actress. It is a measure of Yeats's growing mastery that her language is flexible enough to accommodate the variety of her moods.

The final stage in her development is signalized by her staggering over to the Musicians [*CPl* 198], from where she has to answer Conchubar's demand, surely impausible at this juncture:

> Come to my house now, Deirdre,
> For he that called himself your husband's dead.
>
> [*CPl* 198]

She has to face reality now: Naoise's death, Conchubar's ruthless-ness, her own solitariness. But in that solitariness she finds her strength and, like Cleopatra left alone against Caesar and ultimately outwitting him, beats Conchubar at his own game with the only weapon left to her, her femininity. But it is a femininity that has become so 'marble-constant' that it can turn his own deceit back on his own head. And she uses not only deceit, but flattery, scorn, and mockery, as she raises the stakes in her final game of bluff. Himself now trapped in the cage of his own limited vision of the kingly role, and in his own self-importance, so different from tragic pride, Conchubar, incapable, like King Guaire in *The King's Threshold,* of the imaginative gesture that will lose him a rich prize but gain him a more valuable one, is cheated of his quarry. Her last words are to the Musicians who, resuming their role as commentators, now know how to give expression to the end of Deirdre's story:

> Eagles have gone into their cloudy bed.
>
> [*CPl* 202]

Yet the play ends on an unsatisfactory note. Conchubar, revealed as a deceitful plotter and, what is worse, like Caesar, 'ass unpoliced', must surely, on a naturalistic level, have lost all credibility in the eyes of Fergus and his 'thousand reaping-hooks and scythes' [*CPl* 202], who would certainly make short work of Conchubar's dark-faced body-guard. Yet Yeats, eschewing a naturalistic logic to events, dispenses with their protection, and gives Conchubar sufficient authority to repel their menaces. Why? It is not convincing to argue that he retains the authority of his kingly office, since it is clear that he has subordinated the demands of office to his personal desires. It is no part of an ageing king's duty to insist on marrying a young woman and then go to the lengths of betrayal and murder to fulfil them.

Bushrui remarks [*YVP* 157] that *Deirdre* was the last of Yeats's short verse-plays 'in the traditional grand manner'. This is true, but it also contains stylistic and formal elements that foreshadow the visionary *Plays for Dancers*. Its position as a transitional piece is at the root of its unsatisfactory nature. As a play 'in the traditional grand manner', based fundamentally on psychological naturalism, perhaps a more appropriate ending would have been a tableau in the *Hamlet* manner, with Conchubar destroyed, and the dead lovers illuminated in the radiance of their love. But such a scheme would leave no room for the Musicians, whose role as commentators on and participants in the action is unfortunately confused. As commentators they look forward to the non-naturalistic choric musicians of the dance plays, but this aspect of their role is not consistently handled in *Deirdre*. They move between narrative exposition of the action, through participation in it, to lyrical

comment and back to narrative reporting, though they do show signs
of unifying the metaphorical structure of the language, what Yeats
was later to call 'playing upon a single metaphor.' Corroborating
in lyric verse the passion that is acted out by Deirdre and Naoise,
they concentrate the theme of superhuman love in their song 'Love
is an immoderate thing', which in one way would be more
appropriately placed as the lovers' epitaph and the play's epilogue.
On the other hand they are unable to act the role of lyric
commentators entirely detached from the action. Since it is of the
essence of the play that no matter how strong the sense of a
predetermined end to the story is, they cannot foresee the precise
form it will take, they have to wait until Deirdre has acted it out
for them, and their waiting involves them in the action. This
involvement is clearest in the episode in which they allow Deirdre
to snatch the knife which she conceals on her person and pretend
not to have given it to her. As lyrical commentators pure and simple,
standing right outside the action, they would need no justification
for their presence in the play, just as the Musicians in the later dance
plays need no justification. But because they do in fact participate
in the action, which is conducted primarily on a naturalistic plane,
they therefore need more justification for their presence in the guest-
house than they are given. This uneasy mixture of naturalism and
lyricism is revealed in other areas of the play. Some examples of
implausibility have already been cited. Others are the gagging and
removal of the captured Naoise unseen and unheard by Deirdre. It
is a too-insistent naturalistic detail that injects a jarring note into
the general run of the verse in Deirdre's image of her vulnerability
now that she is alone. 'a single woman'

> Lacking array of servants, linen cupboards,
> The bacon hanging . . .
>
> [*CPl* 199]

Flitches in the larder and sheets in the bottom drawer do not go well
with Libyan dragon-skins, ivory of the fierce unicorn [*CPl* 175],
or with miracle-working stones [*CPl* 183] sewn in the curtains of
a marriage four-poster. But incongruities apart, *Deirdre* is a
significant step on the road that led Yeats to that kind of drama
which Moore has brilliantly defined as one that

> 'purifies' character into symbol, transforms scene into emblem, and
> condenses action into epiphany.
>
> [*MLD* 279]

THE CENTRAL ACHIEVEMENT

At the Hawk's Well, The Only Jealousy of Emer, The Dreaming of the Bones, The Cat and the Moon, Calvary, The Resurrection, The Words Upon the Window-Pane, The King of the Great Clock Tower, A Full Moon in March.

All these plays, with the exception of *The Words Upon the Window-Pane,* reveal features that are characteristic of Yeats's mature drama – the use of verse or a mixture of verse and prose, chorus, mask, dance. These elements are combined in a form that is Yeats's unique contribution to drama. Even *The Words Upon the Window-Pane,* which reverts to the naturalistic drama of illusion, has affinities in theme with many of the verse plays. All were written after Yeats had come into contact with the Pound-Fenollosa version of Japanese Noh plays, in which he found features that confirmed and corroborated his own ideas about drama as they had developed over the years. It would be idle to speculate on the sort of drama that Yeats might have produced had he not read the Pound-Fenollosa plays, but it would be stupid to assert that he would have produced what he did without reading them. He took from Noh drama what suited him.

Broadly speaking what distinguishes these plays from their predecessors is a movement away from naturalism, whether of character, action and its setting in place and time, towards a drama of psychic essences acted out in what Yeats called the deeps of the mind. This movement towards non-naturalistic drama is necessitated by the demands of his subject-matter. This, more and more, is concerned with that moment, necessarily independent of time and place, when the individual by heroic action, greatens, to modify Yeats's phrase [*E&I* 245], until he becomes humanity itself. The moment of this achievement becomes timeless, the place spiritualized.

Since such an action is always that of a hero or is one that makes a person into a hero, more and more Yeats grounded his actions in a world that is populated by heroic figures from myth or legend, such as Cuchulain, Emer and Christ, or by archetypal figures out of timeless folklore, such as Queen and Swineherd, or by figures who suggest generalized qualitities, such as Fool and Blind Man. The

109

Noh, with its concentration, its fusion of language, music and movement, its stylization of character, its ritualization of action, its unity of imagery, helped him to hammer out the kind of drama that was appropriate to his concept of tragedy. He is not concerned to produce a play in which the action, no matter to what extent it supports a structure of conflicting values and attitudes, is designed to present characters whom we are attracted to by pity or repelled by in terror. His dramatic actions are not reflections, not analyses, but epiphanies, dramatizations in terms of speech, movement and visual effects, of spiritual essences and their conflicts, which, simply because they are expressions of the life of the eternal spirit, cannot be confined to the world of finite place and time. For that reason place becomes important either as an externalization of a state of mind, as in *At the Hawk's Well* and *The Dreaming of the Bones,* or as a symbolization of the point where two worlds, human and superhuman, meet – for example, land and sea in *The Only Jealousy of Emer,* the temporal room into which the eternal irrupts in *The Resurrection,* 'the bare place', an abstract area, of *Calvary.* The technique established in the early *The Land of Heart's Desire* and developed in *Deirdre* is brought to fruition. Stage space has become an integral part of dramatic meaning. He is concerned with an action that must lead to a moment of 'passionate intensity' which is its own justification. The frustrating limitations of the temporal world are superbly, contemptuously overcome, in a gesture which at the same time illuminates that world, showing it up as mean and despicable, lacking in the creative wisdom of the imagination.

Of the three main elements that Yeats employs to create his dramatic effect, Mask, Chorus, Dance, it is the Mask that has the most immediate impact. By its very nature it embodies that sense of the changeless beneath the temporal, the general beneath the particular, that is so essential a part of Yeats's vision. Anyone who has had experience in the theatre of masks, or of the carved faces of marionettes, knows the uncanny effect of life-likeness they create in the way that they appear to vary their expression while remaining all the time essentially unchanged. It was Craig and his superb designs for the Fool and the Blind Man more than the Noh convention that opened Yeats's eyes to the dramatic possibilities of the Mask. As Craig wrote [*NDY,* 165]:

The advantage of a mask over a face is that it is always repeating unerringly the poetic fancy, repeating on Monday in 1912 exactly what it said on Saturday in 1909 and what it will say on Wednesday in 1999. Durability was the dominant idea in Egyptian art. The theatre must learn that lesson.

Yeats learned the lesson because he saw that the nature of his vision required the Mask. His masks serve a particular dramatic purpose, not, as in the Noh, an ideal concept of beauty permanent and valid for always and in all circumstances. He permits the grotesque and the ugly because his plays demand them, something which the Noh does not allow.

Yeats wrote in *Certain Noble Plays of Japan* that he had gone to Asia 'for a chorus that has no part in the action' [*E&I* 226], and certainly the choruses of these plays, composed after he had read the Pound-Fenollosa versions, are less involved in the exterior action than that of *Deirdre*. In *Deirdre* the presence of the chorus in the play is to some extent justified naturalistically. They are wandering Musicians who have come by chance to the guest-house where the action is played out. They participate in it. Deirdre snatches the knife with which she kills herself from them and gives them a bracelet with which to commemorate their part in the interior action, which is primarily concerned with the eternalizing power of art. In the latter plays Yeats develops one of the functions of the *Deirdre* chorus – the creation in image and image-clusters of a poetic reality which is supported by mask, costume and movement. The chorus, by poetic intensity and concentration – sometimes, as in *The Only Jealousy of Emer,* by so much concentration as to produce obscurity – by embodying the sovereignty of words over all else, compels us to create a dramatic world in the imagination and thus lead us to the deeps of the mind where the interior action takes place. The chorus is an anti-illusionist dramatic device. It is integral to Yeats's purpose, not a mere experimental gimmick. As such it has many functions. It sets the scene, but nearly always primarily in the mind. Yeats rarely permits himself three-dimensional scenery, such as the bed in *The Only Jealousy of Emer,* the throne in *A Full Moon in March* (two in its predecessor *The King of the Great Clock Tower*), and the cross in *Calvary*. It directs and defines emotion – the awe of the supernatural as it invades the Guardian of the Well in *At the Hawk's Well,* the fear of the Young Man and his terror at the presence of the supernatural in *The Dreaming of the Bones,* the ecstasy of tragic fulfilment at the end of *A Full Moon in March*. It comments – not always solemnly, as in *The Cat and the Moon* – on the action and in commenting extends and enriches it. It serves dramatic and practical economy by speaking as other characters, and in its ritual of the folding of the cloth both helps to create the right theatrical atmosphere and serves a practical function in allowing stage figures to take their place behind it in the acting area unseen by the audience. As Musicians the chorus contributes the musical element to the plays.

This is not nearly so carefully organized as in the Noh tradition, being vaguely impressionistic, merely supportive of movement, or, of course, providing the accompaniment to the climactic dance. Yeats himself said in *Certain Noble Plays of Japan* that *At the Hawk's Well,* the first of the dance plays, was made possible by the Japanese dancer Michio Ito, who danced the part of the Guardian at the Well, but was not himself trained in the Noh tradition. Even though, according to Hiro Ishibashi, a final dance 'is not a fixed rule in the Noh' [*YN* 142], there is one in each of the four plays for dancers (*At the Hawk's Well, The Only Jealousy of Emer, The Dreaming of the Bones* and *Calvary.)* Yeats grasped instinctively that at the heart of the Noh there was an art of rhythmical movement, a movement of the whole body. He perceived that, to quote Richard Taylor's excellent and succinct account of Noh drama

the projection of emotion depends largely on elements of mimetic dance, and every motion of the body is measured in time and space; none are imitations of normal human motions, but are rather expressive movements of abstract purity and restraint which approach the condition of dance, introduce elegant ritual action, and suggest universality.

[*YT* 138]

Thus, for the climactic dance to be successful in performance it must appear as an extension of the norm of movement on the stage, not as something alien superimposed upon it or introduced into it. The dance must grow out of, even as it intensifies, the normal mode of movement.

These features of mature Yeatsian drama, verse composed at various levels of intensity and spoken accordingly, the combination of verse and prose, chorus, mask, dance and stylized movement, all combine to breakdown prosaic illusionism and to achieve that distance from life which Yeats felt was necessary if we are to enter those deeps of the mind where eternally valid spiritual conflicts, which constitute the stuff of his drama, rather than contests of character and character, are worked out.

But Yeats also realized that the deeps of the mind 'can only be approached through what is most human' [*CNPlJ, E&I* 225], so that, however condensed and abstract the plays may be, and however obscure some of the choric writing may be, as indeed it is in *The Only Jealousy of Emer, Calvary* and *The Resurrection,* he generally provides an accessible point of departure from which the audience can begin its journey into the spiritual interior. And frequently he provides, in the chorus, a transition back to the recognizable world of time and space. In *At the Hawk's Well* and *The Only Jealousy of Emer*, as in the earlier *On Baile's Strand* and *Deirdre*, the departure point is psychological naturalism — the conflict between the young and the old, the tensions in the relationships of a man with different sorts of women. In *The Dreaming of the Bones* it is an identifiable historical time and place. *Calvary* and *The Resurrection* are based on traditionally accepted Christian story. *A Full Moon in March* and its inferior predecessor, *The King of the Great Clock Tower*, use easily identifiable archetypal figures who need no explication. Indeed the number of passages that do require explication in terms of Yeats's 'system' is very small. Yeats's drama has suffered from the charge of obscurity, as if its meaning could only be revealed to those who already possess some previously acquired arcane body of knowledge. But the charge cannot be sustained. For example, in *The Dreaming of the Bones, Calvary* and *The Words Upon the Window-Pane,* as well as in the later *Purgatory,* Yeats is at pains to give his audience all the information they need. It is not so much their obscurity that threatens their success on the stage as failures of presentation: for example, the failure to achieve in performance a sense of organic unity whereby action culminates naturally in dance, or the failure to project the full force of the tragic gesture which is the play's dramatic climax. Sometimes the cause of this latter failure is to be laid at Yeats's door. In *At the Hawk's Well* Cuchulain's achievement of heroic individuality is inadequately verbalized, though something can be done in performance to get round this weakness. In *The Only Jealousy of Emer,* on the other hand, Emer's gesture is superbly prepared for and established: the difficulty lies with Eithne. In *The Dreaming of the Bones,* two tragic climaxes must be established and balanced against each other, the frustration of the ghosts and the obdurate rigidity of the Young Man, both leading to the pessimistic and negative conclusion expressed by the chorus. In *A Full Moon in March,* however, there is a continuous crescendo which extends beyond the climactic dance of the Queen with the severed head of the Swineherd into the final chorus, in which death or desecration is transmuted into positive and fructifying joy.

In these plays Yeats achieves a form in which all the aspects of the dramatic vocabulary, speech, movement, décor, are integrated and put to the service of his unique vision.

At the Hawk's Well

This is the first of the plays that Yeats wrote which were the product of the impact on his own views of drama as they had developed over a long period of time of the Japanese Noh drama. What the Noh confirmed in him was his view that the aural and visual aspects of drama were of prime importance and that gesture and movement should not be an imitation of normal bodily actions but an idealized condensation of them. It is this concept of an idealized movement of the body that lies behind his instruction that the characters in this play should move like marionettes. The preface that he wrote for the play's first publication in *Harpers Bazaar,* March 1917, stresses his departure from naturalistic illusionism. All is subordinated to the need to create in the imagination, where alone they can exist, types of permanence. Hence painted scenery and individualized faces yield to verbal pictures and unchanging mask, 'keeping always', as he wrote, 'an appropriate distance from life' so that 'those profound emotions that exist only in solitude and silence' may be aroused in the deeps of our minds.

Although the most impressive feature of the dance plays is the cohesiveness of all the elements of the dramatic vocabulary taken together – the abstract setting, which is not simply a backdrop but part of the symbolic structure of the play in question (in this instance the binding metaphors of bare mountainside, well and thorn-tree), stylized movement, chorus, mask – it is the mask which was probably the most important for Yeats, for already, under the influence of Gordon Craig, he had become interested in masks and had used them before 1916 when *At the Hawk's Well* was first performed in Lady Cunard's drawing-room. As Nathan rightly says:

The significance of the mask . . . is twofold: first, it suggests the superhuman; second, as a stylization or abstraction of nature, it reduces human character to some essential quality.

[*TD* 169]

Nathan is right, too, when he draws a distinction between those figures which are fully masked and those which are only made up to resemble masks:

114

The function of the masks is to simplify the principals to some essential and intense quality defined by the fate that formulates itself in [the] tragic moment of choice. The faces of the muscians and the Guardian of the Well are painted to resemble masks; the muscians are not primarily participants in the action but human observers, and the Guardian is also human until daemonically possessed.

[*TD* 183]

The same distinction is also carried through into *The Only Jealousy of Emer, The Dreaming of the Bones, Calvary,* and *The Cat and the Moon.*

The device of the folding and the unfolding of the cloth serves an obviously practical function as a substitute for a proscenium curtain, but primarily to induce a ritualistic atmosphere within which the audience can be drawn into the imaginative world of the play. This world must be created by the audience in its imagination, and in performance everything must be done to assist this creation. The Musicians, in evoking the scene, also establish the polarities within which the play moves: the passive, debilitating, barren acceptance of age, and the active, productive energies of heroic youth. These contradictory impulses in the human psyche are defined in the contrasting couplets of the First and Second Musician:

> The boughs of the hazel shake. . .
> The heart would be always awake
>
> The sun goes down in the west. . .
> The heart would turn to its rest.

[*CPl* 209]

If these couplets are sung, then the music should also reflect this contrast. After this, the First Musician, in unrhymed, neutral verse that should be differentiated in the speaking of it from the rhymed verse, evokes the Well on the mountainside half-choked by the withered leaves fallen from the hazel tree, protected by the impassive, enigmatic Guardian. The Second Musician, in a frantic human outburst, defines the terror that ordinary unheroic man feels as he anticipates some crisis that he is forced to face:

> I am afraid of this place.

[*CPl* 209]

Then both Musicians singing together reiterate the active, energetic theme.

The different functions of the Musicians are reflected in the

different metres of their verse: first, that of commentators in their
rhymed lyrics; then as mediators between the human and the
supernatural in their unrhymed descriptive passages beginning 'Night
falls' [*CPl* 209] and 'That old man climbs up hither' [*CPl* 210]
and 'He has made a little heap of leaves' [*CPl* 210]. After this last
passage the choric framework is completed by the quatrain beginning
'O wind, O salt wind, O sea wind' [*CPl* 210], expressing the passivity
and apathy of age. This balances antiphonally the earlier quatrain
beginning 'Why should I sleep, the heart cries' [*CPl* 209], which
expresses the opposite qualities of activity, energy and enterprise
embodied in youth. The vocal delivery of all these passages must
be differentiated, or paralleled where necessary, and must all,
including the unrhymed lines, be distinguished from the blank verse
of the Old Man and the Young Man.

While the Musicians reiterate the active, energetic theme

> 'Why should I sleep?', the heart cries,
> 'For the wind, the salt wind, the sea wind,
> Is beating a cloud through the skies;
> I would wander always like the wind'
>
> [*CPl* 209]

the Old Man enters through the audience, bent double like a wind-
warped thorn-tree, providing a dramatic contrast. That both he and
the Young Man make their entries through the audience may be
intended to suggest that they are emanations of the collective mind,
but it is doubtful whether this is the effect they produce. Their dress
and their masks immediately set them apart. The Old Man certainly
has more in common with ordinary men in that most of us share
his inability to make a heroic gesture, but it is precisely this capacity
that puts Cuchulain into an extraordinary category. It is more likely
that their entries emphasize their relationship. Cuchulain's opposition
to the Old Man is not merely that between youth and age, energy
and passivity, but is grounded in the perception that he is confronting
the living embodiment of what he fears to become. The Old Man
is the antithesis of those qualities that Yeats was to celebrate in such
late poems as 'An Acre of Grass' and 'Why Should not Old Men
be Mad?' He lacks frenzy, he has succumbed to the temptation to
be quiet. Such a relationship should be suggested both in their masks
and in their clothes – the Old Man's mask suggesting an aged, the
clothes a shabby Cuchulain.

It is in the handling of the language and the characterization of
these two figures that Yeats shows some uncertainty, understandable

in what was his first essay in a more consistent working-out of his theories than any attempt he had made hitherto. The language and the conflict of attitudes between the two characters, their psychological differences, are expressed in terms that, however, heightened, are in essence naturalistic. The induction into a spiritual realm, which has been effectively achieved by the remote lyricism of the Musicians' passages, is not consistently sustained. The Old Man's language, appropriately stripped though it is of metaphorical richness, as the hazel tree is stripped by the wind, and therefore an acceptable analogue of his spiritual barrenness, is too blatantly the language of an old man whose basic cowardice is marked by his testy ill-temper. By the same token the Young Man's language is overfull of the brashness, the impulsiveness of an overconfident young man. Yeats leaves it to dramatic action, not words, to express the play of forces in the deeps of the mind. Thus, in order to convey the interior action to an audience, the Old Man's collapse into sleep must not be lost in the first movements of the Guardian's dance. It must be prepared for during and after his lines.

> I cannot bear her eyes, they are not of this world,
> Nor moist, nor faltering; they are no girl's eyes.
>
> [*CPl* 216]

His movements here, culminating in the covering of his head, must be seen as his response to the challenge that she represents. Similarly with the Young Man's transformation into the principle of heroism as he goes out, *'no longer as if in a dream'* [*CPl* 218]: his cry, 'He comes! Cuchulain, the son of Sualtim comes!' [*CPl* 218], is insufficient in itself to establish this transformation; it must be supported by convincing movement.

The Guardian of the Well, however, is fully abstract. To begin with, when she is covered with a cloak, she is a woman, but neutral. For the Old Man she is sexless and unattractive, a reflection of all the negative qualities that inhere in him. For Cuchulain she is a woman too, but one who arouses his sexual appetite, which is also an aggressive impulse. She is also the means of access to immortality. Then, in her neutrality, she becomes the agent through which the superhuman manifests itself to the human world. Like a medium she becomes possessed by the Woman of the Sidhe. This is a gradual process and ought to be presented as a frightening one too, lasting from her second cry of the hawk [*CPl* 215] to the moment when she throws off her cloak of neutrality and reveals herself in all her dangerous fascination. It is essential that an audience should

understand that she is being possessed by the superhuman and is
being transformed from woman to hawk, and that in her
transformation she exercises, even before her dance, a sensual
fascination over the Young Man, to which he must respond. The
terrifying nature of this transformation is articulated by the panic-
stricken cry of the First Musician in his role of ordinary unheroic
man:

> O God, protect me
> From a horrible deathless body
> Sliding through the veins of a sudden.

[*CPl* 217]

This cry confirms the First Musician's earlier premonition:

> I am afraid of this place.

[*CPl* 209]

In the context of the play the hawk is both an appropriate image
of superhuman power and, as Bjersby points out [*ICL* 87–93], a
composite image of nobility, bravery, and proud defiance —
dangerous but at the same time attractive to mortals. The dance itself
should express erotic attraction and also menace. In the war of
orders, the superhuman against human, godhead against man, the
terrestrial condition against the condition of fire, the Woman of the
Sidhe as hawk has tried to thwart the Young Man in his approach
to the Well, but he has not only resisted it but is determined to defeat
it, to bring it down and hood it.

> As I came hither
> A great grey hawk swept down out of the sky,
> And though I have good hawks, the best in the world
> I had fancied, I have not seen its like. It flew
> As though it would have torn me with its beak,
> Or blinded me, smiting with that great wing.
> I had to draw my sword to drive it off,
> And after that it flew from rock to rock.
> I pelted it with stones, a good half-hour,
> And just before I had turned the big rock there
> And seen this place, it seemed to vanish away.
> Could I but find a means to bring it down
> I'd hood it.

[*CPl* 214]

Having failed to destroy or even subdue him, she must allure. She takes on the role of the daemon who leads man to that moment of choice by which individuality is both defined and transcended. The Old Man, faced with the intolerable challenge of her unmoistened eyes, relapses into the passivity, defined by the Musicians in their choric lyric as 'a pleasant life / Among indolent meadows' [*CPl* 219], that he has in fact already chosen. He does warn the Young Man, however, of the consequences, the curse that will follow for those who choose to confront that challenge:

> That curse may be
> Never to win a woman's love and keep it;
> Or always to mix hatred in the love;
> Or it may be that she will kill your children,
> That you will find them, their throats torn and bloody,
> Or you will be so maddened that you will kill them
> With your own hand.
>
> [*CPl* 215]

Whether or not this is interpreted in terms of Yeats's own personal frustrations, the curse is the suffering that is involved in all wisdom, that of the Old Man or of the Young. As the Musicians sing in the closing song:

> Wisdom must live a bitter life.
>
> [*CPl* 219]

But the Young Man not so much rejects the warning consciously as dismisses it as an ineffectual threat from a kind of scarecrow. Instead, after a display of magnanimity towards the Old Man in his offer to share the life-giving waters with him, he becomes as possessed as the Guardian as she rises in her predatory beauty, and determines to impose his will on the superhuman:

> Run where you will,
> Grey bird, you shall be perched upon my wrist.
>
> [*CPl* 217]

His possession must be projected to the audience in his movements, which in a way constitute his 'dance'. The moment of his possession is the moment when the waters of eternal life flow, but the waters are not the same for everyone. Helen Vendler is right when she says:

one finds one's own species of immortality at the well and tree. For
Cuchulain it is battle and not the water, but he had to come to the well
to find this out.

[*YV* 215]

The dance must also suggest, therefore, the conflicting attractions
of the hawk and the Well. We know through the first Musician in
his role as commentator that Cuchulain hears the plash of the water:

He has heard the plash;

We learn too that he ignores it:

Look, he has turned his head.

[*CPl* 217]

and we see that he rejects it, as, equally possessed by the divine spirit,
the Young Man follows his daemon. That this is the moment of
choice must be made clear to the audience. The Well is the kind of
immortality he thought he was looking for and which the hawk
prevents him from achieving. In a sense he, too, is cheated. But the
deceit of the hawk leads him to reject the destiny of ordinary men,
as defined by the Musicians:

He might have lived at his ease,
An old dog's head on his knees,
Among his children and friends.

[*CPl* 217]

and embodied in the Old Man, who, now that the supernatural no
longer confronts him, has come awake again. Instead the hawk leads
him to discover the kind of immortality which is the fulfilment of
his heroic being. He re-enters, still possessed by the hawk, but left
alone, since as far as he is concerned the Old Man may as well not
be there, to make his choice of heroism. That choice demands a total
commitment of the self and this can only be given by the self choosing
in isolation. The Musicians' cry of 'Aoife' and the clash of arms
awaken him to full consciousness. He ignores the Old Man and
confirms his choice, this time no longer as if possessed or in a dream,
but in full, ecstatic consciousness. His final cry, in the third person,
as if the Young Man has now seen his role and decided to fuse himself
to it, 'He comes! Cuchulain, son of Sualtim comes!' [*CPl* 218], is
an objective definition of an achieved identity. This is the climactic

moment of the play, the transition from trance to full waking
consciousness, and must be fully realized in performance, though
it is a pity that the effect is somewhat spoiled by the earlier
announcement of his identity.

The final lyric expresses in equivocal terms the equivocal themes
of the play. The first three stanzas (before the folding of the cloth
behind which the Old Man must leave the acting area) are a reflection
of the Old Man's attitudes and evoke the cocoon of unadventurous
familiarity in which energy dwindles into indolence and the exalting
challenge of immolation is reduced to an exercise of barren
destructiveness. If the last two stanzas are taken as an objective
comment by a chorus that 'has no part in the action' [*E&I* 226],
representing ordinary life and regarding any form of commitment,
heroic or otherwise, as a kind of idiocy or folly, then their praise
is highly ambiguous, issuing as it does from an 'empty well' and a
'leafless tree'. The choric framework returns us from the spiritual
stage on which the action has been played out in the deeps of the
mind to the mundane world, but now it is a world that has been
illuminated and transfigured by Cuchulain's heroic gesture.

The Only Jealousy of Emer

Yeats employs the same general dramatic devices in this play as in *At the Hawk's Well* though with greater rigour. The three Musicians retain their role as commentators and mediators between the natural and supernatural worlds, and they are kept rigorously out of the action. The characters that participate in the action as spiritual essences are masked. Yeats tell us that the faces of Emer and Eithne Inguba can be either masked or made up to resemble masks, presumably because they are to be thought of as both spiritual essences and at the same time recognizably more human than the other figures, Bricriu, Cuchulain and Fand, though even Fand, the Woman of the Sidhe, reveals human characteristics. In performance masks would be preferable for them too, though they could be modelled more naturalistically than those of the supernatural figures. This ambivalence, this interpenetration of the two worlds of the human and superhuman, is at the core of the play, which, though acted out in the deeps of the mind at the point between land and sea where they meet, is nevertheless given naturalistic solidity firstly in visual terms by the un-Noh-like bed on which Cuchulain lies in a condition of suspended animation, secondly in aural terms by the directness, the colloquialism even, of much of the language, and thirdly by the psychological verisimilitude of the characterization.

On the surface the action takes place in the house of some 'fisher' and beyond it lies the sea − the same situation as in *On Baile's Strand,* and *The Green Helmet,* and parallel to that in *Deirdre* and *The Land of Heart's Desire,* where the values of domesticity and conventional codes of behaviour are contrasted with those of some world beyond them, suggested by wood, hills, or sea. Ideally this contrast should be made visually apparent to an audience by the depth of the stage-space, something which the Abbey Theatre did not have. Cuchulain has just fought the sea and his body has been brought in from it. Bricriu and Fand both come from the sea. One clear meaning of the sea is that it represents that dimension to which humanity can only gain access by some heroic act of self-immolation, the very thing that Emer wants to save Cuchulain from − 'the enchantments of the dreaming foam' [*CPl* 286] – and from which she does in fact save him, though in the process allowing Eithne to think that it is she who has achieved this:

> *Eithne:* And it is I that won him back from the sea,
> That brought him back to life.
>
> [*CPl* 294]

But more than that, as the opening lyric suggests, it is primordial creative energy, in Yeats's terminology, the *Anima Mundi*.

Structurally the play is defined not only by the six episodes of which it consists, but also aurally by different poetic levels. The six episodes are: (1) opening lyric and setting, (2) Emer and Eithne, (3) Emer and Bricrui, (4) Cuchulain and Fand, (5) Emer, Eithne and Cuchulain, (6) closing lyric. In aural terms the opening and closing songs are, as it were, pure, disembodied lyrics, rhymed and beautifully balanced. They are contrasted not only with the unrhymed but also with the more or less naturalistic blank verse of episodes two and three. When the action recedes furthest into the world of essences, in episode four, the scene between Fand and Cuchulain, there is a change to the remote and abstract stylization of rhymed tetrameters. After that the level returns to blank verse in episode five before the final lyric song. These differences of level must be marked in performance by differences in the vocal delivery of the lines.

Leaving aside for a moment the opening and closing lyrics, much of the play is intelligible on a purely human level, though it is not, as we shall see, confined to it. The setting is evoked with the compelling clarity and economy of what appears at first hearing to be naturalistic detail:

> I call before the eyes a roof
> With cross-beams darkened by smoke;
> A fisher's net hangs from a beam,
> A long oar lies against the wall.
> I call up a poor fisher's house;
>
> [*CPl* 282]

The characters are introduced, again at first sight as human beings: Cuchulain in a trance (Yeats never says that he is irrevocably dead), his wife Emer, and Eithne his young mistress. Their characters are established at the human level. In the second episode, the scene between Emer and Eithne, Emer explains in a reference back to the main action of *On Baile's Strand* how Cuchulain comes to be lying

on the bed, dead or swooning. At the same time the even tenor of
her speech establishes her character: queenly, dignified, and full of
pride in Cuchulain:

> Although they have dressed him out in his grave-clothes
> And stretched his limbs, Cuchulain is not dead;
> The very heavens when that day's at hand,
> So that his death may not lack ceremony,
> Will throw out fires, and the earth grow red with blood.
> There shall not be a scullion but foreknows it
> Like the world's end.
>
> [*CPl* 283–4]

She is convinced he is not dead. She and Eithne tell the audience
all they need to know in terms of folk-belief:

> *Emer:*   It may be
> An image has been put into his place,
> A sea-borne log bewitched into his likeness . . .
> *Eithne:*   Cry out his name.
> All that are taken from our sight, they say,
> Loiter amid the scenery of their lives
> For certain hours or days, and should he hear
> He might, being angry, drive the changeling out.
>
> [*CPl* 284–5]

But she knows that her settled and unwavering devotion may not
have the force of the younger woman's passion:

> *Emer:* It is hard to make them hear amid their darkness,
> And it is long since I could call him home;
> I am but his wife, but if you cry aloud
> With the sweet voice that is so dear to him
> He cannot help but listen.
>
> [*CPl* 285]

At one level they are two sides of the eternal triangle, two different
types of women fighting for a man. Emer here represents the claim
of ordinary life — domesticity, hearth and home, the recognizable
moral world where guilt, remorse and loyalty operate, a world in
time where love has grown from momentary violent passion to settled
devotion, where the past can be evoked by memory and the future
anticipated in hope. Emer tries to prevent the irruption of the
supernatural into this primarily natural world. She symbolically
fosters the hearth fire and tries to counter the tug of the sea by pulling

the curtains of the bed:

> *Emer:* I'll cover up his face to hide the sea;
> And throw new logs upon the hearth and stir
> The half-burnt logs until they break in flame.
> Old Manannan's unbridled horses come
> Out of the sea, and on their backs his horsemen;
> But all the enchantments of the dreaming foam
> Dread the hearth-fire.
>
> [*CPl* 285–6]

Urged on by Emer, Eithne first calls on Cuchulain, then kisses the figure on the bed. But Emer's efforts to ward off the supernatural are in vain. The figure on the bed is now Bricriu, the actor playing Cuchulain having changed his mask behind the drawn curtains.

Bricriu's function is to test Emer's capacity for heroism. The bait he dangles before her (in a sense he is a fisher fishing for her soul) she will not at first rise to:

> [*Bricriu*]: You spoke but now of the mere chance that some day
> You'd be the apple of his eye again
> When old and ailing, but renounce that chance
> And he shall live again.
>
> [*CPl* 288]

To this she replies passionately, 'No, never, never' [*CPl* 289]. Eithne Inguba poses no threat to that hope because she herself and Emer both know that she is no more than the passing fancy of a 'violent hour' [*CPl* 285], to be discarded eventually, and therefore does not arouse jealousy. Bricriu tests Emer further by opening her eyes to the appeal that Fand has for Cuchulain, which *does* arouse her jealousy but at the same time provokes her to her gesture of renunciation. This gesture, which, as Ure said, is also 'her greatest act of love towards him' [*YTP* 74], is the climax of the play, and in making it Emer is recognizably human. But what is Bricriu's motive, or, to put the question in another way, who is Bricriu?

He announces himself as 'Maker of discord among gods and men' [*CPl* 287], and certainly, though this is clearer in the earlier version printed in *FPFD,* he is an enemy of the goddess Fand. His withered arm and his distorted mask are the opposite of Fand's 'mathematical, Babylonian' beauty [*A Vis* (*B*) 268]; his daemonic malevolence, his malice, are opposed to all forms of love, be it married devotion or the passion of lovers, and to Cuchulain's only too human vacillation. Like Iago, the beauty of others makes him ugly. But he is more than this.

Being of the world of the spirit, he, like Fand, testifies to the truth
of that world, whether it be conceived as a world that is different
from and hostile to the natural one, or as one in which life is
continued beyond the grave through a purgatorial process to the point
where consciousness and memory are completely purged away, or
in terms of the power of the imagination, conceived as vision or
dream, to create reality. When Fand appears [*CPl* 290], Emer thinks
of her as nothing but a woman. Bricriu responds that she has
dreamed herself into that shape in the hope of hooking Cuchulain
with the bait of dreams. But to Emer dreams (vision or imagination)
are a lie. Bricriu replies with a succinct account of Yeats's theory
of the purgatorial process that the spirit goes through, unwinding
the mummy-cloths of remembered experience until it reaches a
condition of total purity, when dreams (vision or imagination) are
extinguished. When that happens contact with the natural world is
severed:

> The dead move ever towards a dreamless youth
> And when they dream no more return no more.
>
> [*CPl* 290]

Further, the inhabitants of the spiritual realm, more holy because
uncontaminated by the mire and blood of human veins, only manifest
their presence to the natural world in vision:

> And those more holy shades that never lived
> But visit you in dreams.
>
> [*CPl* 290]

But Emer lacks the imagination to respond to this. To her Fand
remains obstinately human, merely another dangerous temptress who
she thinks has a body that can be physically assaulted.

> I know her sort.
> They find our men asleep, weary with war,
> Lap them in cloudy hair or kiss their lips;
> Our men awake in ignorance of it all,
> But when we take them in our arms at night
> We cannot break their solitude.
>
> [*CPl* 290]

And she proceeds to attack her. Again she has to be educated:

> [*Bricriu*]:   No knife
> Can wound that body of air.   [*CPl* 291]

In the end Emer accepts the reality of the spirit world, recognizing the power of vision to the extent that she makes a sacrifice to save Cuchulain from it. Lastly Bricriu incarnates the very spirit of paradox and conflict that permeates the play, the contradictory tensions lying at the heart of those creative energies suggested in the opening lyrics, the conflicts between the human and superhuman worlds, the hostility of the superhuman world of the Sidhe towards the human, and the conflicts within each: Fand opposed to Emer; Emer opposed to Eithne; Bricriu opposed to Fand; Cuchulain opposed to Bricriu; Cuchulain torn between Fand, Emer, and Eithne. He gives Emer second sight because he knows that though knowledge may give her wisdom it will not bring her peace. But ironically he is also the means by which she is stretched to the limit of her humanity by the act of sacrifice, 'a sacrifice of herself to herself' [*FPFD* 46], that paradoxically establishes personality. When she is given second sight she witnesses the confrontation between Cuchulain and Fand which leads to her final gesture. (According to Yeats's directions the crouching ghost of Cuchulain has been near the front of the acting area right from the beginning and visible to the audience. It would surely be less confusing if he were not visible at the beginning and only revealed at this point.)

With the introduction of Fand and the Ghost of Cuchulain the action recedes further into the deeps of the mind. Mark van Doren remarked in reference to *The Tempest* [*S* 323] that any set of symbols, when moved close to it, lights up as in an electric field. The same is true of this play, whether those symbols be interpreted as aesthetic (Fand as Muse), or philosophical (Fand as Pure Being), or autobiographical. An interpretation that sees the play in autobiographical terms, with Cuchulain representing Yeats, Emer Mrs Yeats, Fand Maud Gonne and Eithne Iseult Gonne, not only distorts the order of events in Yeats's life but also trivializes it. Looked at from the point of view of Cuchulain, Fand is Pure Being, that perfection which he strives to attain, the Image, the Muse to which he would give his entire allegiance, the absolute to which he must respond. From the point of view of Emer she is the eternal siren, one of those who

> find our men asleep, weary with war,
> Lap them in cloudy hair or kiss their lips.
>
> [*CPl* 290]

From the point of view of Bricriu she is simply his enemy whose will he must thwart, since the conflict of opposites permeates the superhuman world too, whose inhabitants, out of the malevolence which is one aspect of their nature, will certainly use human relationships in their own causes. With her appearance the eternal triangle becomes a quadrangle, with Fand at one level standing for the *idea* of the *femme fatale,* a Lorelei who lures men away from their commitment to humdrum reality by their appeal to some ultimately unattainable perfection or beauty. Such is her appeal to Cuchulain, considered as a still living human being. More esoterically, her appeal to him as a dead spirit is that she offers him release from 'the toil of the dead to free themselves from an endless sequence of thoughts' [*M* 353–4]. On an even more abstract level she expresses Absolute Beauty, or indeed any Absolute, Pure Being. This aspect of her should be made clear enough even to an audience innocent of Yeats's 'system' by her cold metallic appearance and her non-human movements, but it is a pity that he chose to burden it with what must sound to the uninitiated a puzzling reference to the fifteenth phase of the moon. This could be explained to a theatre-audience in a programme-note such as Yeats himself provided when he published the play in *FPFD.* There he explained that the fifteenth phase was one of the greatest possible bodily beauty but not visible to the human eye nor having human characteristics. Such beauty is the result of emotional toil in past lives. The essential point about Fand then is that she represents first the perfection, symbolized by the full moon – the toil, the discipline, of the opening lyric – secondly, the eerie and inhuman quality of that perfection once reached, and thirdly, the impossibility of that perfection holding to a permanence in a kinetic universe. Pure Being can only be conceived in terms of Becoming. Even the moon must change. Considered absolutely she embodies not only the cold stasis of that perfection but also the agonizing knowledge that such pure perfection is incomplete, imperfect in its separation from human reality. She is both an unmoved mover and herself moved by longing. She needs Cuchulain as the Muse needs the poet. There is no point in being Inspiration if there is no-one to inspire.

These paradoxes and contradictions should be reflected in her appearance and in her dance, which, though alluring, should not be exclusively erotic. It culminates in the demand for a kiss, the moment in which spirit must be united with body, body with spirit:

> Then kiss my mouth. Though memory
> Be beauty's bitterest enemy
> I have no dread, for at my kiss
> Memory on the moment vanishes:
> Nothing but beauty can remain.

> [*CPl* 292]

Though the Sidhe may cheat others, they do not deceive themselves, for she knows that the kiss will bring for her only an imaginary completion and for Cuchulain only an illusory escape from time-bound memories:

> Time shall seem to stay his course;
> When your mouth and my mouth meet
> All my round shall be complete
> Imagining all its circles run;
>
> [*CPl* 292–3]

But there is no holding back the cycle: pure subjectivity must complete its round into impure objectivity as the moon moves from fullness back to three-quarter light and finally to darkness again. Nevertheless the offer is all but irresistible to Cuchulain, who is only restrained from his desire for Fand by memories of Emer, by his human love, his remorse and his guilt. This conflict in him must be reflected in his movements too, until, like the Woman of the Sidhe in *At the Hawk's Well* she lures him offstage to the moment of his choice. Attraction and repulsion must be in them, the appeal of the sheer beauty of aesthetic perfection, but at the same time the terror of achieving it at the cost of all the complexity, the mire and blood, of his humanity. We must see the conflicting emotions as first he is drawn to Fand with the repeated cry 'Your mouth!' and then back to Emer, 'O Emer, Emer!'

Fand is such a brilliant image theatrically that it is probably right to say with Helen Vendler that she steals the show, but it is equally true to retort with Ure that that does not make the play hers. We feel no pity for Fand since in so far as she is non-human she is bound to act in a way that expresses what she is: she has no choice. It is for Emer that tragedy, which depends upon choice, is wrought to its uttermost. Bricriu brings her to her decision, made in full knowledge of the consequences already foretold:

> 'He'll never sit beside you at the hearth
> Or make old bones, but die of wounds and toil
> On some far shore or mountain, a strange woman
> Beside his mattress.
>
> [*CPl* 289]

Tension rises as Bricriu, in the shape of the Figure of Cuchulain, urges Emer:

> [*Bricriu*]:   . . . cry out, cry out!
> Renounce him, and her power is at an end.
> Cuchulain's foot is on the chariot-step.
> Cry −
> *Emer:* I renounce Cuchulain's love for ever.
>
> [*CPl* 294]

The tragic irony of this decision is the climax of the play. The human qualities in Cuchulain are still strong enough to cause him to respond to her renunciation and to awaken him to the terror of submission to the remote Absolute, but the appeal of that Absolute is also strong enough to compel him to seek for it in its nearest temporary embodiment, the arms of Eithne Inguba.

When Yeats revised the play he cut out at this point a slack speech of Emer's as well as conversations between Fand and Cuchulain and between Fand and Bricriu. These excisions do make for a tauter dramatic structure, but dramaturgically they are weak. Eithne's return is very abrupt. It would marrry word and visual image more effectively if, instead of having left the stage when she cowers away from Bricriu at the beginning of the play and returning here, she were to recede into darkness in the first instance and then reappear on the bed ready to take Cuchulain in her arms. Further, after her gesture of renunciation, Emer does not have enough to say. It is the stage picture alone that has to convey the meaning. Somehow it must suggest what Nathan calls 'that calm exaltation that Yeats felt to be the quality of heroic transcendence − it should not be inferred that she is reduced to dumb pathos' [*TD* 239]. For her it will bring the cold consolation of the hearth; for Cuchulain a life of wounds and toil, vacillating between the beckoning enchantments of the dreaming foam and the weight of guilty memories; for Eithne the indignity of being flung into some corner like old nut-shells; for Fand rejection. These are the sort of reflections that should be aroused by the final tableau − Cuchulain in Eithne's arms with Emer looking on, a dignified, silent statue with the heart of a woman. The supernatural figures have receded: we are returned to the human world.

It cannot be said that the opening and closing lyrics of the Musicians are likely to make converts for Yeats the dramatist, for even the most committed Yeatsians admit their difficulty. In the context of an actual performance they can seem so impenetrable as almost to justify Yeats's nonchalant dismissal of them as irrelevant in his introduction to the simplified prose dance-drama he made of the play, *Fighting the Waves*. Yet they are clearly not irrelevant, not simply because as prologue the first leads us into the world of essences, into the deeps of the mind, and the last as epilogue leads us back to the everyday world. They are more than framework: they are integral to the play and like a sounding-board amplify the range and depth of its resonances.

The first lyric evokes not only a woman's beauty, its fragility, its exquisite uselessness, and so seems relevant to Eithne Inguba, but loveliness itself; and behind that the energies of mind and imagination that create it, energies that are self-generated, in the paradoxical interpenetration of quietude and violence, stillness and movement, attraction and repulsion.

One may agree with Helen Vendler when she calls the closing lyric an example of Yeats at his most maddening [*YV* 230], but it is very difficult to follow her in her distribution of the song among the Musicians speaking now as Emer, now as Fand. There is no indication in the text of the play that they sing other than collectively, whether they are referring to Fand or voicing their own reaction (and thus directing our responses) to what has been witnessed. If they refer to Fand, then the first stanza presents the miracle of her as inhuman statue yet at the same time possessing a human beating heart:

> Why does your heart beat thus?
> Plain to be understood,
> I have met in a man's house
> A statue of solitude,
> Moving there and walking;
> Its strange heart beating fast
> For all our talking.

And its last line becomes a plea for our compassion for her suffering from the sense of her incompleteness:

> O still that heart at last.
>
> [*CPl* 295]

The first refrain then suggests that that suffering will continue to compel our astonished sympathy, so powerful has been the impact she has had upon us, even though it is a dumbfounding experience of something beyond the tomb:

> O bitter reward
> Of many a tragic tomb!
> And we though astonished are dumb
> Or give but a sigh and a word,
> A passing word.

[*CPl* 295]

If the first stanza refers to the Musicians themselves, and thence to us, then it reflects our own heart's fascinated fear when confronted with the experience of the miraculous, and its last line to our instinct to avoid it.

The second stanza does seem to refer primarily to Fand, unless we take the statue now to be extended beyond her to the inhuman beauty of any abstraction:

> Although the door be shut
> And all seem well enough,
> Although wide world hold not
> A man but will give you his love
> The moment he has looked at you,
> He that has loved the best
> May turn from a statue
> His too human breast.

[*CPl* 295]

The third stanza brings us back to the moon images already associated with Fand. At full moon complete subjectivity is achieved, but such a state is not possible for human beings, even though they are eternally attracted to it. The cycle must continue, both for us and for Fand, to the phase of total darkness when both moon and stars are extinguished. This recurring process will not be halted even at the moment of completion. For us, in our natural imperfection, there always will be the danger of rejecting the appeal of the Absolute, which man nevertheless needs if his spiritual nature is to find fulfilment, and for Fand there always will be the cold solitude of an abstract self-absorption, isolated from materiality, and also the desire to complement that abstraction by involvement in and with the body. Spirit must be united with flesh. To recognize that each requires the other is to admit that each by itself is incomplete. Such bitter knowledge is its own reward. This concluding note of resignation in the face of ineluctable forces heroically acknowledged balances the urgent assertion and insistent questioning of the opening lyric.

The two songs together frame antiphonally the dignified, and in the event ironically statuesque, silence of Emer.

The Dreaming of the Bones

The Dreaming of the Bones provides strong evidence with which to rebut the charge so frequently levelled at Yeats both as dramatist and poet that an approach to the understanding of his work can only be made through some previously acquired knowledge, some initiation into the arcaneries of his beliefs and attitudes. For here, for those prepared to listen, are all the data out of which the play's conflicts are constructed. These, whether we agree with them or not, constitute the framework, to which we can give imaginative assent in the same way that we can accept Shakespeare's or Milton's acknowledgedly unscientific cosmology, within which the play's concerns are worked out.

Whatever interpretative differences have been exhibited by critics, all have acknowledged the close parallelism of the play to the Noh' play of spirits', *Nishikigi,* which Yeats read in the Pound-Fenollosa translation. But no esoteric knowledge is required from the audience. Yeats puts it all before us: we are told that places are haunted by the ghosts of the dead:

> *Stranger:* For certain days the stones where you must lie
> Have in the hour before the break of day
> Been haunted.
>
> [*CPl* 436]

This idea the Young Man acknowledges as a traditional belief:

> My Grandam
> Would have it they did penance everywhere;
> Some lived through their old lives again.
>
> [*CPl* 436]

Such penance is seen as conducted on various levels of purgatorial punishment, dependent upon the gravity of the sin committed in life, ranging from physical torment:

> . . . some for an old scruple must hang spitted
> Upon the swaying tops of lofty trees;
> Some are consumed in fire, some withered up
> By hail and sleet out of the wintry North . . .
>
> [*CPl* 436–7]

133

to the spiritual agony of living through their old lives again until
their sin is either burnt away or forgiven. Within the category of
spiritual sufferers, there are at least two groups: those who sinned
out of a 'momentary impulse' [*CPl* 439] or 'the commandment of
some petty king' [*CPl* 439], who will finally achieve peace in the
obliteration of the memory of former deeds, and those, in this
instance Dermot and Dervogilla, whose sin has sentenced them to
accursed, barren loneliness (the image is central to the play) in which
they are isolated not only from their countrymen but from each
other. For them there is no assurance of peace in the obliteration
of memory, for memory of the past keeps them in the form of ghosts
haunting actual places in the present. Their consciousness of guilt
manifests itself as night winds, clouds, the sound of music, images
which seem to condense into liquidity, mounting up the arid valleys
of County Clare as wine fills a cup. Such memories are self-
perpetuating because the act which is their source is one that has
consequences which involve the whole history of Ireland to the
present day, from which the originators cannot be released by their
own will, but only by the choice of others, in this case the Young
Man. Yeats further establishes this purgatorial process in the
metaphor of a dream, not only in the play's title but in the dialogue.
The spirits that live through their old lives again do so 'in a dream'
[*CPl* 436]. Those who, as human flesh and blood

> Once lay warm and live [= alive] the live-long night
> In one another's arms

are now, as shadows

> . . . but of the people of dreams.
>   [*CPl* 441]

One level of punishment is appropriate for Donough O'Brien and
his followers, who rebelled against the king of Thomond, and
another for those who were 'callers-in of the alien from oversea' [*CPl*
439]. The distinction is based on the motive of love, an eternal self-
justifying value, for the consequences of which forgiveness is begged.
This information is an integral strand in the dramatic texture of the
play and is introduced quite naturally. The very first line of the first
choric lyric — 'Why does my heart beat so?' — immediately
establishes the atmosphere of supernatural terror appropriate to a
Noh play of spirits, in which the typical adventure is 'often the
meeting with ghost, god or goddess at some holy place or

much-legended tomb' [*E&I* 232]. The basic images are introduced, the night, the dreams of the barren bones of the dead, the power of passion. These are later to be complemented by the vitality of the cock, the red bird of March and the dawn. As the Musicians set the scene:

> The hour before dawn and the moon covered up
>
> [*CPl* 434]

an atmosphere is created which is an apt preparation for the confluence of two planes of experience, spiritual and physical, supernatural and human, and for the congruence of past and present. This is enacted at once by the almost simultaneous entries of the Ghosts and the Young Man, each trapped in their own isolation, as the birds cry in their loneliness. His tough mind, understandably concerned with his own situation, has no use either for metaphysical speculations or historical excuses. His dismissive rejection of what he sees as no more than an old wives' tale, reflected in his contemptuous 'My Grandam . . .' not only strikes the keynote of his unimaginative character − he cannot foresee the consequences of his own fanaticism any more than the Ghosts could of their own passion − also leads to his refusal of forgiveness. He moves on one plane, the Ghosts on quite another.

Structurally the play consists of an opening lyric, three episodes and an epilogue. The opening lyric in rhyme is followed by an unrhymed passage that evokes the setting. In the first episode the Young Man meets the Ghosts. A second passage evokes the changed scene as the actors symbolically climb up the mountainside to the near summit. In the second episode the past is revealed. After a second symbolic climb, this time up to the summit of the mountain, the third episode both presents the present as a direct consequence of the past and reveals the identity of the Ghosts. The temptation to forgive them − its rejection has already been adumbrated at the end of the second episode − is now confirmed and the Young Man strides off into the future, whose bitter complexities are evoked in the concluding choric lyric.

Within this structure Yeats works out the interpenetration of the two planes, literal and allegorical, on which the action moves. The literal time is 'the hour before dawn and the moon covered up' and the literal site of the action is an area near the desolate Burren hills in County Clare, of which one of Cromwell's generals is reported to have said that there is no tree on which to hang a man, no water in which to drown him, no earth in which to bury him. The historical

associations of the area with rebellion are strengthened by the fact
that it was the site of much bitter fighting during the 1916 period.
The objective reality of the place is established by the use of place-
names, the village of Abbey, the ruined Abbey of Corcomroe,
Muckanish, Finvara, Bailelevelehan, and the description of the
landscape, with its sheep paths leading up the mountainside now
denuded of trees by the enemy English, past the shallow well and
the flat stones fouled by watering cattle, through the long grassy field
and past the ragged thorn-trees to the stones and the scarce grass
where, near the summit, stands the ruined Abbey, where feathered
cocks crow at dawn, and beyond that to the summit itself from which
can be seen

> The Aran Islands, Connemara Hills,
> And Galway in the breaking light . . .
>
> [*CPl* 443]

But at the same time this *paysage* is *moralisé*. The paths that the
Ghosts know are also those traced by the souls of the dead as they
re-live their lives backwards, tracing events to their source; and the
climb up the mountain is an approach to that ultimate purgation
which they are not permitted to attain:

> the sleep
> That lingers always in the abyss of the sky,
> Though they can never reach it.
>
> [*CPl* 444]

a dreamless sleep never again to be troubled by the memory of their
passionate crime flowing up between them, spilling out from their
personal situation to the condition of Ireland, from the past
immediate source to the present moment, and even beyond that to
its imagined consequences in the future, imaged as dreams
overflowing the hills like wine mounting in a wine-cup. The time
is the hour of dawn, near the dark of the moon, when a new
dispensation, heralded by the vigorous cocks of the new solar year
that begins in March, may be revealed. The empty landscape of
barren rock, ragged thorn and briar is an externalization of that
spiritual wasteland inhabited not only by the Ghosts but also by the
Young Man, who, caught in the cold snows of an abstract political
fanaticism, fed on and perpetuated by a kind of automatism of mind,
though momentarily drawn to an alien and antithetical experience,
is in the last analysis incapable of compassion, love, or forgiveness.

Into this ambiguous landscape comes the Young Man, to be confronted by two terrors. One is knowable, manageable and ultimately controlled, as the natural fear of a man on the run. The Stranger's first question to the Young Man, 'But what have you to fear?' [*CPl* 435], shows this. The actor must be on edge here. And he is jumpy at the sound of 'an old horse gone astray' [*CPl* 436]. The other terror is less easily identifiable − 'Why should the heart take fright? [*CPl* 437], the First Musician asks. This terror is caused by the confrontation with an experience that both transcends and stretches the limitations of his imaginative perceptions, questions their validity and finally demands a response to it which has to be made in the misty uncharted air of individual choice, where solidities of dogma and attitude are threatened with dissolution, values with reappraisal or modification, certainties with frightening disintegration. In this atmosphere even conventionally accepted heroic behaviour − the Young Man fought at the Post Office in the 1916 rebellion, so *must* be a hero − can be seen as criminal, the patriot as rogue or rascal, the red beckoning glory of a new day merely the continuation of old savage violence. But conversely the lonely exclusiveness of a private passion, no matter to what extent its power may be acknowledged on crowded roads or unpeopled hills, can become a dizzy dream, a sweet snare. This cloudy terror is close to that 'terror of the supernatural' that *The Resurrection* enacts.

The first terror, wholly natural in the circumstances − the Young Man exhausted (it is a long way from Dublin to the west coast of County Clare), in an unknown eerie landscape, encountering two half-perceived figures dressed in the costume of the past − linked as it is with the historic episode of the Easter 1916 rebellion (the play is specifically set in 1916), is designed to involve an audience, and especially an audience aware of the merest outline of Irish history, in the identifiably naturalistic element in the play and through that into its wider implications. Literally and figuratively in the dark, uncertain of the way he must take, the Young Man puts his destiny in the hands of the Ghosts, just as they are to put theirs in his. In the first episode he is blind to their identity, scornful of their power and indeed of the very notion that events extend beyond the boundaries of their commission into a timeless world of the conscience. Indeed it is part of the play's economy of structure that the Young Man finds himself involved in the past of the Ghosts, and hence in the consequence of their actions, which include the Easter 1916 rebellion, even before their identity is revealed to him. His scorn is expressed in terms that are somewhat incongruous with his generally unelevated language − one of the few weak passages in the play:

> Well, let them dream into what shape they please
> And fill waste mountains with the invisible tumult
> Of the fantastic conscience.
>
> [*CPl* 437]

That is Yeats speaking, not the Young Man, whose voice takes over more appropriately:

> I have no dread;
> They cannot put me into gaol or shoot me.
>
> [*CPl* 437]

The first episode establishes not only the dramatic situation but also the antinomies of the protagonists, but with the second choric lyric the sharp distinctions between the two begin to be blurred. There is something terrifying in this encounter, something repellent but also attractive that draws the obdurate heart towards the condition of loneliness:

> The bitter sweetness of the night
> Has made it but a lonely thing.
>
> [*CPl* 437]

The Young Man and the Ghosts are linked together within their loneliness: he is on the run, they have been sent to a kind of spiritual Coventry:

> *Young Girl:* Until this hour no ghost or living man
> Has spoken, though seven centuries have run
> Since they, weary of life and of men's eyes,
> Flung down their bones in some forgotten place,
> Being accursed.
>
> [*CPl* 440]

But the pull of attraction provokes the converse tug of rejection, as the violent, assertive image of the red bird of March takes over, scorning the atmosphere of cloud, darkness and shadow in which the Ghosts have their being:

> Red bird of March, begin to crow!
> Up with the neck and clap the wing,
> Red cock, and crow!
>
> [*CPl* 437]

But that atmosphere has had its effect. In a cloud of uncertainty, the only course seems to be to hang the consequences, to cling to the perpetuation of the past:

> *First Musician:* My head is in a cloud
> I'll let the whole world go;
> My rascal heart is proud
> Remembering and remembering.
> Red bird of March, begin to crow!
> Up with the neck and clap the wing,
> Red cock, and crow!
>
> [*CPl* 438]

This sounds very like what Juno in *Juno and the Paycock* may well have called your poetical Republican this and your Diehard that marching towards a red future, but Yeats demonstrates the interaction of the two worlds by having the dreaming bones make the same cry. The lovers too, in their subjectivity, create the calamity that is not only their own hell − the *huis clos* of their eternal and inescapable torment ('No shade however harried and consumed / Would change his own calamity for theirs' [*CPl* 441]) but also the calamity that they conferred upon Ireland. For them the cock could bring release from their dark night of suffering into the clarity of day:

> The dreaming bones cry out
> Because the night winds blow
> And heaven's a cloudy blot.
> Calamity can have its fling.
> Red bird of March, begin to crow!
> Up with the neck and clap the wing,
> Red cock, and crow!
>
> [*CPl* 438]

The second episode twists the two strands more tightly together as the Stranger's mention of the past of the now ruined Abbey evokes the memory of destruction more recently wrought among the big houses in Clare, Kerry and Connacht. The story of the rebellion against the King of Thomond of Donough O'Brien, whose body lay in a tomb in the Abbey, both calls out the Young Man's tough-lined obduracy:

> It was men like Donough who made Ireland weak −
> My curse on all that troop
>
> [*CPl* 439]

but also leads on to the story of Diarmuid and Dervorgilla. It begins
the long process of temptation which does not reach its climax until
the dance of the two Ghosts in the third and final episode. The
temptation is not so much stated as *enacted* in the way in which the
Young Man is compelled by the Ghosts' intensity to become more
and more involved in the story they have to tell. Their eerie beauty
(it is significant that Yeats keeps them both young and beautiful,
as if their sin did not create a monstrous image and as if they were
upon the threshold of that beatitude imaged in 'Shepherd and
Goatherd' [*CPl* 159] as a Blakean childhood of innocence), their
language and their movements, create a verbal and visual snare in
which he is half 'moidered'. It is essential that the actor playing the
Young Man should convey to the audience his intense involvement
in their story, that he has indeed 'fallen into the mood' [*CPl* 443].
But sadly for the Ghosts their very intensity excites his, with the result
that the foundations of his final rejection of them are once again
strengthened:

> O, never, never
> Shall Diarmuid and Dervorgilla be forgiven.
>
> [*CPl* 442]

Nevertheless their influence can be felt in the run of the Young Man's
verse, which takes on much of the movement of theirs:

> You have told your story well, so well indeed
> I could not help but fall into the mood
> And for a while believe that it was true,
> Or half believe;
>
> [*CPl* 443]

until it is checked by the brutal

> but better push on now.
>
> [*CPl* 443]

Once at the symbolic summit, where the truth of the past combines
with the present to shape the future, the Young Man speaks again
in his own voice in his passionate indignation at the destruction
caused by English troops – and Yeats is lucky in the fortuitous irony
of its reference to the later confusions of the Civil War:

> there too
> The enemy has toppled roof and gable,
> And torn the panelling from ancient rooms;
> What generations of old men had known
> Like their own hands, and children wondered at,
> Has boiled a trooper's porridge.
>
> [*CPl* 443]

But the comparison that follows, between Galway and 'any old admired Italian town' [*CPl* 443] is pure Yeats, and the two lines on environmental pollution, whether Yeats's or the Young Man's, dramatically a disaster.

The temptation of the Young Man is continued mimetically in the dance of the Ghosts, which should have an almost hypnotic effect on him, as he is caught up not only in the strangeness but in the sweet arabesques of their movements, performed, surely, to that 'music of a lost kingdom', that wandering airy music, that sweet wandering snare in which a man may be 'lost of a sudden' [*CPl* 445]. In choreographic terms he should be caught up in their movements just as historically he is caught up in the consequence of their past actions. But the outward attraction is suppressed by the inner subsconscious rejection: the Ghosts in their dance anticipate his final refusal of forgiveness. Rajan suggests that the play's weakness lies in the fact that the Young Man

> faces no conflict and in the end makes no choice. He looks back into the past but his attitude to it is already decided. He is too much its victim to be able to redeem it.
>
> [*YCI* 103]

This is to make the Young Man too much the centre of dramatic interest. The comment is true in respect of the Young Man's relation to the past, but it does not take account of the way that choice is in fact presented — mimetically, as it was in Fand's dance around the wavering Cuchulain. If it were not, there would be no point in his final lines:

> I had almost yielded and forgiven it all —
> Terrible the temptation and the place!
>
> [*CPl* 444]

The terror must and can be transmitted to the audience in movement. Moore's comment is just:

If he did forgive them, he would indeed take on a stature for which Yeats
had not prepared us . . . But he is no Cuchulain; he is a hot-blooded young
Irish patriot on the run for his life. Caught up in a moment of cloudy vision,
he is compelled to admit the wild sweetness of a side of existence he had
never previously imagined.

[*MLD* 234]

That he cannot rise to the heroic level of a Cuchulain is precisely
Yeats's point – again corroborated visually by the detail that it is
the Ghosts who wear heroic masks. The Young Man remains
obstinately and inadequately human, his face not even made up to
resemble a mask, as if the gap between the two dimensions, heroic
and human, past and present, is tragically unbridgeable. The Young
Man's failure to respond to the Ghosts' compassion towards him
with his own towards them is a tragedy for Ireland. Ireland is
incapable of making the kind of decision that will redeem the past
and direct the future away from the blight of hatred that the final
song sees as withering its life:

> Our luck is withered away,
> And wheat in the wheat-ear withered,
> And the wind blows it away.

[*CPl* 445]

The play belongs neither to the Young Man nor to the Ghosts. His
tragedy is that in spite of his temporary response to the subjective,
mysterious world of the Ghosts:

> My heart ran wild when it heard
> The curlew cry before dawn
> And the eddying cat-headed bird

[*CPl* 445]

he remains imprisoned in his vision of a future sustained only by
the violence of the past. Theirs is that they remain locked in their
torment, since there is no-one heroic enough to release them from
it, as Emer at her own cost was capable of releasing Cuchulain from
bondage to Fand.

Young Man and Ghosts are figures in a dramatic scenario which
is completed by the Musicians, who are not merely commentators
but themselves part of its imaginative expression. The play moves
towards the kind of drama that has to be accepted in the totality
of its action, language and visual impact, as an epiphany, in this
instance, of the spiritual condition of Ireland trapped in the

consequences of its own history and unable to break out of them. It is almost a gloss on the lines:

> We had fed the heart on fantasies,
> The heart's grown brutal from the fare;
> More substance in our enmities
> Than in our love.
>
> [*CP* 230–1]

No wonder Yeats thought that in its contemporary political references the play when performed might be 'too powerful' [*L* 626].

The Cat and the Moon

Yeats tells us in *The Cat and the Moon and Certain Poems* that he intended the play to be 'what the Japanese call a "Kyōgen" [brief farces in colloquial language, introduced early in the development of Noh drama as interludes between the more serious ritualistic plays], and to come as a relaxation between, let us say. "*The Hawk's Well*" and "*The Dreaming of the Bones*" ' [*VPl* 805], and although it is doubtful that Yeats knew very much about actual Japanese *Kyōgen,* the play, like others that approximate to the same genre, such as *The Pot of Broth* and *The Green Helmet,* even though these were written before his contact with Noh drama, does reflect the general spirit of Japanese *Kyōgen* as described by Taylor:

Kyogen are not merely farces used for comic relief, however, but present the lives of common folk and the comedy of human imperfection as a contrast to the exalted subjects of the more sombre and ritualistic No. . . Kyogen sets out to expose human frailty, but within a frame of reference determined by self-knowledge, joy and reconciliation. It is a celebration of warmth and human nature, and the buffoonery is often delicious, however slight . . . While No makes one aware of an ideal reality through its presentation of ennobled human experience, Kyogen underlines the comic insignificance of everyday life.

[*DWBY* 77]

If Noh presents us with an image of life magnified to heroic proportion, *Kyōgen* looks at it through the reverse end of the telescope. Although *The Cat and the Moon* is written from this generally reductive angle of vision, the image it gives us is charmingly without any tinge of satire, parody or travesty. It is mock-heroic without being derisive, totally lacking in anything approaching Swiftian contempt. Again Mark van Doren comes to mind. Of Shakespeare's mockery of pastoral romanticism in *As You Like It* he wrote:

When Rosalind has made her last curtsy and the comedy is done, the pastoral sentiment is without a leg to stand on, yet it stands; and not only stands but dances.

[*S*152]

144

The equivalent is true of *The Cat and the Moon*. There is mockery, but the thing mocked survives. In the Noh Yeats found a form in which to express some of his most profound convictions. In the *Kyōgen* he found a dramatic vehicle for that vein of mockery and irony that is an integral part of the dialectical movement of his mind. Here, seen through the reductive lens of comedy, are all the familiar Noh features — the spiritual quest (by two far from noble heroes), the encounter with the supernatural (an invisible saint upon an ash-tree), the moment of choice (cure or blessing, like a Hallowe'en 'trick or treat'), the climactic dance (two, in fact: a walloping for one and a crippled pirouette for the other), the binding metaphors (a nursery moon and a pantomine cat, a metaphysical Felix who keeps on walking).

Just as *Kyōgen* is acted out in a recognizable down-to-earth world, so *The Cat and the Moon* for all its symbolic overtones, is grounded in naturalistic detail. Minnaloushe was a real Persian; the Well, sacred to St Colman, was within two miles of Thoor Ballylee, Yeats's tower; there were 'bits of cloth torn from a dress, hairpins and little pious pictures' at its side; the Gaelic League had organized processions to it where 'somebody . . . was cured of a lame leg or a blind eye' [*Comm. Pl* 174]; Kiltartan river is mentioned, so are the villages of Kiltartan and Ardrahan in County Galway; and County Mayo is not far away, for those who catch the references associated with Edward Martyn and George Moore [*Comm. Pl* 176]. Yeats grounds not only the language in the speech of familiar figures, only too familiar in the Irish landscape of the period, more successfully than in *The Pot of Broth,* though without the flavoured bite of his model, Synge, but also the characterization in the plausibility of human behaviour. This characterization is, of course, rudimentary, — in a piece as short as this, what else could it be? — but it is going too far to say that the personages are mere simulacra of human forms, without individuality. Indeed this naturalism, of speech, setting and behaviour, is probably the best path along which an audience can be led into the symbolic meanings that the personages, as projectors of the fable's meanings, act out. For unlike the earlier 'peasant' play, *The Pot of Broth,* which does not mean anything more than what it says on the surface, *The Cat and the Moon* invites, however vaguely, multiple interpretations, even without the guidance of Yeats's notes.

These show that Yeats had in mind, even though he puts only 'the vaguest suggestion of it into the play', that 'the blind man was the body, the lame man was the soul' [*Comm. Pl* 174], and that when 'the Saint mounts upon the back of the Lame Beggar he personifies a certain great spiritual event' [*Comm. Pl* 172], acted out in the setting of the Well of Immortality and the Tree of Life, below a moon whose changes symbolize

all the cycles; the soul realising its separate being in the full moon, then, as the moon seems to approach the sun and dwindle away, all but realising its absorption in God, only to whirl away once more.

[*Comm. Pl* 174–5]

Thus Lame Beggar on Blind Beggar's back suggests the interdependence of body and soul. Conversely their separation is a condition of their individual self-fulfilment. In this context the cat, says Yeats, is 'the normal man', and the moon is 'the opposite he seeks perpetually' [*Comm. Pl* 174] – sensuality both accused by asceticism and seeking it, hot animal blood excited by cold purity and rebuked by it, absolutes both antithetical and kindred, whose synthesis, in which fulfilment is achieved, is never fixed in stasis but always subject to the kinesis of change. The symbolic meanings are enacted in the play's dialogue, in what physical action there is, and in its visual imagery. But these enactments themselves contribute to the meanings. It is a mistake to import into the play symbolic meanings which have been derived from outside it as if they were immutable data. It is better to proceed from inside, from what the play presents us with, outwards to whatever significance it may suggest beyond the surface impact.

The first thing we are presented with is the opening choric song, which in the delicate, almost playful, fantasy of its verse both complements and forms a contrast with the more earthy prose of the central action. There is something less than serious in this symbol of normal man, belly to the ground and pupil to the sky, creeping around aimlessly seeking his opposite in a moon that spins round like a child's top. It is surprising that no-one has remarked upon the traditional Irish symbolism of the black cat as the devil's familiar or the source of ill-luck as reported by Lady Wilde [*AL* 151 ff.], though Wilson, to my mind rightly, links 'Black Minnaloushe' with man's unregenerate nature. Certainly both Blind Beggar and Lame Beggar are unregenerate in themselves. The Moon, its changes reflected in the changing pupils of Minnaloushe's eyes, dominates the play, and if I were producing it, I would at the risk of offending purists require a stage setting in which the moon, complete with a man-in-the-moon, would spin round, coming to rest at the beginning of the central action, waxing as the Beggars enter, reaching the full at the point when the Saint offers them their choice, and remaining so until the end of the Lame Beggar's dance, then waning for the concluding choric song, when we are told it 'Has taken a new phase' [*CPl* 471]. The entire action, including the choric songs, takes place below this comic moon and is illuminated by it. Two of the Musicians, since only one of the three is required to sing as Chorus or to speak as Saint, could mime, as front and hind legs of a pantomime cat, the dance of Minnaloushe.

The grotesquerie of the Beggars maintains this comic tonality, though on a different dynamic level as it were, and moreover maintains it throughout the play. Yeats tells us that

when the Saint mounts upon the back of the Lame Beggar he personifies a certain great spiritual event

[*Comm. Pl* 172]

but our imaginations, compelled to respond to this in the terms that Yeats has used – terms that present man as a grotesque, impoverished, flawed, crippled, though ultimately not a despicable creature, must surely apprehend it as something less than a solemn heroic transcendence.

Both Wilson [*YI* 153] and Taylor [*DWBY* 147] interpret the counting of the steps in terms of an historical and spiritual approach to unity, but with so little corroboration from elsewhere in the play that it is almost certain that no audience would take such a point. Even a Yeats *aficionado,* with the thousand-year units of the Magnus Annus at the back of his mind (when the heavenly bodies were to return to their original relative positions) is likely to lose grip on it in the very effective theatrical shock of this gothically comic entry. (Is the omission of 'thousand and eight' from the counting sequence an opportunity for a bit of comic 'business' from the actors?) The beggar at the crossroads, considered within the prevailing tone of the play, seems to suggest not so much Wilson's solemn '*conjunctio oppositorum*' or Unity of Being, as a comic reduction of the Daemon figure who directs the hero to the place and moment of his decision. The two Beggars are simply following the instructions given them – 'one thousand paces from where he stood and a few paces over' [*CPl* 462].

Their joint entry, one on the back of the other, of course embodies visually the notion of incompleteness of either taken separately, and the necessity of their interdependence, the fusion of opposites. Considered separately, they exhibit opposite qualities which lead

them to independence — though of different kinds — and
consequently their separation. But they are not merely opposed to
each other in some respect. Each contains contradictory qualities
within himself, manifested as recognisably human traits of character.
Blind Beggar is bad-tempered, selfish, domineering and suspicious
— rightly as it turns out. One side of his nature, the materialistic,
can see the practical disadvantages and advantages of being cured:
the risk of not getting the money that people are prepared to give
to the blind, but also the opportunity to stop others from stealing
his own goods, and finally the chance to achieve independence from
Lame Beggar. It is this side of his nature that prevents him from
seeing the Saint. He is blind, not to all spiritual experience, but only
to certain kinds of it. He is anti-clerical, anti-conventional piety, but,
like Crazy Jane, he has his own brand of secular spirituality. Below
his crusty exterior there is a reservoir of folk-wisdom, fed by his
experience from the age of ten, of 'hearing and remembering the
knowledges of the world' [*CPl* 465], his blindness having imparted
to him an inner knowledge of 'the heart of man' [*CPl* 464]. This
is what Lame Beggar, for all his physical sight, lacks. Blind Beggar
recognises the kinship of this mysterious wisdom with Lame Beggar's
but at the same time asserts its difference. Like Cat and Moon they
are kindred but opposite. He admits that he has been egged on by
Lame Beggar's 'flighty talk' [*CPl* 463], but questions the wisdom
of doing so. His inner wisdom rejects the transcendence of the Saint,
finding his own form of blessedness in the natural, secular world,
where things and people have the natural egalitarian innocence of
their simple existence, where love is neither pity looking down upon
its object, nor a moral force directed at converting it, but what Yeats
called in a letter to Lady Dorothy Wellesley 'a form of the eternal
contemplation of what is' [*DWL* 126]. It is this natural, non-moral,
life-affirming wisdom, heretical to the conventionally pious Lame
Beggar, that prompts Blind Beggar to suggest that the Saint is not
at all interested in their prayers, nor even in the 'holy company
kneeling at his will on holidays and Sundays, and they as innocent
maybe as himself' [*CPl* 465], but only in talking to sinners because
he would not have them different from what they are:

Now the Church says that it is a good thought, and a sweet thought, and
a comfortable thought, that every man may have a saint to look after him,
and I, being blind, give it out to all the world that the bigger the sinner
the better pleased is the saint. I am sure and certain that Saint Colman would
not have us two different from what we are.

[*CPl* 466]

But is is quite in accord with his mixed nature that he is incapable of carrying through into argument the apparently sweet concessionary reasonableness of this approach. He answers Lame Beggar's contradiction 'I'll not give into that' [*CPl* 466] by a blow with his stick. At this moment, when the differences between them have reached a critical point, they encounter the supernatural. The Saint intervenes, offering them their choice of cure or blessedness. Blind Beggar chooses cure and at once his restored sight becomes the agent of his inner vision in a description of the external world that clearly reflects not only Synge's pagan delight in nature but also Yeats's own idea that ultimately the blind, having been excluded from practical activities, become artists and find content in 'the praise of life' [*E&I* 278]:

I see it all now, the blue sky and the big ash-tree and the well and the flat stone, – all as I have heard the people say – and the things the praying people put on the stone, the beads and the candles and the leaves torn out of prayer-books, and the hairpins and the buttons. It is a great sight and a blessed sight . . .

[*CPl* 468]

What is this but a prose gloss on the Self's Blakean cry in 'A Dialogue of Self and Soul',

We are blest by everything
Everything we look upon is blest.

[*CP* 267]

But such vision, whose source lies in 'the knowledges of the world', though it may reward him with worldly information, does not change his essential nature. His eyes confirm what his instincts had already suspected, namely that Lame Beggar is a thief, and his response to the situation is true to his nature, unregenerate and unconverted, yet at the same time superbly indifferent to material considerations. There is nothing in the text to suggest that he is faintly interested in recovering his stolen sheepskin: in the light of his new-found spiritual enlightment such things are immaterial. The two sides of his nature, animal and spiritual, are wonderfully exhibited in the ambivalence of his infuriated question, 'Where'll I hit him, for the love of God, where'll I hit him?' [*CPl* 469]. But the God he serves is his own God, and again like the Self in 'A Dialogue of Self and Soul' he enters upon his own secular beatitude, symbolized by the

ritual dance. This begins with his physically asserting his domination
over Lame Beggar but ends with his choosing the loneliness of his
own individuality, of self-fulfilment, of separation. The Saint, out
of a kind of kindred fellow-feeling — 'I am a saint and lonely' [*CPl*
466] — does not commit himself to consigning him to conventional
perdition, as Lame Beggar does:

> *Lame Beggar:* That is a soul lost, Holy Man.
> *First Musician* [*as Saint*]: Maybe so.
>
> [*CPl* 470]

Ambivalence lies at the core of the play, encompassed by a benign
Chaucerian inclusiveness that expresses itself in the joyful acceptance
of God's plenty, warts and all.

Lame Beggar is every bit as much a specimen of man's
unregenerate nature as Blind Beggar. He is a cheat, a liar, and a
thief, quite ready to shift the burden of moral choice onto his
companion:

> you are a bitter temptation to many a poor man, and I say it's not right,
> it's not right at all. There are poor men that because you are blind will be
> delayed in Purgatory.
>
> [*CPl* 464]

He is conventionally pious, certain that the Saint will not listen to
them 'without an Ave or Paternoster to put before the prayer or
after the prayer', [*CPl* 464] and sure that he would be put out by
their ignorance of ecclesiastical Latin. He is anxious that Blind Beggar
should not put his soul in mortal peril:

> Forty years we have been knocking about the roads together, and I wouldn't
> have you bring your soul into mortal peril.
>
> [*CPl* 469]

To him Blind Beggar's view of sainthood is heretical. But, like Blind
Beggar's, his nature is mixed. Intelligent enough to realize the
material advantages to his companion of sight, he is stupid enough
not to realise that if sight is restored to him Blind Beggar will see
through his deceit over the sheepskin:

Lame Beggar: Haven't I been telling you from the peep o' day that my sheepskin is that white it would dazzle you?
Blind Beggar: Are you so swept with the words that you've never thought that when I had my own two eyes, I'd see what colour was on it?
Lame Beggar [*very dejected*]: I never thought of that.

[*CPl* 468–9]

On the material level he takes orders from Blind Beggar, but spiritually he finds at least part of his own way. For all his conventional piety, for all his roguery, it is he who sees and responds to the kind of disembodied spirituality that the Saint, invisible and weighing no more than a grasshopper, represents. But even so his response is far from pure. It is true that he rejects the material advantages of a cure in favour of the possibly superior advantages of blessedness:

It would be a grand thing to have two legs under me, but I have it in my mind that it would be a grander thing to have my name in that book.

[*CPl* 467]

But there is an element of calculation, what Wilson calls 'spiritual cupidity' [*YI* 143] in his choice, which is balanced by his spiritual timidity, his unwillingness to accept, after the first taste of it at the end of Blind Beggar's stick, the full burden of sainthood, which includes martyrdom. The inner contradictions of Lame Beggar's nature are summed up in the word 'flighty', used six times of him. It bears not only the connotations of 'unstable', 'untrustworthy', even 'stupid' − 'wise though you are and flighty though you are' [*CPl* 464] − but in much the same way as the same word sums up the ambivalent qualities in Decima in *The Player Queen,* it also suggests a superior quality, the capacity of the imagination to take flight into a spiritual atmosphere. As Yeats keeps on telling us, there is no impassable gulf between higher and lower, between body and soul, pagan and Christian, saint and sinner. Lame Beggar's crippled nature does become the vehicle of Christian miracle, but not until after the Saint has made him participate in the pagan ceremony of the blessing of the natural world by bowing to the four cardinal points of the compass. His unregenerate nature remains with him: he still cannily wants to be assured of the calculated rewards of blessedness, and he still plays second fiddle, only this time to the Saint, who gently pushes him towards his beatitude.

And what of his 'great spiritual event'? Just as his 'martyrdom' is diminished by the terms of its expression − a ritualistic beating-up in which the blows, like the collisions in custard-pie comedy, do not hurt — so his dervish dance of beatitude, however ecstatic, is reduced in significance both by the play's inherent comic qualities and by being placed in the framework of the choric songs. The comic qualities reside in the following elements: firstly, the pervasive grotesquerie already referred to, which a reader, lacking the visual impact of drama, is apt to forget, but which an audience is continually reminded of by the players' masks; secondly, *pace* Moore [*MLD* 244] the fact that Lame Beggar remains lame, his lameness being emphasized by the clashing of cymbals whenever his lame foot touches the ground [*CPl* 471], the miracle lying not in his losing his lameness but in being able to dance at all, though it is a far from graceful performance; thirdly, the fact that although he thinks that the Saint has completed his being by getting up on his back, there is actually no-one there. There is something absurb in the way in which he thinks the Saint is on his shoulders, accepts like a child the assurance and the directions of the First Musician, becomes, in fact, the butt of his gentle humour as he propels him to the dance. But although he is made a fool of, he is not derided. His folly is that of 'The Child of God' [*AV(B)* 182], impervious to ridicule or criticism.

The First Musician, having discarded the role of Saint, now completes the framework of the play with the closing choric song, which echoes and confirms the tone of the others. The first has been discussed already. The second, sung while Blind Beggar with Lame Beggar on his back move grotesquely on their symbolic journey towards spiritual enlightenment, strengthens the note of mockery already sounded in the first:

> Minnaloushe runs in the grass
> Lifting his delicate feet.
> Do you dance, Minnaloushe, do you dance?
> When two close kindred meet
> What better than call a dance?
> Maybe the moon may learn,
> Tired of that courtly fashion,
> A new dance turn.
>
> [*CPl* 462–3]

This stresses the connection between the ungainly movements of the linked pair and the comically graceful movements of Minnaloushe, and also anticipates the central action. Now, in the last song, the creeping cat runs, the fusion of opposites 'When two close kindred

meet' will be fit subject for a dance, a dance not confined to courtly
aristocrats but one that will be appropriate to the beggars who are
at the opposite pole of society yet complete it. The last song realizes
the ironies implicit in the other two:

> Minnaloushe creeps through the grass
> From moonlit place to place.
> The sacred moon overhead
> Has taken a new phase.
> Does Minnaloushe know that his pupils
> Will pass from change to change,
> And that from round to crescent
> From crescent to round they range?
> Minnaloushe creeps through the grass
> Alone, important and wise,
> And lifts to the changing moon
> His changing eyes.

> [*CPl* 471–2]

Minnaloushe is back where he started, creeping on the ground; the
moon has learnt a new dance tune; the cycles have turned, the moon
has taken a new phase; soul has separated from body; each has found
its own ecstasy, having gone its own way, alone, content with its
own wisdom, sure of its own value. But in the moonlit illumination
of sanctity, which would seem to offer an escape from the endless
round of change, does man know that every movement of his thought
or life, even his own transcendence, is but a microcosmic reflection
of the macrocosmic cycles? Whether he does or not, he cannot escape
the contradictions of his own nature. Alone, important, wise – there
is a kind of affectionately mocking irony in the application of these
urbanely poised, weighted epithets to the humanly fastidious animal
Minnaloushe, and beyond him to those two squalid, tatterdemalion
specimens of humanity who are at the same time his opposites and
his kindred, while overhead in the endless sequence of its phases,
the comic moon continues to inspire and mock man's transient
enterprises. My man-in-the-moon would end this play with a wink.

Calvary

The source of the play is Oscar Wilde's austere anecdote told to Yeats by an actor, which impressed him by its 'terrible beauty', though he regretted the 'verbal decoration' that Wilde gave to its later form when he published it as 'The Doer of Good'. The actor's version is as follows:

Christ came from a white plain to a purple city, and as He passed through the first street He heard voices overhead, and saw a young man lying drunk upon a window-sill. 'Why do you waste your soul in drunkenness?' He said, 'Lord, I was a leper and You healed me, what else can I do?' A little further through the town He saw a young man following a harlot, and said 'Why do you dissolve your soul in debauchery?' and the young man answered, 'Lord, I was blind, and You healed me, what else can I do?' At last in the middle of the city He saw an old man crouching, weeping upon the ground, and when He asked why he wept, the old man answered, 'Lord, I was dead, and You raised me into life, what else can I do but weep?'

[A 286]

Yeats abandons the rather shallow *fin-de-siècle* concern with sin, but follows the episodic structure of Wilde's anecdote while at the same time making it the basis of an intellectualized version of what he saw as a Noh play, with its Musicians, choric songs, actors generalized by masks, climactic dance and binding images. It is the episodic nature of its base that makes one question the validity of its dramatic structure, for although the episodes in themselves dramatize intellectual or emotional attitudes, they are not related to each other in terms of dialectical argument, in the manner of a Shavian cut-and-thrust debate leading to some conclusion whether explicit or implicit. One wonders why the episodes occur in the order that they do, though one can acknowledge the effectiveness of the concluding tableau as yielding a kind of theatrical *frisson*. Two considerations emerge in this respect: one is that the very absence of a dramatic structure that can be formulated in logically related terms is in itself a dramatization of one of the ideas implicit in the play, namely God's chance, or, as the second Roman Soldier remarks:

154

> Whatever happens is the best, we say,
> So that it's unexpected.
>
> [*CPl* 456]

The other is also related to a possible reading of the play which sees the despair of Lazarus unable to find the freedom he desires, the abrogation of choice by the Marys, the betrayal by Judas as a means of establishing his separate identity, the indifference of the Soldiers, and Christ's own decision to abrogate human choice in favour of submission to the Divine Will, all these acts as ultimately unfree. They are in themselves gestures in the direction of individual identity and freedom, but they are in fact conditioned by the inescapable circular movement of destiny. Everyone, including Christ, is at the centre of the whirling wheel. Imaginatively the structure of the play can be seen as circular, in which, because all the events have to happen, it does not matter in what order they occur. It may be significant that Yeats in his note talks of *surrounding* Christ with images of those He cannot save. This creates problems of dramatic form since drama is essentially sequential, with one event not only following but developing from the preceding, but it may support those who, like Wilson, see the play as moving to a climax in the final dance, whose function is

> that of all the dances in Yeats's drama: to isolate, and to present in a concentrated form, the central emotion of the play.
>
> [*YI* 200]

If this is the case, then the imaginative centre of the play are the choric songs, round which the other elements of the play revolve, and to which they are related not only by contrast but by shared imagery. For example, Lazarus is related to the imagery of the solitary birds of the first song and to the height and the depth of the third (the 'blue deep of the upper air' [*CPl* 457]); the Marys to the

> eagle, swan or gull,
> Or a drowned heron's feather
>
> [*CPl* 453]

of the second; Judas to the heron ('When I planned it / There was no live thing near me but a heron' [*CPl* 454]); the Soldiers more remotely to the notion of solitude ('There's no-one here but Judas and ourselves' [*CPl* 455]) and to the heron-bone flute whose music, as in *The Herne's Egg,* announces the presence of divinity. It is the instrument of Choice but is now down-graded into a sheep's thigh-bones from which dice, the instruments of Chance, are fashioned. The contrast is effected, as Ure pointed out [*YTP* 117], by the more than usually sharply defined differences of style and feeling between the 'impersonal, remote, and symbolic' qualities of the songs on the one hand and the individual, almost naturalistic, language of the episodes.

Within, and in terms of this circular structure, Yeats works out his themes. The most readily identifiable, and one which scarcely needs the assistance of Yeats's elaborate note [*Comm. Pl* 166–7] is, in Ure's formulation 'the powerlessness [of Christ] to save those who can live without salvation' [*YTP* 115]. This is worked out first in the Lazarus episode. Lazarus has sought his own chosen peace in the oblivion of death, but has been deprived of it by what to him is Christ's totally gratuitous and unacceptable act of bringing him back from the dead. The intensity of his revulsion is reflected visually in his 'Death-stricken and death-hungry' mask [*CPl* 453], and verbally in the toughness, the crudeness even, of his image:

> You dragged me to the light as boys drag out
> A rabbit when they have dug its hole away.
>
> [*CPl* 452]

The notion that Christ, through his voluntary sacrifice, has cancelled death, is seen by Lazarus as an imposition upon his own free choice:

> But now you will blind with light the solitude
> That death has made; you will disturb that corner
> Where I had thought I might lie safe for ever.
>
> [*CPl* 452]

For Lazarus it is no justification that Christ is merely the agent of His Father's will; that, too, is a despicable denial of individuality. Consequently he has no option but to go on searching in an agony of despair for a peace that he can no longer find in an historical era that is bound to be infected by the consequences of Christ's choice until the cycles bring it to an end. As a corollary Christ has no option but to accept the responsibility for that despair.

Lazarus, who attempts to preserve self-hood by keeping Christ at arm's length, is followed in the second episode by those who are the complete antithesis of him, Martha, the three Marys, and 'the rest / That live but in His love' [*CPl* 453], that is, those who have so completely sunk their own individuality in His love that they have become anonymous units, their lives expressed in a mime of corporate humility. Unlike Judas and Lazarus, they have no personalities. Significantly they are given nothing to say.

These are followed by Judas, who has not only resisted absorption in the will of God but has attempted to master it by the assertion of self in an extreme act of choice. In *A Vision* Judas is an example of the Hunchback 'who commits crimes . . . because he wants to feel certain that he can', whose

greatest temptation may be to defy God, to become a Judas, who betrays, not for thirty pieces of silver, but that he may call himself creator.

[*AV(B)* 177–8]

Even if the betrayal of Christ had been decreed by a supreme destiny ruling over everything, including Christ's fate, the actual mode of its operation was determined by Judas:

It was decreed that somebody betray you –
I'd thought of that – but not that I should do it,
I the man Judas, born on such a day,
In such a village, such and such his parents;
Nor that I'd go with my old coat upon me
To the High Priest, and chuckle to myself
As people chuckle when alone, and do it
For thirty pieces and no more, no less,
And neither with a nod nor a sent message,
But with a kiss upon your cheek. I did it,
I, Judas, and no other man, and now
You cannot even save me.

[*CPl* 454–5]

Although the 'chuckle' image links him with Lazarus:

And when I sickened towards my death I thought,
'I'll to the desert' or chuckle in a corner,
Mere ghost, a solitary thing.'

[*CPl* 452]

he is different from him in the way he confronts Christ with the energy of an intellectual argument, to which in the end Christ has no answer but to attempt to banish him to the solitude of that freedom which Judas sees as the reward of 'Whatever man betrays Him' [*CPl* 454]. To Christ his presence is intolerable and therefore he must be banished. But the cycle of events does not permit this. Taylor is surely right in saying [*DWBY* 159] that with the entry of the Roman Soldiers who make Judas hold up the cross, 'necessity routs reflection'. A force larger than the human will, larger, even, than Christ's will, takes over.

In the last episode the Roman Soldiers present a third way of asserting independence from Christ's will: they declare their total disinterestedness towards Him and His agony. They do not seek either the oblivion of Lazarus, or the anonymity of the Marys, or the egocentric authority of Judas. They worship whatever life brings, and in their good natured tolerance offer Him the ironical comfort of the knowledge that He can do nothing for them, which of course is the last thing He wants to hear:

> One thing is plain,
> To know that he has nothing that we need
> Must be a comfort to him.

> [*CPl* 456]

This and their symbolic dance, in which antagonisms are resolved not by individual decision but by chance (the throw of the dice), which in its gaiety is in itself a mimetic representation of the cyclic revolutions of destiny, elicits from Christ his agonized torment at His failure:

> My Father, why hast Thou forsaken me?

> [*CPl* 456]

For even an uninitiated audience this dramatic core of the play is not difficult to discern, though Yeats's 'programme-note' could be drawn upon to dot the Is and cross the Ts:

I have surrounded Him with the images of those. He cannot save, not only with the birds, who have served neither God nor Caesar, and await for none or for a different saviour, but with Lazarus and Judas and the Roman soldiers for whom He has died in vain. 'Christ' writes Robartes, 'only pitied those whose suffering is rooted in death, in poverty, or in sickness, or in sin, in some shape of the common lot, and he came especially to the poor who are most subject to exterior vicissitude.' I have therefore represented in Lazarus and Judas types of that intellectual despair that lay beyond His sympathy, while in the Roman soldiers I suggest a form of objectivity that lay beyond His help . . .

> [*Comm. Pl* 167]

What is more difficult to grasp is the complex of ideas with which Yeats surrounds this central core, expressed in terms of loneliness and the initiation of the Christian era in the cycles of history.

Types of loneliness are defined as subjective and objective, the former metaphorically in terms of certain birds, especially, as Yeats's note informs us,

Such lonely birds as the heron, hawk, eagle, and swan are the natural symbols of subjectivity . . . while the beasts that run upon the ground, especially those that run in packs, are the natural symbols of objective man. Objective men, however personally alone, are never alone in their thought, which is always developed in agreement or in conflict with the thought of others and always seeks the welfare of some cause or institution, while subjective men are the more lonely that more they are true to type, seeking always that which is unique or personal.

[*Comm. Pl* 167]

Those who are subjectively lonely are those who are completely absorbed in their own being, who have totally divested themselves of the love of created beings, of all contact with the external world, who have descended into the depths of the self-contained soul in order to reach the heights of absorption in God. Those who are objectively lonely are those who, however isolated as individuals from the community of men, however much they appear to be 'loners', nevertheless seek their identity in relation to the outside world. Yeats's symbol for the first type, for pure subjective being, is the heron illuminated in the light of the full moon. The heron is lost in contemplation of his own image. He rejects the ephemeral appeal of externalities, being self-sustained by the passive energies of his own inactivity, but terrified, like the mystic in the penultimate stage of his quest, the dark night of the soul, at the apprehension of the total isolation of the self from everything, even from God:

> Motionless under the moon-beam,
> Up to his feathers in the stream;
> Although fish leap, the white heron
> Shivers in a dumbfounded dream.

[*CPl* 449]

The dream not only has the terror that accompanies any quest for a self-annihilating spirituality (the kind of terror that the Young Man was confronted with in the meeting with the Ghosts in *The Dreaming of the Bones*), but also by virtue of its total detachment from the exterior world, renders the subjective man dumb, as the Soul is rendered dumb at the moment of its total absorption in spirituality in 'A Dialogue of Self and Soul' [*CP* 265]. However, the opening lyric seems to indicate that the state of mystic self-absorption is not eternally static: the full moon is a symbol of complete subjectivity, but equally the moon must change. In the kinetic nature of things, in the inevitable movement of the cycles, the appeal of the objective external world will reassert itself over the subjective, otherwise the heron would not be able to sustain itself. It would die, and become the diet of fishes instead of itself feeding upon them. Eternal energies need to be sustained by the products of time:

> But that the full is shortly gone
> And after that the crescent moon,
> It's certain that the moon-crazed heron
> Would be but fishes' diet soon.

> [*CPl* 450]

To some extent all the figures in the play partake in a degree of subjectivity. This is why the heron/bird/eagle image relates to all of them. It relates to Lazarus, in his assertion of the right of the individual to his own kind of solitude — the finality of death in a desert or a corner; to the Marys and their followers in their total surrender of self — they are truly 'dumbfounded' in that they say nothing; to Judas, in the vehement assertion of his own subjective will; to the Soldiers in their total surrender to the vicissitudes of Chance; and finally to Christ Himself in his total, subjectively willed surrender to the will of His Father.

But equally all are caught up in objective loneliness, in the degree to which their subjectivity is related to the thought of others. First the Heron — and here one should make a distinction between the Heron as natural bird, like swans, gulls and eagles, part of the order of Nature which knows neither spirituality nor secular civilization ('have served neither God nor Caesar' [*Comm. Pl* 167]) and which remain solid birds in the accuracy of Yeats's observation of them in the final lyric — and the Heron as symbol. The Heron's subjectivity is not self-sustained. It is even crazed by the moon and could be supplanted by the emergent objective cycle, as it is drowned in the bitter spray of the sea of objective life even though the moon is at the full. Similarly Lazarus cannot escape from the influence of Christ, which reaches beyond and destroys the sought tranquillity of the grave. The Marys and their followers are wholly dependent upon Christ. Judas cannot avoid the task of holding up the cross for the Saviour whose efficacy he has denied. In the end the circling

Soldiers become the symbol for the objective world that can only
turn round Him. Christ Himself, in so far as His love is expressed
as pity for those rooted in the common lot of death, suffering,
sickness or sin, is essentially related as Man to that objective world.
It is within the tug of these polarities that the play is worked out,
so that Helen Vendler is right in saying that

the play is concerned with the interaction of objective and subjective life,
the double interlocking gyres [of History].

[*YV* 173]

though I find nothing in the *play,* whatever Yeats may have written
about Him elsewhere, to support her view that He is the creative
imagination.

The double interlocking gyres of History emerge, less insistently,
in the symbolism of the lunar phase in which Yeats expresses his
view of the historicity of Christianity. The birth of Christ initiates
an objective age, in which heroic transcendence becomes less and
less possible as it moves away from a condition of pure subjectivity
to its disintegration, in lunar terms from the full of the moon to
its dark, phase 15 back to phase 1. It is Christ's torment not only
to witness but to participate in this movement. Nathan aptly
comments:

His human nature, derived from the dying subjective cycle, experiences the
agony of a man out of phase and deprived of the possibility − in His isolated
state − of completion. He is a protagonist agonizingly fixed in His historical
role and has no hope of a fulfilling tragic experience. Living His experience
over again means only *that,* not a purgatorial cleansing. Appropriately the
play ends on a note of unmitigated horror.

[*TD* 204]

Thus the play can be thought of in terms of concentric, circular
movements revolving round a centre which is not, however, rigidly
fixed, as it oscillates between subjectivity and objectivity. At the
centre of pure subjectivity stands the heron and the aspect of Christ
in the perfection of His self-hood which He has achieved in the
voluntary and paradoxical surrender of His self in the will of His
Father. This is the dominant element in His nature, as Yeats presents
Him. Though He has in His life expressed His love towards others,
He remains curiously remote from them, a figure of marmoreal
stillness, rigid like the figure in an icon. Outside that circle and
moving round a point of objectivity are those who are subjective by

nature but, having been born into an objective era, cannot entirely escape from the influence of Christ's pity, however much they reject it. These are Lazarus, who responds emotionally, Judas, who responds intellectually, and the Soldiers who respond unthinkingly, all imagining that their indifference to Christ is a passport to freedom from His influence. But it is not. Bloom is right in saying that 'to be indifferent is not to be self-sufficient; it is only not to know that one is dependent' [*Y* 312]. Martha, the Marys, and their like are the complete antithesis of Lazarus and Judas in that they totally abandon their selfhood in the objectivity of Christ's love, a gesture which Yeats seems to treat as a degradation of personality. Their mimed acts of humility come close to abasement:

> He holds His right arm out, and on His arm
> Their lips are pressed and their tears fall and now
> They cast them on the ground before His dirty
> Blood-dabbled feet and clean them with their hair.
>
> [*CPl* 453]

In the same way Christ's gestures of pity for Lazarus and Judas are described in terms that not only reflect the antithetical animal imagery of objectivity, but also the coarseness of the animal world — Lazarus dragged out of his hold like a rabbit, Christ whistling to Judas as one whistles to a dog:

> I could not bear to think you had but to whistle
> And I must do.
>
> [*CPl* 454]

But outside that circle is yet another, which revolves round Christ Himself, completing a pattern in which, caught between His subjective nature and His objective pity, He is fixed in the endless Calvary of His knowledge that for some, at any rate, His passion has been in vain. His subjectivity is reflected in the action, in His self-absorbed passivity. He does nothing by Himself, everything that happens is a reflection of Him. In this He resembles the moon-crazed heron. Verbally this passivity is reflected in the almost static impersonality of His austere statements. His objectivity is reflected in the way in which His response to the final agony of recognition that He has failed is a devastatingly human outcry from Himself as Man. That tableau of Christ crucified on the cross supported by Judas with the Soldiers dancing around it is indeed a genuine and theatrically vivid climax, which suggests that the revolving cycles encompass all, that neither Lazarus nor Judas can get free of Christ, that the Soldiers' indifference is no release from Him, and finally that He cannot escape the consequences of His own actions, that He is both isolated from and at the same time related to them. In this connection it is difficult to account for Lazarus's absence from the scene, and I find Taylor's suggestion of keeping him on stage throughout very attractive. The Musicians are left to assert the force and beauty of the drive towards subjectivity, in the lonely sea-bird, the ger-eagle content with his savage heart, the flight of cygnets (new breed from a dying generation as the cycles turn) towards absorption in their own kind, but at the same time the bleak denial that God impinges on them. In the end God has not only not died for the white heron, He has forsaken it too.

A major problem in the presentation of the play is how to make the audience see that the action does not take place on the actual day of Christ's Calvary, but in His mind, as He is compelled to re-live the events of His past. Everything that happens is the product of His dream-vision, but He initiates no exterior action, remaining passive. He is, of course, a central figure, the axis on which the dance turns, but so too are the Musicians who also move into the centre in so far as in their lyric (subjective) songs and in their descriptive/narrative (objective) passages they reflect the interaction of the subjective and the objective life. They are not to be regarded as mere commentators on the circumference. The way in which the action is basically internalized in Christ's mind and thus held at a distance from the exterior world – a quality that Yeats saw in the Noh convention and sought to uphold in his dance plays – is best realized by the use of correspondingly non-naturalistic masks and stylized mimetic movement. With imaginatively sculptured masks, a serene, almost liturgically chanted delivery of the choric songs, and stylized movement and gesture, devices that draw the action into the deeps of the mind, with these set against the more naturalistic language of Judas, Lazarus and the Soldiers, and their immediately apprehensible relevance, in terms of psychology and action, to a plausible exterior world, something of that interaction of the stasis of subjectivity with the kinesis of objectivity which is Yeats's central concern may be translated into theatrical terms, and the play produce a greater impact on the stage than a reading of it would suggest.

The Resurrection

The Resurrection can be contrasted with *Calvary* in many ways, in respect of its content and its dramatic procedures. Whereas *Calvary* left one in doubt as to the universal validity of Christ's sacrifice, *The Resurrection* presents it as having an impact that is not only shattering but generative in the world in which it occurs. That world can be interpreted externally in terms of social and political structures, or internally in terms of philosophical and religious attitudes, or, indeed, of the functioning of the creative imagination as new images are created in the death of the old. Even though this impact is set within a choric framework which absorbs it into the same kind of universal process of destruction and renewal that was adumbrated in *The Unicorn from the Stars,* the imaginative core of the play lies in the presentation of Christ's resurrection, concentrated in a scene of stunning theatrical effectiveness, as a unique temporal event of overwhelming magnitude. Whereas the 'arguments' of *Calvary* revolve round the nucleus of a visual image, literally held up for our contemplation, the argument of *The Resurrection* is developed lineally in the form of a thesis/antithesis structure. This is represented dramatically by the Greek, who believes that Christ was only a God and therefore cannot die, and the Hebrew, who believes that He was only a man and therefore must die. This opposition is not resolved in a synthesis but transcended by an altogether different third category, Christ, who is both man and God. This third category, however, is presented not in the intellectual terms of the other two but as a kind of dramatic epiphany – the entry of the risen Christ. This epiphany links *The Resurrection* with *Calvary*, where it took the form of the tableau of Christ on the cross held up by Judas and surrounded by the dancing Soldiers. But *The Resurrection* differs from *Calvary* in the function of the choric songs. There they were an integral part of the play's dramatic and imaginative structure; here, even though they are subtly linked with the main action, they operate much more as an extrapolation from it. A good deal less of a 'dance-play' than *Calvary* – there is, in fact, no climactic dance – it nevertheless exhibits features derived

164

from Noh practice: the binding images in the choric songs of the beating heart and the fabulous darkness, 'characters' who, without being archetypal, are generalized in so far as they represent points of view, while retaining enough recognizable human qualities to enable an audience to identify with them and so become drawn into the almost naturalistic representational element of the play. It is this representational element, untypical of Noh drama, that Yeats nevertheless uses as a means of magnifying the shock effect of the one feature of *The Resurrection* that derives most obviously from the Noh, namely the introduction of the supernatural, the entry and impact of the risen Christ. For all its aura of the miraculous, this derives its effectiveness from the naturalism of its setting. At the same time it shatters the temporal shell of that naturalism, so that the mind is opened to the wider concerns which are the subject of the closing choric song.

Leaving aside the opening choric song for the moment, the play opens naturalistically enough at a particular moment in time, which we later learn is the third day after Christ's crucifixion, in a particular house where the Hebrew, the Greek and the Syrian have been guarding the disciples. The play ought to be staged with Yeats's original intentions in mind: '*an ordinary stage scene. . . curtained walls, a window and door at back, a curtained door. . .* [*CPl* 579] its mundane boundaries anticipating their fracture by the irruption of the miraculous. Once again, as we have seen in earlier plays, Yeats uses the stage space as a factor in dramatic meaning. The action is set in the natural and measurable world of rational human behaviour. Outside it are the forces that are going to break into it and shatter it. These forces are symbolised first by the two mobs — the followers of the Dionysian rite and the anonymous crowd hunting Christians — and later by Christ Himself. In the same way Yeats exploits the aural resources of drama: laughter, drum-beats (corroborated by the verbal image of 'the beating heart'), rattles, which take the place of his usual Noh-like instruments, the scream, and that most important ingredient in the build-up of tension — silence.

The three 'characters' are generalized to the extent that they represent attitudes more than personalities, though they are not entirely without psychological depth; their nationalities seem to be somewhat arbitrarily selected, except possibly that of the Greek. He does embody some of the qualities so often associated with the Hellenic ideal — a kind of rational, order-loving, logical humanism — but the Hebrew does not appear to represent conventional Hebraism, nor does the Syrian seem to be more susceptible than anyone else might be to the appeal of the mystery of a God who is both God and Man. No reason is given for their willingness to defend the disciples to the death, even when it is revealed that Christ's crucifixion has merely confirmed them both in their existing convictions: the Hebrew that Christ was, after all, not the Messiah but merely a very good man; the Greek that he was never a man but only a God who chose to take on the appearance but not the substance of humanity. Perhaps a point here is that regardless of intellectual convictions, regardless even of human will, the Christian dispensation will inevitably appear, will inevitably acquire its adherents and defenders.

Philosophically the Hebrew's position is quite clear: up to the moment of Christ's crucifixion, when it appeared that He was unable to save Himself as a God could have done, he was prepared to believe that He was the Messiah, born of woman, since

If the Messiah were not born of woman he could not take away the sins of man. Every sin starts a stream of suffering, but the Messiah takes it all away.

[*CPl* 584]

For the Hebrew the Messiah is able to

exhaust human suffering as though it were all gathered together in the spot of a burning-glass.

[*CPl* 584]

But His death destroyed that belief:

He was nothing more than a man, the best man who ever lived. Nobody before him had so pitied human misery. He preached the coming of the Messiah because he thought the Messiah would take it all upon himself. Then some day when he was very tired, after a long journey perhaps, he thought that he himself was the Messiah.

[*CPl* 583–4]

As an ordinary man, unwilling like most of us to make the spiritual effort necessary to submit oneself entirely to the divine will, to lose subjective individuality in the objectivity of God's love, the Hebrew is glad that that condition is not likely to be realized. The cost would have been too great:'

It must be a terrible thing when one is old, and the tomb round the corner, to think of all the ambitions one has put aside; to think, perhaps, a great deal about women. I want to marry and have children.

[*CPl* 585]

The Hebrew reveals his humanity both in its frailty and its decency. It is he who describes in plain matter-of-fact terms the simple, natural human activities of the disciples in the next room:

James brought a loaf out of a bag, and Nathanael found a skin of wine. They put them on the table . . .

[*CPl* 581]

Though aware of the claims of the absolute he cannot respond actively to them. Nevertheless he is humble and compassionate enough not to condemn others like him:

Peter told the others what he had done. But when the moment came they were all afraid. I must not blame. I might have been no braver. What are we all but dogs that have lost their master?

[*CPl* 582]

Later, before the actual manifestation of the risen Christ, when the Syrian returns with the news of the resurrection, the Hebrew literally stands in the way of the Syrian carrying it to the disciples. Out of sheer human compassion he tries to protect Peter from the over-whelming burden of the significance of his betrayal:

Peter's misery would be increased. I know him longer than you do and I know what would happen. Peter would remember that the women did not flinch; that not one amongst them denied her master; that the dream proved their love and faith. Then he would remember that he had lacked both, and imagine that John was looking at him. He would turn away and bury his head in his hands.

[*CPl* 589–90]

Nevertheless, when faced with the objective truth of Christ, he acknowledges it, though passively, by kneeling before Him in a moment of silence. (In performance, should Christ make some acknowledgement here?)

The attitude of the Greek is equally clear but totally different. He is primarily an intellectual humanist, rational, urbane, cultivated, something of an aesthete. Philosophically his position is based on the view that Gods and men inhabit totally different dimensions, though the Gods are knowable to man in the act of contemplation. Imaginatively man projects onto them his own qualities, magnified and idealized. He knows that he cannot hope to realize them himself, and that only men of heroic proportions can emulate them. But the

Gods themselves exist in their perfection, independence and remoteness:

When the goddess came to Achilles in the battle she did not interfere with his soul, she took him by his yellow hair . . . They can be discovered by contemplation, in their faces a high keen joy like the cry of a bat, and the man who lives heroically gives them the only earthly body that they covet. . . What seems their indifference is but their eternal possession of themselves. Man, too, remains separate. He does not surrender his soul. He keeps his privacy.

[*CPl* 587–8]

That privacy extends to his own sins: 'nobody else has a right to them' [*CPl* 584]. Here is not only Greek anthropomorphism but Yeatsian subjectivity. For the Greek, Calvary is not so much a tragedy as a laughable failure, for how could anyone in their rational senses imagine that

they were nailing the hands of a living man upon the Cross, and all the time there was nothing there but a phantom?

[*CPl* 583]

He is consistent enough, however, to demand rational proof of this view, and with the courage of a man to whom empirical truth is more important than life, sends the Syrian for it, convinced that he will come back with the only answer he expects or can understand. For him the rites of the worshippers of Dionysos are tasteless and unaesthetic displays of self-abasement in which they merely lose their identity in an attempt to escape from their wretchedness and suffering. In the same way the central Christian symbolism is aesthetically repulsive to him:

That makes me shudder. The utmost possible suffering as an act of worship! You are morbid because your nation has no statues.

[*CPl* 584]

To him the cycle of birth, death and rebirth, whether of Dionysos or Christ, is not an analogue of the cyclical process of destruction and renewal, but merely a reversion to barbarism – 'You talk as if you wanted the barbarian back' [*CPl* 591] – in which order and knowledge, in particular his kind of knowledge, is lost sight of:

The knowledge that keeps the road from here to Persia free from robbers,
that has built the beautiful humane cities, that has made the modern world,
that stands between us and the barbarian.

[*CPl* 591]

In this respect he is not unlike Auden's liberal humanist Herod in
For the Time Being. The situation seems to be making his point for
him. Society seems to be disintegrating in a way that has never
happened before. The Roman authorities are afraid to intervene.
Irrational streams of blood, whether from the dancers of the
Dionysos rite or from the wounds of Christ, are staining the earth;
sexual restraints are abandoned: men and women couple in the street;
aesthetic order is violated: the marble repose of Greek lapidary art,
with the measured certainty of its formal statements, is mocked by
the ambiguous simulacrum of a statue, a boy/girl from the theatre.
The room in which they stand seems to be the only stronghold of
calm rational behaviour in a world given over more and more to
the forces of anarchy, though even this centre is not going to hold
much longer.

Up to the moment of the Syrian's entry it is the tone of the Greek's
words that dominates the dialogue. Deliberately low-keyed in order
to throw into relief the visual and aural imagery of Christ's entry,
it is detached, somewhat amused, even at Calvary – there is almost
a feeling of 'My dear boy, the thing is absurd' – urbane, tolerant,
a tone that passes over into the Hebrew's self-deprecatory 'None of
us are in our right mind today' [*CPl* 585]. Even the actions of the
worshippers are something to be regarded from the outside, as an
artistic spectacle, just like a play, not to be taken too seriously since
the emotions aroused by it are discharged innocuously back into the
performance, and therefore to be tolerated – 'No great harm comes
of it' [*CPl* 586]. He is outwardly protected by the carapace of his
own conviction that truth is only to be discovered empirically.

The Syrian's entry effects a complete change of tone. He returns,
breathless, excited, elated, as spiritually intoxicated as Martin was
in *The Unicorn from the Stars.* The urbane note is maintained, but
only above a stress, intellectual and emotional, that is charged with
explosive forces. The ironic undertones that have been present right
from the beginning of the play, in the first choric song, below and
outside the central action, now begin to thrust towards the surface.
The Syrian brings the news that the women declared the tomb was
empty. The Greek's exclamation indicates, though with something
less than conviction, that this is a proof of his belief that Christ was
never a man. The Hebrew, always more emotional – he would not

even look at the rites of the Dionysos worshippers, dismissing them
roundly as 'madmen' [*CPl* 586] — rejects this evidence as mere
dreaming, but the Greek insists on rational confirmation before any
action is taken, clinging to his certainty, powerfully ironic in the
dramatic circumstances, that 'somebody else' besides the Syrian is
coming with proof, and that that somebody is no more than a
phantom that

can pass through that wall; that he will so pass; that he will pass through
this room; that he himself will speak to the apostles.

[*CPl* 590]

The Syrian counters this with the statement that a great stone placed
over the mouth of the tomb has been physically rolled back. No mere
phantom could do that. The Hebrew, trying to find a way round,
suggests another explanation that will account for the apparently
miraculous: that the Jews had stolen the body from the tomb during
the night. Again the Syrian counters, leaving the Greek in an
intellectual *cul-de-sac,* from which the only escape is by a hitherto
unconsidered route:

> *The Syrian:* What matter if it contradicts all human knowledge? . . .
> What if there is always something that lies outside knowledge, outside
> order?. . .
> What if the irrational return?

[*CPl* 590–1]

The Syrian's laughter, a *mélange* of hysteria and ecstasy,
characteristically condemned as a loss of control by the Greek, signals
the irruption of a new truth which, however, for the moment he is
too terrified to accept. He projects his own hysteria onto the
worshippers outside, whose drums and rattles externalize his own
interior disintegration as the new truth begins to take hold on him:

> *The Greek:* He too has lost control of himself.
> *The Hebrew:* Stop, I tell you. (*Drums and rattles*)
> *The Syrian:* But I am not laughing. It is the people out there who are
> laughing.
> *The Hebrew:* No, they are shaking rattles and beating drums.
> *The Syrian:* I thought they were laughing. How horrible!

[*CPl* 591]

The sound of laughter, which is as much a binding image, though
an aural one, as the beating heart and fabulous darkness, is first

heard as the Greek's intellectual scoffing at the idea of sainthood and the validity of Calvary:

> *The Hebrew:* What makes you laugh?
> *The Greek:* Something I can see through the window. There, where I am pointing. There, at the end of the street. (*They stand together looking out over the heads of the audience.*)
> *The Hebrew:* I cannot see anything.
> *The Greek:* The hill.
> *The Hebrew:* That is Calvary.
> *The Greek:* And the three crosses on the top of it. (*He laughs again.*)
> *The Hebrew:* Be quiet. You do not know what you are doing. You have gone out of your mind. You are laughing at Calvary.
> *The Greek:* No, no. I am laughing because they thought they were nailing the hands of a living man upon the Cross, and all the time there was nothing there but a phantom.
>
> [*CPl* 582–3]

But the laughter also symbolizes, as it is transferred to the Syrian, the mockery of the limitations of hitherto accepted rationality, the ecstatic acceptance of the idea of destruction and renewal. In performance it should be heard for the last time in and through the Greek's final speech:

O Athens, Alexandria, Rome, something has come to destroy you. The heart of a phantom is beating. Man has begun to die. Your words are clear at last, O Heraclitus! God and man die each other's life, live each other's death.

[*CPl* 594]

In between, this personal hysteria is both identified with and widened by the drums and rattles of the worshippers of Dionysos into cosmic significance.

Theatrically Yeats handles his sound-effects with consummate skill, as the turbulence outside reaches its climax in the cry, repeated again and again to the sound of drums and rattle, 'God has arisen', which abruptly turns to an ominous silence, when the dance movements of the worshippers change into steps utterly beyond the range of the Greek's knowledge:

> *The Greek* (*looking out over heads of audience*): The worshippers of Dionysus are coming this way again. They have hidden their image of the dead god, and have begun their lunatic cry, 'God has arisen! God has arisen! (*The Musicians who have been saying* 'God has arisen!' *fall silent.*)
> They will cry 'God has arisen!' through all the streets of the city. They can make their God live and die at their pleasure; but why are they silent? They

are dancing silently. They are coming nearer and nearer, dancing all the while, using some kind of ancient step unlike anything I have seen in Alexandria.

[*CPl* 591–2]

Dionysiac ritual is waiting, indeed requiring, to be expressed in terms of Christian revelation, and all the external tensions are concentrated on the centre of dramatic interest, the room in the house, once the sanctuary of Platonic tolerance and Doric discipline, and, one might add, Hebraic humaneness, now about to become the epicentre of a cataclysm whose energies have their source in both the immolation of Dionysos and the resurrection of Christ. Yeats's mastery of dramatic structure is surely nowhere better revealed than in this moment, when the antithetical strands of the dramatic texture, the prosaic disputations of Greek and Hebrew, the incipient faith of the Syrian, the orgiastic abandon of the mob outside, are woven together to create a tension both of content and of form − something *must* happen now, theatrically and cosmically, that demands release.

The release is effected by Christ's entry, which is a superb translation into theatrical terms of Yeats's belief that 'the sense of spiritual reality comes . . . from some violent shock' [*E* 399]. If I were producing the play I would reinforce the effect, underlining the verbal imagery by having Christ enter literally from 'a fabulous darkness' to the blazing illumination of the Greek's discovery. Argument is carried over into dramatic action and reinforced upon our pulses. The Hebrew can do nothing more than acknowledge its force by passively kneeling; the Syrian, his convictions now confirmed, can stand outside the action and describe it calmly; the Greek, in his intellectual certainty is nevertheless courageous enough to submit himself to his own criterion of objectively ascertainable proof, and is compelled to find it irrelevant. Brought face to face with the miraculous, impossible, or in Kierkegaardian terms, absurd category of God-become-Man, he loses control. His scream reflects Yeats's own view:

The loss of control over thought comes towards the end; first a sinking in upon the moral being, then the last surrender, the irrational cry, revelation − the scream of Juno's peacock.

[*AV(B)* 268]

For him, Christ's resurrection is a destructive act which engulfs not only his own personal attitudes, philosophical and religious, but also a whole era of civilization:

O Athens, Alexandria, Rome, something has come to destroy you.
[*CPl* 594]

For the Syrian and the disciples that same act has created and confirmed a new dispensation. The interpenetration of the antithetical gyres of history, dramatically effected in the central action in both aural and visual terms, is now completed in speech by the last of the choric songs.

Ure was mistaken in thinking that the opening and closing songs are

lyrical meditations on the theme of the play, intelligible in the light of it [but] completely detachable from it, unlike the songs in *Calvary*.
[*YTP* 127]

They are not merely comments on the theme. They expand it.

The first song, as Helen Vendler rightly points out, prepares both for that sense of shock, horror and terror, that 'terror of the supernatural' [*E* 398] which is the climax of the play, and also the idea of the cyclical movement of history in which the Christian dispensation, revolutionary at its inception, will itself be absorbed into a larger cosmic process of destruction and renewal. To an audience primarily attuned to the story of Christ's birth, the opening line, 'I saw a staring virgin stand' [*CPl* 579], would invoke the image of the Virgin Mary. Then, if we know the story of the twice-born Dionysos (see *Comm. Pl* 195], the Christian Virgin Mary becomes identified with her pagan precursor Pallas Athene. The reference here is to the story in which Pallas Athene snatched the heart from the body of Dionysos when he was torn to pieces by the Titans. She brought it on her hand to Zeus, who had begotten Dionysos on Persephone, whereupon he swallowed the heart, killed the Titans, and begat Dionysos again on Semele. Both Persephone and Semele were mortal. Thus there are parallels drawn between Dionysos, offspring of a god and humans, and Christ, begotten by God on the Virgin Mary. The lyric continues:

> And then did all the Muses sing
> Of Magnus Annus at the spring
> As though God's death were but a play.
> [*CPl* 580]

If only the broader connotations of 'Magnus Annus' are accepted, as containing the idea of cosmic renewal (at the Magnus Annus the

planets were thought to return to their relative positions), later to
be echoed by the Syrian's cry, 'What if the irrational return? What
if the circle begin again?' [*CPl* 591], then the sixth and seventh lines
proclaim that the creative imagination exults in it — the rhyme and
the rhythm making the point:

> And then did all the Muses sing
> Of Magnus Annus in the spring.
>
> [*CPl* 580]

God's death is seen as a play which can be both performed again
and again and enjoyed as a spectacle, as the Greek enjoys the
spectacle of the Dionysiac worshippers in which God's part is taken
by an actor from the theatre.

The first two lines of the second stanza emphasize the idea of
renewal, accepted with all the optimism and conviction of Shelley,
and behind him, Virgil:

> Another Troy must rise and set,
> Another lineage feed the crow.
>
> [*CPl* 580]

But the third and fourth lines are by intention shockingly reductive:
the Golden Fleece becomes no more than a flashy bauble, as the
solidities of civilization begin to fragment in the cosmic revolution
of the gyres:

> Another Argo's painted prow
> Drive to a flashier bauble yet.
>
> [*CPl* 580]

The same point is to be made by the Syrian — renewal and
destruction are part of one cosmic process:

> . . . another Argo seeks another fleece, another Troy is sacked.
>
> [*CPl* 590]

The fifth and sixth lines prefigure the loss of rational order and
control (again reflected in the central action in the powerlessness of
the Roman authorities):

> The Roman Empire stood appalled:
> It dropped the reins of peace and war
> When that fierce virgin and her Star
> Out of the fabulous darkness called.
>
> [*CPl* 580]

In the last two lines, the staring Virgin, whether or not we accept the multiplication of identities through the reference to Virgo and Spica (see *Comm. Pl* 196–7) no longer stands outside events looking on, but in her fierce destructiveness initiates them. Bloom rightly refers to the song's ferocity, and in performance that quality should be brought out.

The second choric song is in effect a gloss on the last three lines of the Greek's speech before it:

Three days after the full moon, a full moon in March, they sing the death of the god and pray for his resurrection.

[*CPl* 586]

To the Greek, of course, the god is only Dionysos, the full moon in March the turning point of the year, when winter turns to spring. He is unaware of their ironic application to Christ and His resurrection three days after Calvary. His confident dismissal of the song in his next speech:

I cannot think all that self-surrender and self-abasement is Greek, despite the Greek name of its god

[*CPl* 587]

and his subsequent assertion of the independence of men and gods takes on an ironic force. Here, in the song itself, but as yet outside the room, beyond the stockades of reason and order, outside consciousness and as yet outside history, is the force that is going to shatter civilization. Even if the references to Dionysos and his death at the hands of the murderous Titans are not caught, the song, with its ominous drum-taps, helps to create the atmosphere of terror from which that force is going to emerge. Almost at once, the herald of one embodiment of that force – and it is only one embodiment, since Christianity too will die into another life as the gyres of history revolve – the Syrian, knocks on the door. The Greek, still proclaiming his belief that he will admit only the powers of reason, is confronted by the Syrian, who has entered from the audience as if to show that the action is not so much something that we watch as a play but something that we must experience ourselves.

The closing song's first stanza completes the picture of the historicity of Christianity:

> In pity for man's darkening thought
> He walked that room and issued thence
> In Galilean turbulence;
> The Babylonian starlight brought
> A fabulous, formless darkness in;
> Odour of blood when Christ was slain
> Made all Platonic tolerance vain
> And vain all Doric discipline.
>
> [*CPl* 594]

Christ reaches out in pity for man as he loses control over thought, yet at the same time contributes to that loss of control as miracle is substituted for reason. Galilean turbulence supersedes Dionysiac turbulence, the fabulous formless darkness wheels us back to the last two lines of the first choric song:

> When that fierce virgin and her Star
> Out of the fabulous darkness called.
>
> [*CPl* 580]

Dionysos's blood, Dionysos's death, Dionysos's rebirth yield to Christ's blood, Christ's death, Christ's resurrection. But the stanza deals only with the impact of that particular resurrection in a particular period of history. Helen Vendler's interpretation of the second stanza carries complete conviction as it clarifies the relation of Christ's historical resurrection to Resurrection, which is

a blaze of revelation . . . led up to by a long process of preparation [which] will spend itself slowly in an equally long process of attrition. Man creates his moments of glory out of his own carefully built substance, and suffers in their waning. The great necessity is to prepare for the moment of revelation and rebirth, to welcome it as it comes, and to be willing to exhaust oneself in sustaining it.

> [*YV* 184]

The first stanza reaffirms the cosmic cycles: the winding of one gyre is the unwinding of another. The second asserts that every activity, whether of love, of art, of civilization achieved by conquest or matured in peace, in fulfilling itself destroys the creative energy of its origin.

Everything that man esteems
Endures a moment or a day:
Love's pleasure drives his love away,
The painter's brush consumes his dreams;
The herald's cry, the soldier's tread
Exhaust his glory and his might:
Whatever flames upon the night
Man's own resinous heart has fed.

[*CPl* 594]

But in that very immolation, man, partaking in the miraculous energy of reborn divinity, which both consumes and feeds, reinvigorates that energy, as the beating heart of the God becomes his own resinous heart. The final stanza defiantly proclaims the source of all achievements of civilization, however transient, in what, in the light of the play, we may call the human heart divine.

The Words Upon the Window-Pane

Although *The Words Upon the Window-Pane* is written in the naturalistic mode, which eschews the stylization of Noh drama, it has obvious links with the Noh play of spirits: the meeting with ghosts, the spirit re-living its temporal anguish, the sense of location. These links are forged by the device of the séance, at which spirits of the dead communicate with the living. The device also enables Yeats to dramatize the interpenetration of past and present. Events of the 18th century are re-enacted in the 20th, words written and spoken in the past are cut into the windows of the present. The dramatization is presented on two interconnected levels: one based upon the inner turbulence of Swift's private life, the other, an extrapolation from this, based on the contrast between past and present, the world of the 18th century and the contemporary world, with their fundamentally opposed values and outlooks. Finally, in the brilliantly conceived ending, Yeats compels us to face the shock of the irruption of timeless spiritual forces into the temporal world. And not only face it but evaluate it. Yeats's mastery of dramatic structure is demonstrated by the way in which the skilfully interwoven tensions of the play (the tension of the séance and the tension of Swift's relationships with Vanessa and Stella) lead up to this climactic *coup de théatre*. The naturalistic frame of the play, in which the past appears to be wholly superseded by the present and the spiritual and the mundane kept in separate compartments, is shattered. The past will not be suppressed by the present, the spiritual will irrupt into the mundane. In terms of dramatic structure this means that the play-within-the-play, the séance, bursts out of its frame and assaults us directly. Dramatic form and content are completely fused. This is the core of the play, around which revolve the two circles of the double action, the outer circle of contemporary Dublin and the inner circle of the 18th century as revealed through Swift's relations with Vanessa and Stella. Yet at the same time, as one comes to expect from Yeats, the apparent simplicities in the opposing terms of the dramatic conflicts are blurred by pervasive ironies.

The stage setting — and again one stresses the importance of the

visual element in Yeats's dramaturgy – immediately evokes the
contemporary world, commonplace, *petit-bourgeois,* slightly seedy.
A stage designer should try to catch the run-down atmosphere of
the Dublin of the thirties, where, as *Comm. Pl* notes [222], what
were once the town-dwellings of well-to-do families in the 18th
century had declined into slums. The impression of degeneration
extends to many, if not all, of the characters who are interested in
spiritualism: to Mrs Mallett, an experienced spiritualist it may be,
but one who uses that experience to further her commercial
ambitions. These, however, go no further than the opening of a tea-
shop in Folkstone – she is a kind of latter-day Abel Drugger. It
extends to Corney Patterson (the reductive christian name is both
interesting in itself and in the light of the later *The Herne's Egg)*
who hopes to find in his dealings with the spiritual world first nothing
higher than a means of backing winners at the dogs (*Comm. Pl* fails
to record George Brandon Saul's note that Harold's Cross [*CPl* 599]
is the site of a dog-racing track in the suburb of that name in the
south-west of Dublin), and then a confirmation of his belief that
he will continue to go to the dogs after his death. It extends to
Abraham Johnson, a penny-counting low-church minister from
Belfast, who ascribes greatness to the sentimental pieties of figures
no more exalted than the American 'Evangelists' (surely he means
Evangelicals) Moody and Sankey; to shabby-genteel Miss Mackenna,
the practical secretary of the Dublin Spiritualists Association, still
open to doubts about spiritualism ('I have seen a good many séances,
and sometimes think it is all coincidence and thought-transference'
[*CPl* 605]) but also responsive to its frightening appeal ('Then at
other times I think as Dr Trench does, and then I feel like Job –
you know the quotation – the hair of my head stands up. A spirit
passes before my face' [*CPl* 605]). And finally it extends to Mrs
Henderson herself, poor, uneducated – she has never heard of Swift
– outwardly uncommercial ('it is very wrong to take money for such
a failure' [*CPl* 614]) but nevertheless sufficiently down-to-earth to
assess the takings (a detail that was added at the suggestion of
Mrs Yeats), 'a poor woman', as Dr Trench describes her [*CPl*
598],'with the soul of an apostle', and, one may add, tender-hearted,
but with neither intellect nor imagination. She is quite incapable of
making the whole thing up. To balance the suggestions of suburban
hole-in-corner mumbo-jumbo surrounding spiritualism (the
subject is not fit for intellectual discussion, the doors of the séance-
room must be locked, unwelcome intruders excluded), Yeats gives
us the broad-minded, courteous, intellectually respectable and
imaginatively charitable Dr Trench, whom he uses to expound

the doctrines of spiritualism. These are given in his long speeches on *CPl* 603–4:

The spirits are people like ourselves, we treat them as our guests and protect them from discourtesy and violence, and every exorcism is a curse or a threatened curse. We do not admit that there are evil spirits. Some spirits are earth-bound – they think they are still living and go over and over some action of their past lives, just as we go over and over some painful thought, except that where they are thought is reality. For instance, when a spirit which has died a violent death comes to a medium for the first time, it re-lives all the pains of death . . .

Sometimes a spirit re-lives not the pain of death but some passionate or tragic moment of life. Swedenborg describes this and gives the reason for it. There is an incident of the kind in the *Odyssey,* and many in Eastern literature; the murderer repeats his murder, the robber his robbery, the lover his serenade, the soldier hears the trumpet once again. If I were a Catholic I would say that such spirits are in Purgatory. In vain do we write *requiescat in pace* upon the tomb, for they must suffer, and we in our turn must suffer until God gives peace. Such spirits do not often come to séances unless those séances are held in houses where those spirits lived, or where the event took place. This spirit which speaks those incomprehensible words and does not answer when spoken to is of such a nature. The more patient we are, the more quickly will it pass out of its passion and remorse.

[*CPl* 603–4]

These speeches are dramatically justified not only by the need of the theatre-audience to be made aware of the central doctrines without which the play cannot be understood, but also by the presence of the stage-audience, comprising the sceptical novice John Corbet, who must be informed of them, Mrs Mallet and Abraham Johnson, whose existing knowledge must be refined and extended.

But the setting and its inhabitants, firmly established on the naturalistic plane, like the attic and what it contains in *The Wild Duck,* also exist on the symbolic level. They symbolize the decay which Yeats saw infecting the processes of history since the 18th century. The private house with its stable at the back has now become a common lodging house. Its former notable inhabitants, Grattan or Curran, the friends of Swift or Stella, have now given place to representatives of the petty commerce, the mediocrity, the shallow piety of the contemporary world. Dr. Trench is the only 'gentleman' present. It is tempting, with the support of Yeats's views on Swift and the 18th century expressed outside the play to go on to see the Swift of the play as the embodiment of 18th century attitudes, its stable classicism, its elegant religion, its achievements of intellect and art, its anti-egalitarian political philosophy and to see Swift himself, his political, moral and sexual *mores* rooted in an idealized Roman world, as rejected by but nevertheless imposing his presence as spirit on 'the foul world in its decline and fall', ('*A* Bronze Head' [*CP* 383]). This world, with its low-church evangelicalism, its lack of understanding and artistic taste, its 'levelling, rancorous, rational sort of mind' ('The Seven Sages' [*CP* 272]), is rooted in the mechanistic thought of Locke and the egalitarianism of Rousseau, breathed on by the timid breath of merchant and clerk. But does the Swift we are given in the play embody these 18th century qualities? Yeats himself, in his introduction to the play, where he does deal with Swift in this way, sounds a note of warning. The idea of 18th century Ireland as the fountainhead of Irish greatness is, he tells us, the 'overstatement of an enthusiastic [the adjective implies a Swiftian disapproval] Cambridge student' [*VPl* 959] who is 'full of the unexamined suppositions of common speech' [*VPl* 965]. John Corbet is writing a thesis and is determined to prove his point, namely that:

in Swift's day men of intellect reached the height of their power . . . that everything great in Ireland and in our character . . . comes from that day.
[*CPl* 601]

And further, like so many thesis-writers, he will adapt evidence to suit the demands of his proof. In point of fact the core of the play gives us a Swift in whom there is nothing of the epitome of Augustan rationality, nothing of the man who by heroic choice has achieved fullness of being, nothing of the champion of the oppressed Irish, nothing of the Irish patriot, fighter for Irish freedom, but instead a man helplessly lost in the emotional turbulence of his relations with Vanessa and Stella, a man who has failed to resolve the conflict between the passionate impulses of his body and the chaste energies of his intellect. Swift takes out his failures on Vanessa by cruelly rejecting her, and on Stella by turning her into an image of sexless and selfless devotion, and on himself by damming the natural current of his sexual impulses (in contemporary Irish folk-lore considered strong), producing a backwash that turned personal affection to enmity, love of the common man to misanthropy. Vanessa's response is to point out that in rejecting her he is arrogantly setting himself above the limits in which ordinary humanity is subjected to the vicissitudes of chance:

If you had children, Jonathan, my blood would make them healthy.

I will take your hand, I will lay it upon my heart — upon the Vanhomrigh
blood that has been healthy for generations . . . Look at me, Jonathan.
Your arrogant intellect separates us. Give me both your hands. I will put
them upon my breast . . . O, it is white — white as the gambler's dice —
white ivory dice. Think of the uncertainty. Perhaps a mad child — perhaps
a rascal — perhaps a knave — perhaps not, Jonathan. The dice of the intellect
are loaded, but I am the common ivory dice . . . It is not my hands that
draw you back. My hands are weak, they could not draw you back if you
did not love as I love. You said that you have strong passions; that is true,
Jonathan — no man in Ireland is so passionate. That is why you need me,
that is why you need children, nobody has greater need. You are growing
old. An old man without children is very solitary. Even his friends, men
as old as he, turn away, they turn towards the young, their children or their
children's children. They cannot endure an old man like themselves . . .
You are not too old for the dice, Jonathan, but a few years if you turn away
will make you an old miserable childless man.

[*CPl* 610–1]

Stella's response is the rebuke of silence; his own, remorse. Between
them they keep rekindling the purgatorial fires of passion in which
his embittered and tormented spirit must suffer.

Have I wronged you, beloved Stella? Are you unhappy? You have no
children, you have no lover, you have no husband. A cross and ageing man
for friend — nothing but that. But no, do not answer — you have answered
already in that poem you wrote for my last birthday. With what scorn you
speak of the common lot of women 'with no endowments but a face . . . '

'Before the thirtieth year of life
A maid forlorn or hated wife'.

It is the thought of the great Chrysostom who wrote in a famous passage
that women loved according to the soul, loved as saints can love, keep their
beauty longer, have greater happiness than women loved according to the
flesh. That thought has comforted me, but it is a terrible thing to be
responsible for another's happiness. There are moments when I doubt, when
I think Chrysostom may have been wrong.

[*CPl* 612–3]

As Douglas Archibald points out [*YT* 193], it is the image of the
desperate, despairing and disfigured old man that dominates the play.
Corbet's idealized vision of him, in one of its major ironies, is
contradicted by dramatic fact.

Indeed a pattern of ironic contradictions runs through the play.
Comedy is not far below the surface — in the contrast between the
solemnity of the situation and of the theme it dramatizes, whether

it is defined as the relation between a timeless spiritual world manifesting itself as an objective reality in the temporal, or in the historical terms of the decline of a civilization, and in the mild ridiculousness of some at least of the figures involved in it – Corney, Mrs Mallet, Abraham Johnson. Comedy breaks through the surface in the juxtaposition of banal pious hymn and irreverent snore, as the control, whose incongruous child-like language (an echo of the 'little language' of the *Journal to Stella*) provokes laughter in the sceptical Corbet [*CPl* 607].

But below the comedy there is the deeper current of frustration and failure. Neither Dr Trench's compassionate patience nor Abraham Johnson's prayer will help Swift's tormented spirit to find rest from the purgatory of his passion and remorse. John Corbet is convinced that Swift 'sleeps under the greatest epitaph in history', but the play shows that this is not true. Yeats's own version of the epitaph is

> Swift has sailed unto his rest;
> Savage indignation there
> Cannot lacerate his breast.
> Imitate him if you dare,
> World-besotted traveller; he
> Served human liberty.
>
> [*CP* 277]

The epitaph is great, but for Swift death is certainly no sleep: fierce indignation continues to lacerate his heart. The sense of failure is carried over, too, into his private life. His educational policy clearly did not work with Vanessa:

I taught you to think in every situation of life not as Hester Vanhomrigh would think in that situation, but as Cato or Brutus would, and now you behave like some common slut with her ear against the keyhole.

[*CPl* 609]

Swift must stand convicted here of a failure of imagination: there is nothing sluttish in Vanessa's love for him, nothing ignoble in her behaviour. On the contrary his behaviour towards her is that of an intellectual corner-boy. For all his adoption of the role of high-toned moral and intellectual tutor to the women in his life and to history, it is clear that Plutarch taught him nothing. However free his intellect may be from superstition, however great his intellect – and it is only Corbet the thesis-writer who tells us this – it is certainly not immune from male vanity. In matters of human relations he is a spoilt child,

desperately in need of education. Imprisoned in his own arrogance
he is incapable of making that commitment to the unknown future
that on a personal level marriage and the chance of having children
who might or might not inherit his disease means. On an impersonal
level he is trapped in a political and social philosophy that will not
let him plunge into the living stream of history. He becomes a stone
obstructing its fluid movement, as, in Yeats's words, Corbet imagines
that Swift' so dreaded the historic process that it became in [his]
half-mad mind . . . a dread of parentage' [*VPl* 967]. At both levels
he is a hostile force. He is hostile to Vanessa, hostile fundamentally
to love, hostile to the future and its representative Rousseau (though
we have to take Corbet's words for this since the play does not give
us the 'political Swift' directly), hostile to humanity and therefore
hostile to the séance, whose participants meet in an atmosphere of
love, however mawkishly Mrs Henderson creates it (another strand
in the pattern of ironies) in her speech of welcome [*CPl* 606].
Stripped of Corbet's theorizings Swift is presented to us as an
emotional and intellectual bully, forced to suffer passionately for
the rejection of passion, forced to face the consequences of both
denying fulfilment of body and mind with Vanessa, and asserting
it in soul only at the expense of body with Stella. The consolations
proffered in Stella's poetical acquiescence are at worst illusory, at
best temporary: at the end of the play suffering is renewed and
intensified:

> You taught how I might youth prolong
> By knowing what is right and wrong;
> How from my heart to bring supplies
> Of lustre to my fading eyes;
> How soon a beauteous mind repairs
> The loss of chang'd or falling hairs;
> How wit and virtue from within
> Can spread a smoothness o'er the skin.

                                                          [*CPl* 613]

In the event youth is prolonged merely into dirty senility; intelligence
and virtue are no defence against boils, against disease, against bodily
decrepitude, against madness. The comforts that she offers him do
not materialize:

Mrs Henderson [*in Swift's voice*]: Then, because you understand that I
am afraid of solitude, afraid of outliving my friends – and myself – you
comfort me in that last verse – you overpraise my moral nature when you
attribute to it a rich mantle, but O how touching those words which describe
your love:

> 'Late dying may you cast a shred
> Of that rich mantle o'er my head;
> To bear with dignity my sorrow,
> One day alone, then die tomorrow.'

Yes, you will close my eyes, Stella. O you will live long after me, dear Stella, for are still a young woman, but you will close my eyes.

[*CPl* 613]

Stella does not, in fact, live to close his eyes. Dr. Trench suggests that release from such purgatorial suffering of dead spirits is, as in *Purgatory,* God-given only:

In vain do we write *requiescat in pace* upon the tomb, for they must suffer, and we in our turn must suffer until God gives peace.

[*CPl* 604]

But there is little sign of peace. It is difficult to see Swift's last cry, 'Perish the day on which I was born', as other than an expression of Job-like despair, of a Lear-like *hysterica passio* (the words are recorded as having been spoken by Swift in his madness) at the recognition of the dead-end to which all his energies, moral and intellectual, have led him. His discarnate spirit is trapped in the exploration of the events of its incarnate life which it must live through, a process which will bring him ultimately to the knowledge of their moral and intellectual origins in the 'foul rag-and-bone-shop' of his own responsible heart; then to the knowledge of their consequences, as in *Purgatory,* both on himself and on others. The treadmill of his agony induces nothing but despair and madness. Purgation and release are no part of our dramatic experience. Just as the Old Man's prayer in *Purgatory* and Johnson's prayer here are not answered, so the response to Swift's passionate prayer:

O God, hear the prayer of Jonathan Swift, that afflicted man, and grant that he may leave to posterity nothing but his intellect that came to him from Heaven

[*CPl* 611]

is renewed affliction. The silence following Swift's tormented cry 'Perish the day on which I was born' is parallel to the dramatic response to Albany's 'The Gods defend her!' of '*Enter Lear, with Cordelia dead in his arms*'.

Ironically it is Corbet himself, the rationalist, who takes this note of failure beyond the point where it applies to Swift himself to where it has general relevance. Corbet is a sceptic who is satisfied by the séance because he sees it not as proof of the existence of an objective spiritual world, but as presenting a theory about Swift's behaviour which he accepts simply because it corroborates his own:

When I say I am satisfied I do not mean that I am convinced it was the work of spirits. I prefer to think that you created it all, that you are an accomplished actress and scholar.

[*CPl* 615]

He adopts the stance taken by Yeats himself, based on G. N. M. Tyrrell's *Science and Psychical Phenomena,* and hinted at by Mrs Mallet and Dr Trench in their brief reference to the conversation of spirits as if they were characters in 'some kind of horrible play' [*CPl* 603]. Yeats wrote:

I consider it certain that every voice that speaks, every form that appears, whether to the medium's eyes and ears alone or to some one or two others or to all present, whether it remains a sight or sound or affects the sense of touch, whether it is confined to the room or can make itself apparent at some distant place, whether it can or cannot alter the position of material objects, is first of all a secondary personality or dramatisation created by, in, or through the medium.

[*VPl* 967]

But Corbet's rational explanation is clearly wrong, since Mrs Henderson lacks the imagination, the knowledge or the intellect to be either creative artist or scholar. This interpretation of the séance 'explains' the psychic phenomena in terms confined to the rational and comprehensible by the intellect. It rejects the idea of an independent spiritual world that can manifest itself in the temporal. Like so many 'explanations' of the inexplicable, in its attempt to explain it merely explains away. But unfortunately the inexplicable will not go away: it returns in the form of Swift's invasion of Mrs Henderson at the final curtain. Further, Corbet's theory of Swift's behaviour includes the proposition that he was

the chief representative of the intellect of his epoch, that arrogant intellect free at last from superstition.

[*CPl* 615]

We have already seen that dramatically that proposition is untenable. The final irony is that it is Corbet, the intellectual pure and simple, who rejects the idea of a spiritual dimension independent of the human imagination (unlike Dr Trench who, though an intellectual, is open to the suggestion that such a dimension is objectively real), who wonders not only whether Swift himself in all the supremacy of his intellect was after all mad, but whether intellect itself is mad too, incapable of explaining any experience that transcends its own terms of reference:

But there is something I must ask you. Swift was the chief representative of the intellect of his epoch, that arrogant intellect free at last from superstition. He foresaw its collapse. He foresaw Democracy, he must have dreaded the future. Did he refuse to beget children because of that dread? Was Swift mad? Or was it the intellect itself that was mad?

[*CPl* 615]

Here is reason questioning its own authority. Is the séance a fake? If it is not, even if it bears witness to a reality impervious to rational explanation, is it a failure? The play never answers the questions unequivocally, perhaps because Yeats intends us to conclude that there are no unequivocal answers.

For Mrs Mallet, who came for one purpose and found another, it is a failure. For John Corbet, who did find in it what he was looking for, it is a success. For Corney, who did not find what he came for, did not get a return on his stakes, it was just a bad bet. For Mrs Henderson, who hoped to satisfy her clients but was prevented from doing so by the intrusive spirit of Swift, it was a failure. The charitable Dr Trench seems to regard it as a failure, though an honourable one:

You did your best and nobody can do more than that.

[*CPl* 614]

Miss Mackenna is thrilled for a moment out of her mundane practicality. Abraham Johnson, for all his earlier hostility, is moved enough to ask God to bless and protect the séances. Dramatically, for the theatre-audience, the scales come heavily down on the side of the séance as evoking a reality. No-one, except the audience, is present to hear the final unconscious testimony to the frightening reality of the spirit-world, which is all the more powerful for occurring outside the séance, outside the play-within-the-play. The sceptic does not hear it, nor do the faithful, and the medium, the unconscious and ignorant link between the natural and supernatural worlds, does not understand it. We are left alone with mystery, the terror of the supernatural. Everything must be done in performance to produce the same reaction in the audience as that which Mrs Mallet describes to John Corbet [*CPl* 606]. When Swift's voice speaks through Mrs Henderson at the final curtain, our hair should be made to stand up too.

Post-script

It is a pity that a performance of this, one of the best and certainly the most approachable of Yeats's plays, should run the risk of failure by the inherent difficulty of finding an actress with sufficient technical expertise to render the four voices required of her: the high soprano of Lulu, and Mrs Henderson, and the male voice of Swift. Such an actress *can* be found, but the play might be performed more often if the difficulty could be circumvented. It would be an interesting experiment, for example, to stage the play-within-the-play as physically enacted in the séance-room by other actors. Swift, Vanessa and Stella could materialize and recede as required dressed in 18th century costume, with Swift made up in the way he appears to Mrs Henderson's inner eye – his clothes dirty, his face covered with boils, one eye swollen. This would leave the actress playing Mrs Henderson with the lesser problem of coping with the unseen Lulu. The ironic contrasts would be heightened, the interwoven tensions between present séance and past events tautened, the function of Mrs Henderson clarified as the unconscious and ignorant channel through which timeless spiritual forces impinge upon the temporal world. It might lose the sense of the simultaneity of past and present, but such a loss might well be compensated by a gain in theatrical impact, in that the audience would be provided with a scene in which the inner drama is played out before their own eyes on which to focus their attention rather than create it in their own imagination. The invasion of the temporal world by a physical embodiment of the timeless spiritual world would hammer Yeats's main point home, and the manifestation of a Swift suffering in body and mind would stress the ironies inherent in the play.

The King of the Great Clock Tower

This is one of Yeats's least satisfactory efforts, and in view of his much more convincing reworking of the material as *A Full Moon in March,* it is difficult to see why he permitted this version to survive, all the more so since to anyone inclined to play it he recommended the prose version, which is not included in *Collected Plays* at all, though it is reprinted in *VPl.* The central weakness, as Yeats himself perceived, is that the character of the King is unnecessary. Therefore, in order to preserve the fable's intensity, he cut him out of *A Full Moon in March.* But there are other weaknesses too: it is full of inconsistencies, of half-realized effects, of uncertain emphases. Yeats said that it imitated the Japanese model in that it climaxes in a dance and substitutes suggestion for representation. To these features can be added the choric attendants, the lyrics, with their binding metaphors, and the masks. It certainly does move in the direction of abstraction in that its characters seem more like participants in a rite than living persons. The essence of ritual is that what the participants do and say has to be interpreted in terms of the ritual action as a whole, not in terms of naturalistic behaviour. As Ure pointed out:

If the priest plucks out the victim's heart, or drains the cup before the altar, explanations in terms of his cruelty or his thirst are plainly out of court.
[*YTP* 160]

But the King's behaviour, his all too human anger with Queen and Stroller and his sense of outrage at finding his regal authority insulted, is inconsistent with his ritual obeisance, itself inadequately justified, to the Queen. It is the lyrics, not the action, that bear the main burden of the theme, yet Yeats himself seemed testily uncertain about their function:

The orchestra brings more elaborate music and I have gone over to the enemy. I say to the musician 'Lose my words in patterns of sound as the name of God is lost in Arabian arabesques.'
[*Comm.Pl* 254]

190

It would not matter that the words were drowned by music if they were not the channel through which the theme runs; but if they are, then let them be not only heard by an audience but also intelligible to it. The first stanza of the opening lyrics is intelligible enough, but the second is intelligible only to those already initiated into *The Wanderings of Oisin* and *The Wind Among the Reeds*. Judging by the printed texts, the handling of masks too is uncertain. The Queen is described as wearing 'a beautiful impassive mask' [*CPl* 633] appropriate enough for one who does not speak in her own 'character', but there is no indication of whether the King should wear one too. If he does, this would raise him to a symbolic level, but in doing so would conflict with his obviously human behaviour. The Stroller wears a 'wild half-savage mask' [*CPl* 633], but this animal aspect of him is not supported by his language. Yeats's own suggestion that the theme of the play is 'the old ritual of the year; the mother-goddess and the slain god' [*Comm.Pl* 255] is hardly borne out. There is nothing of the mother in the Queen; the Stroller invites his own destruction, and there is no sense of seasonal recurrence. The final tableau, reinforced by the last lyric, suggests an experience that has opened a gap into eternity, not into the cyclical renewal of the seasons or of anything else.

The juxtaposition of eternity and temporality is the theme of the first lyric, with its contrasting metaphors of the eternal paradise of the Celtic Tir-nan-oge and clock time symbolized by the bell that strikes at midnight 'when the old year dies'.

> *Second Attendant:*
>   They dance all day that dance in Tir-nan-oge.
> *First Attendant:*
>   There every lover is a happy rogue;
>   And should he speak, it is the speech of birds.
>   No thought has he, and therefore has no words,
>   No thought because no clock, no clock because
>   If I consider deeply, lad and lass,
>   Nerve touching nerve upon that happy ground,
>   Are bobbins where all time is wound.
>   [*CPl* 633]

When the central action begins to unfold, this theme appears to be reflected in the hostility of the King to the Queen, and in his total incomprehension of what she represents. They exist on different planes: in no sense can they symbolize the perfect union that the first verse of the opening lyric has suggested. In fact it is very difficult to see what their marriage can mean on any level.

Naturalistically it is plainly absurd:

> *The King:* A year ago you walked into this house,
> A year ago tonight. Though neither I
> Nor any man could tell your family,
> Country or name, I put you on the throne.
> And now before the assembled court, before
> Neighbours, attendants, courtiers, men-at-arms,
> I ask your country, name and family,
> And not for the first time. Why sit you there
> Dumb as an image made of wood or metal,
> A screen between the living and the dead?

[*CPl* 634]

Symbolically they seem antithetical to each other and for such a relationship marriage is just as absurd a symbol. There is nothing in the King's language or behaviour to sugggest that he is Zeus to the Queen's Cybele, as Wilson would have it [*Y&T* 70]. He comes perilously close to the archetypal jealous husband of comedy, totally out of place in a play of this nature, as Yeats came to realize. The trouble with the King in this version is that he is not given dramatic substance either as human being or as representative symbol. Neither his jealousy of the Queen nor his anger at being insulted by the Stroller has anything to do with the substance of the fable, which is fundamentally concerned with the Queen's union with the Stroller. Equally his ritual obeisance to the Queen at the end is inadequately explained. This is much clearer in the prose version, when he cowers in terror at the supernatural as the severed head begins to sing. Like the Greek in *The Resurrection* he is compelled to admit the authority of what hitherto he had been opposed to and was unable to comprehend. In the prose version the authority to which he makes obeisance is more easily recognizable as the miraculous power of the imagination to create images that transcend time. These are the product of a union of Poet and Muse which exceeds by far any temporal sexual union, and which in its integrity opens up a gap into eternity that time cannot close. The First Attendant, as the head, then goes on to sing of the deathless images that form the substance of 'The Alternative Song of the Severed Head', removed from this version.

The Queen and the Stroller, however, are much more consistently treated. Helen Vendler and others are surely right in examining them in terms of the fundamental relationship between poet and muse, artist and image. The Queen is first an aloof and solitary object of worship, the remote subject of the poet's song, the Image; but during the dance and the kiss, she unites with the poet, causes him to sing through her inspiration, and at this point may rightly be named the Muse.

[*YV* 145]

In her mysterious and, on the King's human level, understandably infuriating aloofness, she is

> Dumb as an image made of wood or metal.
>
> [*CPl* 634]

The Stroller, who is plainly identified as a poet [*CPl* 635], comes to see the Queen in order to test the truth of his own images of her, and even when he finds her 'Neither so red, nor white, nor full in the breast' [*CPl* 636] as he had thought, still proclaims the validity of the image in his head. In fact he is prepared to die for it. Like Septimus in *The Player Queen* he will never insult that. As poet he is like 'sacred Virgil,' the *vates*, in touch with a truth that is corroborated by the Gods. His fructifying union with the Image is divinely ordained:

> I ran to the Boyne Water
> And where a sea-mew and the salt sea wind
> Yelled Godhead, on a green round hillock lay;
> Nine days I fasted there — but that's a secret
> Between us three — then Aengus and the Gods
> Appeared, and when I said what I had sworn
> Shouted approval. Then great Aengus spoke —
> O listen, for I speak his very words —
> 'On stroke of midnight when the old year dies,
> Upon that stroke, the tolling of that bell,
> The Queen shall kiss your mouth . . . '
>
> [*CPl* 637]

The Queen and the Stroller, unlike the Queen and the Swineherd of *A Full Moon in March,* who are opposites, couple out of spiritual consanguinity. The idea that such a union is also a desecration for the Queen was once present in the prose version of the play, but was removed from this version and only restored in the reworked *A Full Moon in March,* where it is corroborated by visual and verbal imagery — 'Crown of gold and dung of swine'; the Queen descends, the Swineherd ascends. In the later play the Queen puts herself at risk, inviting her own desecration by issuing the challenge to which the Swineherd responds. In *The King of the Great Clock Tower* he seeks her of his own free will. The suggestion of the underlying element of primitive instinctual savagery in sexuality is hardly established, except by the Stroller's mask and his association with beggars. But even so, Yeats's beggars are not Synge's — they are more an idealization of the vitality of the imagination. The Stroller is almost as 'pure' as the Queen herself. Their union is imaged as a death because for the artist art is only achieved in the immolation of personal experience on the altar of form, and for the divine Muse, when, in Helen Vendler's words, she enters 'into a fleeting relation with humanity' [*YV* 151]. The sacrifice of the artist, made explicit in the prose version ('it is plain that he wishes to sacrifice his life, to lay it down at your feet' [*Comm. Pl* 262]), is here merely implied by his silence and accepted as inevitable: 'I go; but this must happen' [*CPl* 637].

The second lyric prefigures the Queen's complementary part in the necessary union in terms of the sexual act. This involves the death of the body and the consumption of beauty, but it is also a creative act:

> He longs to kill
> My body, until
> That sudden shudder
> And limbs lie still.
>
> O, what may come
> Into my womb,
> What caterpillar
> My beauty consume?
>
> [*CPl* 638]

Strictly speaking, she jumps the gun here, since until she has entered into a relation, however fleeting, she remains abstract and cannot have a body to kill. As what will issue from this union will be either a deathless image or an image of deathlessness, the King, who is bound by time, finds her words incomprehensible and can only see her dance as mockery of the Stroller. But ironically it is he who is mocked, he who is the fool:

> *The King:* I do not know the meaning of those words
> That have a scornful sound.
> Sing, Stroller and fool.
> Open that mouth, my Queen awaits a song.
> (*The Queen begins to dance*)
> Dance, turn him into mockery with a dance!
>
> [*CPl* 638–9]

The third song, though poetically fine, is theatrically weak for two reasons: first, Yeats's chronic tendency to load more intellectual ore into its rift than a theatre audience is likely to be able to handle, and secondly because it seems to anticipate the moment of union symbolized by the dance that follows:

> Clip and lip and long for more,
> Mortal men our abstracts are;
> *What of the hands on the Great Clock face?*
> All those living wretches crave
> Prerogatives of the dead that have
> Sprung heroic from the grave.
> *A moment more and it tolls midnight.*
>
> Crossed fingers there in pleasure can
> Exceed the nuptial bed of man;
> *What of the hands on the Great Clock face?*
> A nuptial bed exceed all that
> Boys at puberty have thought,
> Or sibyls in a frenzy sought.
> *A moment more and it tolls midnight.*
>
> What's prophesied? What marvel is
> Where the dead and living kiss?
> *What of the hands on the Great Clock face?*
> Sacred Virgil never sang
> All the marvel there begun,
> But there's stone upon my tongue.
> *A moment more and it tolls midnight.*
>
> [*CPl* 639–40]

If the Queen and the Stroller have already consummated their union in the place 'Where the dead and living kiss' – and the line 'Mortal men our abstracts are' seems to suggest this – then there is no need for the dance. The inexpressible joy of the 'there', which far exceeds in pleasure the nuptial bed of man, and in knowledge and vision anything that the interpenetration of human and human or of human and divine can bring, and of which their mortal counterparts are mere 'abstracts', is nevertheless set against the inexorably effacing movement of the hands of the Great Clock, expressed in the threatening refrain lines. (In performance the point would be clearer if these were assigned to the Second Attendant.) When they reach midnight, as Helen Vendler says,

the ultimate union is consummated. The union is brief because the tolling
of midnight will bring it to an end — time will intervene and break the trance
— but for the moment during which it lasts the absorption is complete.

[*YV* 147]

After this, the Queen's second dance is bound to lack tension,
because its meaning has already been anticipated, and because she
represents no such kinetic force of attraction and repulsion, allure
and refusal, as her counterpart shows in *A Full Moon in March*.
Yeats wrote to Olivia Shakespear that her dance was 'a long
expression of horror and fascination' [*L* 827]. This may be true of
the Queen's dance in *A Full Moon in March*, but not of this dance.
The Queen is emotionally neutral. She is entirely abstract, entirely
without feeling for either King for Stroller. Outside the dance she
exists only at second-hand, her meaning mediated only through the
First Attendant. All her dance does is to corroborate in movement
what the fable has already established in words and action. Its
justification in the play is secured only by Aengus's prophecy that
on the stroke of midnight the Queen will kiss the Stroller's mouth.
Her union with the Stroller always was inevitable: there is no
resistance to it, hence no sense of conflict or tension between them.
If there is tension it exists between the two of them together and
the King, and the dance represents their joint victory over him.

The final song both confirms and qualifies this victory. In its
theme, the juxtaposition of eternity and temporality, it refers back
to the opening lyric. One of its two metaphorical spokesmen, 'the
rambling shambling travelling-man', binds it to the Stroller in so far
as he is associated with beggars; the other, 'the wicked, crooked,
hawthorn tree' (why 'wicked'?), is new, and seems somewhat
arbitrary. Unlike the same image in *At the Hawk's Well*, it is not
integrated into the visual pattern of the play. Their assertions
contradict each other. One spokesman, however much he may be
himself a rambling, shambling travelling man in time and space,
nevertheless sees in the lighted Castle Dargan an image of the
temporal transformed into one of permanence:

> *First Attendant:* O, but I saw a solemn sight;
> *Said the rambling, shambling travelling-man;*
> Castle Dargan's ruin all lit,
> Lovely ladies dancing in it.

[*CPl* 640]

The other counters with a vision of transience:

Second Attendant: What though they danced! Those days are gone,
Said the wicked, crooked, hawthorn tree;
Lovely lady or gallant man
Are blown cold dust or a bit of bone.

[*CPl* 640]

In the third stanza the shambling travelling-man replies with the paradoxical assertion that life may be transitory, but that nevertheless it is man's creative imagination that constructs images that achieve permanence:

O, what is life but a mouthful of air?
Said the rambling, shambling travelling-man;
Yet all the lovely things that were
Live, for I saw her dancing there.

[*CPl* 640]

The Queen, who *'has come down stage and now stands framed in the half-closed curtains'* [*CPl* 641], is one such image. But the visual assertion is qualified by the suggestion of uncertainty in the final stanza concerning the relation between time and eternity:

Nobody knows what may befall,
Said the wicked, crooked, hawthorn-tree.
I have stood so long by a gap in the wall
Maybe I shall not die at all.

[*CPl* 641]

Yeats wants it both ways. But the upshot is a failure on two counts, in that the terms of his conflict are neither formulated with sufficient clarity, nor adequately embodied in his dramatic protagonists. Both weaknesses were remedied in the reworking of the play as *A Full Moon in March*.

A Full Moon in March

Everyone agrees that Yeats's own criticism of *The King of the Great Clock Tower* is just:

In *The King of the Great Clock Tower* there are three characters, King, Queen and Stroller, and that is a character too many; reduced to essentials, to Queen and Stroller, the fable should have greater intensity. I started a fresh and called the new version *A Full Moon in March*.

[*Comm. Pl* 246]

Not everyone, however, has perceived that in gaining the greater intensity that he sought he also shifted the emphases and re-drew the lines of its dramatic pattern. The removal of the King from the play, the insertion of a new opening lyric on a totally different theme, the redesigning of the role of the Queen from a passive to an active force, the transformation of the Stroller into the Swineherd, whose essence lies in his savage absolutism, the substitution of the March moon for midnight as the climactic moment, all these changes combine to shift the theme away from that of the intersection of the timeless with time to one of the familiar Yeatsian paradox of creative death. What is common to the two plays — they are so essentially different that it is wrong to refer to them as two versions of the same theme — is the archetypal folk-tale element of humble Suitor winning the hand and kingdom of the Princess, and of course, the Noh-like treatment.

The basis of the tragic pattern is a dying into life, as much Keatsian as Heraclitan, expressed as a ritualistic cyclical movement, a dialectical struggle both between opposites and within them. Not only are Queen and Swineherd thesis and antithesis, but the energy that impels them to their union derives from the contradictory qualities within each of them. The Queen is driven to sacrifice her purity to the hateful force that alone can ensure the fulfilment she desires, the Swineherd, desiring his opposite, has to sacrifice his essential vitality, his fundamental 'livingness', in order to attain it. This driving energy is seen both as a force operating on them from outside – the inevitably recurrent pattern of the year focused on the climactic moment of the spring solstice when the old year dies into the new – and from within. Whereas in *The King of the Great Clock Tower* the Stroller just happened to confront the Queen as a result of hearing by chance that the King had married 'a woman called / Most beautiful of her sex' [*CPl* 635], now she *chooses* the confrontation by means of her challenge, and the Swineherd has to answer it: the moment has now come in the inevitable movement of time, the full moon in March, when she must be won:

> You must be won
> At a full moon in March, those beggars say.
> That moon has come, but I am here alone.
>
> [*CPl* 624]

The challenge, replacing Aengus's vague and unsatisfactory prophecy in *The King of the Great Clock Tower*, and originating in the Queen's internal self-destructive impulses, is the first step that leads to her inevitable desecration. And she takes it herself. She is not the passive Queen of the earlier play, who simply waits for something to happen to her. She is, as Nathan says,

an active agent . . . clearly defined as a virgin goddess, cruel and beautiful, needing human love to achieve her full identity, needing, in fact, all that is opposite to her virgin beauty. Thus, the Stroller becomes a filthy arrogant Swineherd, whose sacrifice 'fertilizes' the Queen's barren virginity so that it can achieve fulfilment at the full moon in March.

> [*TD* 195]

The twain must converge since both Queen and Swineherd desire their destructive consummation.

Fundamentally the play dramatizes a stark dialectical conflict in a dramatic vocabulary, verbal, visual and mimetic, which is correspondingly stark and brutal. What should be aimed at in performance is not only the absoluteness of the opposition between the antithetical terms of the conflict, but also the inevitability of their fusion, expressed as a build-up of tension to the explosion-point of the climactic dance with the severed head. As a dramatic paradigm it is Yeats's most abstract play, but at the same time his richest, in that the terms of its central conflict can be interpreted in a number of ways. These are cumulatively complex and not mutually incompatible. In this respect it has a mythic quality for which the Noh-like treatment, stylized and generalized, is admirably appropriate.

For those furnished with the sort of esoteric lore that Whitaker
exhumes from Hermetic and alchemical sources [*S&S* chap. 12],
it can be read in these terms. But not much will be lost by those who
are not. Other approaches are possible, such as the philosophical
one of Nathan given above, or that of Wilson [*YT* ch. 2], even
though they may not command consent in all their details. Wilson's
comments to the effect that the Queen's cruelty and coldness are

the mark that Godhead itself is imperfect when divorced from the spirit which
has gone out into matter: heaven is incomplete in its separation from man,
the timeless in its separation from the world of time

[*YT* 92]

and that

heaven is no heaven until it has been fertilised by its opposite, the energy
which is the property of time

[*YT* 92]

are just. But his view that the Swineherd is brutally oblivious of the
Queen's divine nature is disputable, since it is precisely her qualities
of coldness and cruelty which the Swineherd is aware of and which,
far from preventing him from desiring her, are what attracts him
to her. The aesthetic approach, in which the Queen is identified with
the Muse and the Swineherd with the Poet, seems, as we have seen,
less appropriate to this play than to *The King of the Great Clock
Tower*. What distinguishes the Stroller from the Swineherd is the
element of savagery. In *The King of the Great Clock Tower* there
is nothing inherently savage about the Stroller: his savagery is only
visually suggested by his mask and does not characterize his language.
In this play, however, the Swineherd's savagery is basic: it is in his
appearance, his speech and his action. But there is no compelling
reason why savagery should characterize the Poet. He seems less like
the Poet than an irreducible primitivism which lies at the root of
civilization ('kingdoms' [*CPl* 625]) and of the culture ('song' [*CPl*
625]) it produces. But the play suggests that such primitivism must
be acknowledged and must impregnate its opposite if that civilization
is to be preserved and recreated. The Swineherd snaps his fingers
at the thought of kingdoms, and to him culture – beauty and songs
– are nonsense:

> *The Swineherd:* What do I know of beauty?
> *The Queen:*   Sing the best

> And you are not a swineherd but a king.
> *The Swineherd:* What do I know of kingdoms?
>   (*Snapping his fingers*) That for kingdoms!. . . . .
> But first my song – What nonsense shall I sing?
>
>   [*CPl* 625]

But the way to the analogical lies through the literal, so that if the play is to function effectively in the theatre on a level of abstract generalization (alchemical, aesthetic or metaphysical), as a psychic drama acted out in the deeps of the mind, an audience must be provided with an entry point that will lead them into these depths. In the Queen and the Swineherd Yeats has created masterful images, of the essential duality he sees at the heart of life, but, to change the metaphor, ladders to these masterful images, as Yeats discovered, begin in the foul rag-and-bone shop of the human heart. Such a point of access Yeats has provided by the way in which he makes his 'myth', his fable, also relevant to recognizable human behaviour. For all its non-naturalistic character, the play 'works' if not *at* then not far *below* the naturalistic level. As Newton pointed out in *Essays in Criticism* VIII, 1958, the theme of sex-antagonism in it relates it to Strindbergian naturalism. On this level the play can be regarded as an extended gloss on the thought at the basis of 'Crazy Jane Grown Old Looks at the Dancers' [*CP* 295], which Yeats told Olivia Shakespear was 'Blake's old thought, "sexual love is founded upon spiritual hate" ' [*L* 758]. Even Moore, who suggests that 'everything is mythical; nothing historical or "real" ' [*MLD* 268], acknowledges that we do get a sense of the Swineherd's 'character' – his 'honesty, courage, and a naive and therefore invincible resolution' [*MLD* 269] – even though these are qualities associated with the archetypal third son of folk-tales who achieves what his older brothers cannot. These two aspects, the human and the abstractly archetypal, are fused together more effectively in the Swineherd than they are in the Queen, perhaps because in her Yeats emphasizes their separation more clearly. The song of the First Attendant, who sings as the Queen, 'Child and darling, hear my song' [*CPl* 628], insists on the distinction between herself as woman and her role as cruelty. Peter Ure pointed to the inconsistency in Yeats's treatment of her when she considers herself insulted by the Swineherd:

> All here have heard the man and all have judged.
> I led him, that I might not seem unjust,
> From point to point, established in all eyes

That he came hither not to sing but to heap
Complexities of insult on my head.

[*CPl* 625]

But, wrote Ure,

. . . this Queen needs no excuses for her cruelty or witnesses to her justice.
It is the dramatist who has needed the insult-motif as an excuse to keep his
story unfolding; he 'must have severed heads', and he must somehow contrive
that the Queen shall behead the Swineherd in order to organize his central
symbol. A touch of human motivation is introduced into the rite.

[*YTP* 161–2]

Ure wrote that he had seen

no interpretation . . . which makes it clear why the Queen should be
considered or should consider herself insulted by the Stroller/Swineherd's
somewhat tepid commendations of her beauty when at last he beholds it.

[*YTP* 161]

If there is inconsistency here between the Queen's reaction as woman
and the rest of her behaviour as impersonal participant in a rite, it
is doubtful whether it is noticed in the theatre. It is absorbed by the
expectations already set up by the arbitrariness of the 'Catch–22'
situation she has already created:

> *The Swineherd:* But what if some blind aged cripple sing
> Better than wholesome men?
> *The Queen:*   Some I reject.
> Some I have punished for their impudence.
> None I abhor can sing.
> *The Swineherd:*   So that's the catch.

[*CPl* 623]

But is there really inconsistency here? Does she not feel insulted as
a woman just because she has not yet achieved her full unity of being?
The phrase 'complexities of insult' suggests the 'complexities of mire
and blood' associated with the human condition in *Byzantium* [*CP*
290]. When that achievement occurs, when abstract virginity accepts
human desecration, the cruelty turns to tenderness, insult to
adoration. At this human level the play makes a powerful impact
– even Bloom concedes it 'a nasty power' [*Y* 341] – as a dramatic
epiphany of the archetypal human situation, whether we define it
with Bentley as one in which 'if we are to live, our wintry and saintly

virginity must descend into the dung of passion' [*PY* 222], or with Moore, 'the human use of beauty demands its desecration' [*MLD* 271].

In whatever terms this basic duality is interpreted, they are integrated into the complex vocabulary of the play, which comprises visual, verbal and mimetic effects, and is contained within a form which expresses the theme's fundamental aspect, the inevitability of the congress of the two components of the duality. This form is appropriately ritualistic, since the essence of ritual is its inevitability, in which there is no room for the manœuvring of individual choice, everything being fore-ordained. This congress is a process, a coming together, a movement in time, not a static meditation: it needs an action to express it. In the world of Yeats the centre is not a still hub, round which the circumference revolves: it is always itself seeking the circumference and the circumference always seeking the centre.

A pattern of inevitability is established by the very title of the play, since the moon is bound to reach its full at the vernal equinox, winter is bound to die and a new spring is bound to be born. The Attendants ground the play obviously in duality – Young Man opposed to Elderly Woman, base to soprano. Also, but by implication, they ground it in inevitability. They dispense with an introduction since, whatever form it takes, what it introduces is bound to happen anyway:

> *First Attendant:* What do we do?
> What part do we take?
> What did he say?
> *Second Attendant:* Join when we like,
> Singing or speaking.
> *First Attendant:* Before the curtain rises on the play?
> *Second Attendant:* Before it rises.
> *First Attendant:* What do we sing?
> *Second Attendant:* 'Sing anything, sing any old thing', said he.
> [*CPl* 621]

This staccato dialogue lays the foundations of the play's linguistic decorum. The pattern of inevitability continues through the play in a series of prolepses. The Queen's 'stretching and yawning' [*CPl* 622], used elsewhere by Yeats to suggest the lassitude that follows sexual intercourse, anticipates her final union with the Swineherd. As *Comm. Pl* says (249), their relation is determined by the necessary relationship of opposites, that they should seek fulfilment in their interpenetration. The trembling of her limbs [*CPl* 625] anticipates the shivering of her body in her final dance. Her revulsion at the thought of taking a severed head in her hands, of blood begetting a child in bridal sleep [*CPl* 626] anticipates what actually happens. The line in the First Attendant's song as the Queen, 'Great my love before you came' [*CPl* 628], implies that the whole process of the interpenetration of the two is pre-ordained. She knows, too, even before he appears, that someone has come. Her descent from the throne (which should be designed to have reference to the 'emblematic niches' of the final song), the dropping of her veil, both point forward to her desecration. All these prolepses should be projected to the audience by parallel movements.

The first lyric announces the duality — wisdom and stupidity, yob and egg-head, crowned head and swineherd, gold and dung, and above them the anarchic, absolute, force of love indifferent to all else but its object. As a result of Yeats's reshaping of his material, the themes of the songs are interwoven with the action, not, as in *The King of the Great Clock Tower,* left as comments on it. The scene that follows, between the Queen and the Swineherd, enacts both that which divides them, his carnality and her purity, and also that which binds them together, the uncompromising absolutism with which each maintains his position. There are no pretences on either side: he is utterly foul and ragged, she is utterly cold and cruel. He knows exactly what she is and the nature of what he wants and the cost of getting it. She knows that if she has him, she must

> . . . leave these corridors, this ancient house,
> A famous throne, the reverence of servants

and that she will gain only

> the night of love,
> An ignorant forest and the dung of swine.
>
> [*CPl* 625]

He wants her as she is, in the beauty of her body and in the coldness of her cruelty, a point that is made more directly in the earlier manuscript versions printed by Curtis Bradford:

> When I shall touch your body I shall touch that cruelty, and my desire for one is as my desire for the other.
>
> [*YW* 276]

His desire is divorced from the idea of the rewards of conquest. Whether her features are beautiful or not does not matter: they are what they are and do not require the flattery of either simile or hyperbole. A song in praise of her beauty is ultimately irrelevant. The material wealth and power that are her attributes are not worth the snap of a finger. She has rejected other suitors because she has seen in their songs only a reflection of their own desires; in him she is brought face to face with a force of love that is literally self-less, that does not desire to change its object, of love, that is, as Yeats wrote to Lady Dorothy Wellesley, 'a form of the eternal contemplation of what is' [*DWL* 126]. The assertion of that value he is prepared to bring to the ultimate test of death. He is prepared to trump her ace, laughing at the prospect of his head being severed, but in fact she is already prepared to concede the trick. As yet, however, even though her descent from the throne prefigures her commitment to the Swineherd, and the dropping of her veil her eventual desecration, the Queen does not embrace the implications of her decision. Both his assertion and her knowledge have still to be proved in the fire of experience, still to be translated from intention into action, his by death, hers by surrender.

In the meantime the second song of the Attendant is a kind of analogue to the Queen's attitude, in that it is first a transparently ineffective attempt to deny her responsibility for the Swineherd's death:

> And all men lie that say that I
> Bade that swordsman take
> His head from off his body
> And set it on a stake . . .
>
> They lie that say, in mockery
> Of all that lovers said,
> Or in mere woman's cruelty
> I bade them fetch his head.
>
> [*CPl* 627]

As Helen Vendler suggests [*YV* 154], we suspect that she protests too much. Secondly, it demonstrates that she does not yet desire the Swineherd for what he is. She is prepared to give her body, as other women have done before, but only for the sake of self-gratification, for the abnormal pleasure of standing before a stake and hearing dead lips sing. Not until she is discovered standing with the dropped veil at her side, holding the severed head of the Swineherd (proof that in his case intention has been converted into action), her hands red and her own dress stained with blood [*CPl* 627–8], do we realize that even though others have been agents of his death ('. . . in a moment they will lead you out / Then bring your severed head' [*CPl* 626]), hers is the responsibility. Like Beatrice-Joanna she cannot shift her responsibility onto De Flores, though in the song of the First Attendant as Queen she still distinguishes between herself and her cruelty, still tries to shelter behind her lunar mask.

> Cry that wrong came not from me
> But my virgin cruelty.

[*CPl* 628]

In a sense the Queen tries to remain outside the action as the Queen in the song tries to remain outside the beheading. But she is inevitably forced into it. Unity of being has not yet been reached, though the Queen is moving or is being carried by the inexorable movement of the cycles along the path that will bring her to it in the climactic dance. The measure of her progress so far is marked by the tone and rhythm of this song, which is more than an explanation of her former cruelty. It represents in its confessional and supplicatory tenderness a movement away from it. The snows are beginning to melt.

> Child and darling, hear my song,
> Never cry I did you wrong;
> Cry that wrong came not from me
> But my virgin cruelty.
> Great my love before you came,
> Greater when I loved in shame,
> Greatest when there broke from me
> Storm of virgin cruelty.

[*CPl* 628]

At the end of it she symbolically acknowledges the change of roles, his elevation, her submission, by laying the head upon the throne. The final miraculous transformation of savage time-bound Swineherd to timeless eternal singing star is celebrated in the 'one song', as Ure perceived,

which ought not to have the same character as the others, because it is a part, or fulfilment, of the action in a way that they are not . . . It is the depersonalized voice of phantasmic folk-song and nursery-rhyme, utterly different from the richer and more human note of amazement and longing heard in the Musicians' songs

[*YTP* 162–3]

and, we may add, in the Queen's motherly lullaby. Slain Swineherd becomes risen God. Ritual murder is used here, as coition is later, to symbolize the way in which higher wisdom or ecstasy is attained by the death of self, or, if the aesthetic allegory is pursued, the artefact emerges from the sacrifice of experience on the altar of form. Laughter now becomes a metaphor linking the two — and the point should be made in performance. The Swineherd's laughter at the thought of surrendering his life is echoed by the Queen's as she begins the dance that epitomizes the willing surrender of her cold virginity.

Yeats is careful to remove from the final version of the play the identification of the climax of the dance exclusively with the sexual act, which is explicit in the manuscript that Curtis Bradford prints [*YW* 288]. Not, I think, out of prudishness (which is hardly to be expected from the author of *The Herne's Egg*), but because he wants to use coition not simply as an act in and for itself, but as symbolic of that union of dialectical opposites in which each is destroyed in the conception of something other than themselves. This is the problem the choreographer has to solve, just as the director must solve the problem of the ritual severing of the Swineherd's head, preserving each incident's theatrical shock, which is the conductor of spiritual illumination, without reducing it to either gratuitous horror on the one hand or prurience on the other. Both acts must be ritualized.

Shock and the terror it produces are among the emotions conveyed by the final lyric. This is not the benign summing-up of what has just been witnessed, in calm of mind, all passion spent. It carries onthe dramatic impetus from ignorant amazement to ecstatic enlightenment. The Second Attendant in effect relates ritual action as a projection of generalized psychic reality to ordinary experience. What *is* this mysterious energy that drives Queen from emblematic niches to ignorant forest and dung of swine at the cost of her purity, that impels loutish Swineherd to crown of gold at the cost of his physical being?

> Why must those holy, haughty feet descend
> From emblematic niches, and what hand
> Ran that delicate raddle through their white?
> My heart is broken, yet must understand.
> What do they seek for? Why must they descend?
> [*CPl* 629]

The First Attendant's reply is too frightening at first for the Second, ordinary humanity, to contemplate, since it implies the rending of what appears to be a self-sufficient purity, as fixed and remote as the blank face of the full moon:

> *First Attendant:* For desecration and the lover's night.
> *Second Attendant:* I cannot face that emblem of the moon
> Nor eyelids that the unmixed heavens dart,
> Nor stand upon my feet, so great a fright'
> Descends upon my savage, sunlit heart.
> What can she lack whose emblem is the moon?
>
> [*CPl* 629–30]

But such a rending is necessary if wholeness is to be achieved. As Crazy Jane puts it:

> . . . Love has pitched his mansion in
> The place of excrement;
> For nothing can be sole or whole
> That has not been rent.
>
> [*CP* 295]

The pitchers of eternity must be poured out onto the hill of time, and it needs both a Jack and a Jill together to fetch them. Individual being finds achievement only in union with its opposite, as 'she' merges with 'him' into 'their' desecration and the lover's night, a conclusion that should be asserted in tones of delight and ecstatic conviction:

> *Second Attendant:* Delight my heart with sound; speak yet again.
> But look and look with understanding eyes
> Upon the pitchers that they carry; tight
> Therein all time's completed treasure is:
> What do they lack? O cry it out again.
> *First Attendant:* Their desecration and the lover's night.
>
> [*CPl* 630]

LAST STAGES
The Herne's Egg, Purgatory, The Death of Cuchulain

Two things distinguish these last plays from those of Yeats's mature period: differences of form and differences of tone. Deviations from the Noh-like convention of the dance plays are clear. *The Herne's Egg* has neither chorus, mask, dance nor binding metaphor. Its setting, décor, range of characters, are all much more diffuse. *Purgatory* has no chorus, no masked characters, and no dance. It does have binding metaphors, in the form of house and tree, but these are not presented solely as poetic concepts to be perceived in the mind; they are also physical objects on the stage and thus form part of our visual experience. *Purgatory* is firmly based on psychological naturalism, and in this respect it represents a return to the techniques of the much earlier *On Baile's Strand* and *Deirdre*. But at the same time it shares with the plays of the central achievement the Noh-like subject of the meeting with spirits which takes place in a dimension where past and present mysteriously and, in theatrical terms, boldly meet. The play is worked out both in historical time – the entire action is related to 1916 – and in actual space, which, even if it is not precisely defined, suggests an actual location. It shares, too, the kind of concentration that is found in the dance plays.

The Death of Cuchulain, in that it seems to be a conscious epilogue to his dramatic *oeuvre,* is a rather special case. It has a chorus of sorts, though it is not the same kind of Chorus that appears in *At the Hawk's Well, The Only Jealousy of Emer, Calvary, The Resurrection, The Dreaming of the Bones, The Cat and the Moon,* and *A Full Moon in March.* For one thing, the choric personages are not consistently maintained: the Old Man, who introduces the play, disappears, fading into the Street-Singer; prose becomes song. The characters are not masked, unless it is intended that the Blind Man should wear the same mask that Craig designed for him in *The Hour Glass* and *On Baile's Strand,* thus evoking his impact in those plays. But there are masks, this time conceived in terms of the extreme abstractionism of the parallelograms that represent the heads

209

of Cuchulain and the six warriors who gave him six mortal wounds. There is a dance, but it is by no means clear that it is a climactic dance. The climax seems to lie in the song of the Street- Singer, which is not so much an expansion of the previous action or a comment on it as an extension of it. The contemporary world, in the 'music of some Irish Fair of our day' [*CPl* 704] and the Street- Singer's song, gives its ambiguous reaction to the serenely confident, though tragic gesture of a heroic past. Nor does the dance seem to grow naturally out of the preceding action. It is an interpolation, and furthermore it is danced by a character whom an uninitiated audience would have difficulty in identifying.

Both *Purgatory* and *The Death of Cuchulain* differ from all the plays of the central achievement except *The Dreaming of the Bones* and *The Words Upon the Window-Pane* in that an essential part of their meaning lies in the relation of the heroic or aristocratic past to a degenerate present. The earlier plays exist in a self-contained heroic era; now we are conscious of the relation of that era to the present. As he got older Yeats became more and more concerned with the idea of the moral and spiritual decay of western European civilization as a whole, of which the decay of Irish aristocracy and the decline of the 'Big House' were but local symptons. This is particularly plain in *The Words Upon the Window-Pane* and *Purgatory*. There were earlier signs of this attitude in *On Baile's Strand,* where the Fool and the Blind Man survive in deceit and cupidity to inherit a land alien to heroic virtues, and also in *The Green Helmet,* where, although heroism triumphs comically in the end, we never forget the *petit-bourgeois* materialism and social divisiveness of the contemporary world which it mocks and defeats.

Mockery had already appeared in earlier plays. In *The Green Helmet* it was good-humoured and good-natured. In *The Player Queen* the tone begins to darken. There is a near-cynical bleakness about it that is barely neutralized by the display of human absurdity. The Prime Minister's plans are frustrated, authority is debased. Decima gains one role but loses another, possibly more important. The inspiration of the poet Septimus becomes hardly distinguishable from rant, service to art degenerates into the self-preservation of the artist. No-one is capable of heroism any more. The fact that 'in order to get rid of the play', as Yeats wrote, which he had begun as a tragedy in 1907 concerned with one of his fundamental ideas, 'the finding or the not finding of what I have called the Antithetical Self', he had to turn it into a farce, which he did very quickly, is significant. The veins of mockery in Yeats do not lie very far below the surface of seriousness. But in these last plays this tendency is more pronounced. In *The Herne's Egg* basic concepts are subjected to a reductive process that cheapens them. Heroic intransigence, such as is displayed by Cuchulain in *On Baile's Strand,* becomes stupid and destructive stubbornness in Congal and Aedh. In *The Death of Cuchulain* the final 'heroic' gesture is so muted that doubts are raised about its value. In *Purgatory* the Old Man's gesture is merely savage and fundamentally futile. The denial of that futility is never positively established: the Old Man's prayer is directed to a God who remains dramatically silent. The Old Man is trapped in a degenerate process from which there is no escape either by individual gesture, since such a gesture is coarsened by the very conditions which form it and in which it is made, or by relief in a generalized fructifying renewal. In *At the Hawk's Well,* Cuchulain's gesture, however inadequately it may be expressed in terms of theatrical effect, was positive. It established his heroic status, even if it also involved a life of frustration leading ultimately to death. Such a status is held up as one that creates its own value, a value that both sets it up above mundane concerns, illuminates them and in the last analysis provides the level to which they aspire. The same paradoxical achievement of triumph in defeat is also present in the earlier *Deirdre* and the later *The Only Jealousy of Emer,* and most positively in the ecstatic conclusion of *A Full Moon in March.* Deirdre, Cuchulain, Emer, the Queen and the Swineherd are unmistakable heroes and nothing is done to belittle their stature. *The Dreaming of the Bones,* however, depicts a contemporary world in which the Young Man, whom many would regard as heroic, trapped by the past, is incapable of that gesture which would release the present from the repetition of a murderous vitality. *Calvary* is the first play to hint at the futility of all heroic action, whether self-assertive or self-sacrificial. Both Judas and Christ are prisoners of necessity; but there is no mockery in the depiction of their situation. It is not until *The Herne's Egg* that the hero and the heroic gesture themselves are mocked and trivialized. *The Words Upon the Window-Pane* and *Purgatory* both suggest a world which in its progressive debasement and degeneration either cannot acknowledge the hero, or renders him and his action futile. *The Herne's Egg* building on *The Green Helmet* and *The Player Queen,* takes this attitude further. In *The Green Helmet,* for all its grotesquerie and extravagance, Cuchulain is acknowledged as hero, and in *The Player Queen* even Septimus, for all his romantic *folie de grandeur,* retains a kind of integrity: through him the value of art is, though unsteadily, preserved. But *The Herne's Egg* is dipped in a comic ambiguity that stains its action, its characters, its décor, and, more significantly, the concepts that lie behind it. Conflict, divine reality, whether conceived in terms of flesh or spirit, lust or chastity, the desecration of body or spirit, the hero and his accoutrements of weapons and armour, reincarnation, unknowable transcendent order, all are subject to reductive mockery. All the major symbols of the play, verbal or visual, the herne and its boiled eggs, nursery donkey and its painted creel, table-legs and candlesticks, cauldron-lid, cooking-pot, kitchen spit and skull-cap are inherently absurd. The 'heroes' Aedh, Congal and their followers, and also their antagonists, Attracta and her giggling worshippers, are all at times made to look ridiculous. It is almost as if Yeats were taking refuge, if not in farcical contempt then in comic ambiguity, since laughter can be both aggressive and protective, from despair at the collapse he saw in the world around him of so much that he held dear. In *The Death of Cuchulain,* to this *mélange* of discontent, mockery and defiance, there is added a kind of serene resignation that does not entirely exclude the possibility of either triumph or defeat. The mockery and discontent are there, expressed in the Old Man, who is not so much a dramatized version of Yeats himself and of his views of drama as some critics have held him to be, but a grotesque caricature. The titanic element in the Hero's effort to transcend temporal limitations — the sort of gesture which hitherto has been seen in the young Cuchulain's acceptance of his role, Emer's renunciation, the Swineherd's immolation — is muted. Cuchulain has to be helped to his apotheosis. He has to be assisted to die on his feet, the stance of heroic death, by the ageing Aoife, who winds the 'womanish stuff' of her veil about him. He dies ignominiously at the hands of the materialistic Blind Man. Nevertheless it is typical of the ambivalences of the play that Cuchulain should survive beyond death. He does this, however, not as a Michael Angelo-like, larger-than-life human form, but as an abstract image, a parallelogram among parallelograms. The soul of the tough fighting man dies into its opposite, a soft feathery bird. His conviction that as such it will sing, as indeed it does, in other words that the immortal image of himself that he has created in his death will illuminate the future, is qualified by the song itself, sung to the 'music of some Irish Fair of our day' [*CPl* 704] to the accompaniment of musicians dressed in ragged street-singers' clothes. Yet the serene authority of his vision,

> There floats out there
> The shape that I shall take when I am dead,
> My soul's first shape, a soft feathery shape,

> [*CPl* 702]

and of his belief, 'I say it is about to sing' [*CPl* 702], triumphantly denies the degenerate vulgarity of the contemporary world. That depersonalized image created by the undying imagination may be the inspiration for the re-creation of heroic personality, symbolized by the statue 'By Oliver Shepherd done'. It may also be the measure by which that which has been adored solely in its materiality, its flesh, may be loathed for its rejection of the reality of the spirit, the reality of the imagination:

> Who thought Cuchulain till it seemed
> He stood where they had stood?
>
> [*CPl* 705]

where the 'they' are Conall, Cuchulain, Usna's boys and their modern counterparts, Pearse and Connolly. It may also be the means by which the present, the bodies 'by modern women borne', are seen as inferior to those very inhabitants of the timeless world of myth. Yet at the same time we cannot exclude the possibility that Cuchulain's final noiseless gesture is pointless, as it is drowned by the cacophony of the present.

These last plays of Yeats encompass both belief and the possibility that belief is futile. Truth is not to be found in either attitude: it embraces both.

The Herne's Egg

Yeats described this play as 'the strangest wildest thing I have ever written' [*L* 845], and 'as wild a play as *Player Queen,* as amusing but more tragedy and philosophic depth' [*L* 843]. There is no doubt of its strangeness, its Rabelaisian irreverence, which he thought might provoke riots if the Abbey produced it, and there is also no doubt about its philosophic overtones, in the sense that in its characters and action it echoes ideas that have sounded in other works, both plays and poems. What is not so easy to determine is its tone. It would be easier to assess it if it were either stranger and wilder or more deeply philosophic and tragic. It is the relation between these two elements that is the problem. Nathan sees it as an extension of *The Player Queen,* as 'an extravagant attempt to embody on the level of farce and travesty Yeats's theory of reality' [*TD* 281], but it is not all farce nor is it at all clear what theory of reality it demonstrates. Bloom, while granting it a lasting imaginative power, dismisses it as a squalid parody of Yeats's own mythology, though it is not all that squalid. Rajan rightly points to the strong sense of the absurd in it. But exactly what is absurd? Is it man and his pretensions, his predicament, his heroism in the face of that predicament, heroism itself, or even God? Even Wilson, who takes the play very seriously indeed, is conscious of a 'half-farcical atmosphere' [*Y&T* 122], a 'tragic-comic levity' [*Y&T* 115]. Helen Vendler, who feels that that very levity is 'tiresome and unsuccessful . . . uncongenial to Yeats's temperament' [*YV* 160–1], is right in saying that the question of tone has to be settled before anything can be said about the play. Whatever the philosophic issues the play raises, they are passed through a process of reductive comedy. The significance of character or incident, as in *The Cat and the Moon,* is determined by their mainly comic theatrical representation. More than ever with this play, one must guard against the tendency to import meaning into it from external sources without regard for the dramatic vocabulary in which that meaning is expressed.

The opening scene establishes this tone at once, both visually and by verbal means. It gives us a battle, stylized both in movement

214

('sword and sword, shield and sword, never meet. The men move rhythmically as if in a dance.' [*CPl* 645]), and verbally in the stychomythia of Congal and Aedh. The effect that this produces is not the same as that of the stylization of the earlier dance plays such as *The Only Jealousy of Emer* or *At the Hawk's Well*. There the stylization is a means of drawing us into the deeps of the mind, into a drama of psychic essences. Here the stylization distances the situation and the characters involved in it, producing a detachment in which the seeds of comedy can grow. This is certainly a battle, whether it represents a state of prelapsarian equilibrium, or the empty gestures of a tradition in the final stages of disintegration in Yeats's system, but it is a comic battle, just as Corney's donkey is a comic donkey and the painted eggs in a painted creel comic eggs.

Philosophic issues there are, not the least important being man's relation to God, dramatized as Congal's three bouts against the Great Herne. But what sort of man and what sort of God? There is much in the play to support the view that the Herne is God, that Attracta is His priestess, whose trance indicates that her will has been absorbed by His, that she is His agent. Visually, His image, *'suggested, not painted realistically'* [*CPl* 645], because realism would limit the range of His symbolic significance, dominates the entire action, just as the recurrent music of 'The Great Herne's Feather' attests His immanence, however it is played, on flute or whistled, and whoever plays it, whether it is Corney or one of Congal's men, or Tom Fool. The Herne is impervious to human attack on him by stone and sword. His curse, that Congal shall meet his death at the hands of a fool, in whatever way that it is interpreted, does take effect. The thunder corroborates his power, and it corroborates Attracta's declaration that she knows the punishment he will impose on those who claim that they have lain with her. Even Congal is momentarily terrified. In *Calvary* Yeats had used the heron as a symbol of a type of subjectivity that is sufficient to itself. This must be what Attracta means when she says that in his union with her

> . . . he,
> Being all a spirit, but begot
> His image in the mirror of my spirit,
> Being all sufficient to himself
> Begot himself.
>
> [*CPl* 677]

Narcissistically absorbed not only in the contemplation of his own image, as the heron in *Calvary* is, but in the exercise of his own

will, he shows himself to be arbitrary, absurdly arbitrary, in allowing
his instrument Attracta to attempt to thwart his own plans by lying
with Corney. It is difficult to resist the impression that had Corney
and Attracta been quick enough, his will would have been thwarted.
It is, of course, possible to argue that even Corney's reluctance to
get on with the job is itself part of the Great Herne's will, that indeed
all human choice is exercised within the framework of an overriding
determinism, that Congal and his men are made fools of because
whatever they do, even if they attack him, they are in fact merely
surrogates of the Great Herne's power, and that the joke is on them
because they do not understand this. But is this the impression that
the play as a whole gives? If it is, to some extent, an expression of
man's relation to God, then at least two questions have to be
answered. Is this God totally omniscient and totally omnipotent to
the extent that even man's defiance of Him is futile and self-defeating
because it is an aspect of Himself? Or is He, for all His apparent
self-sufficiency, incomplete, in that He operates in an area of spiritual
subjectivity which denies or is opposed by other areas of subjectivity
which may be just as valid as His? The image of the heron in *Calvary*
implies that the heron is not ultimately the ruling principle of life,
since his continued existence depends upon the renewal of the cyclical
pattern:

> But that the full is shortly gone
> And after that is crescent moon,
> It's certain that the moon-crazed heron
> Would be but fishes' diet soon.

[*CPl* 450]

Attracta's lines quoted below imply that there is an area of
experience, namely the union of spirit with body, which is just as
important as the Herne's self-sufficiency:

> but there's a work
> That should be done, and that work needs
> No bird's beak nor claw, but a man,
> The imperfection of a man.

[*CPl* 677]

In other words, the Herne as God of pure spirituality is incomplete,
a view which is in keeping with Yeats's thought as a whole, and which
he dramatized without any suggestion of grotesqueness in *A Full
Moon in March*. To symbolize Godhead by an arbitrary old bird
standing on one leg whose agents can be seen as a sex-starved virginal

headmistress taking a class of giggling adolescents in the facts of life, a penny-counting Tom Fool, or a half-witted Tweedledum armed with a saucepan-lid, a pot and a kitchen spit, is comically reductive. We never know the answers to the questions that the play as a whole asks, or indeed whether the questions are themselves important. Was Attracta in fact raped by Congal and his six men, or did they only seem to do it? And if she was, were they acting as God's surrogates? Or was she only spiritually united with the Great Herne? All we get are two contrary assertions, both subjective: Congal maintains she was; she maintains she was not. Is Congal a tragic hero or merely a fool, or are tragic commitment and folly two sides of the same coin?

The views of Congal and Attracta seem mutually exclusive and are set in a context that appears stable but is in fact threatened with change. The first scene is more than a curtain-raiser; it is clearly related to scene 4, in which the threat is actualized in undignified violence. Its ritualistic symmetry may represent a prelapsarian equilibrium, but it is an equilibrium that is the product of exhaustion: '. . . war / Has taken all our riches' [*CPl* 646]. It is threatened by the caprice of an arbitrarily asserted subjective will. Congal threatens Aedh with violence unless he completes his story:

> *Congal:* Finish the tale and say
> What kind of dog they bought.
> *Aedh:* Heaven knows.
> *Congal:*   You must have thought
> What kind of dog they bought.
> *Aedh:* Heaven knows.
> *Congal:*   Unless you say
> I'll up and fight all day.
>
> > [*CPl* 646]

This equilibrium is imaged in the reductive terms of a dog's life,

> A fat, square, lazy dog,
> No sort of scratching dog.
>
> > [*CPl* 646]

which Congal in the final scene refers to again, in which 'heroic' man is not so much a soldier as a flea:

> Never be a soldier, Tom;
> Though it begins well, is this a life?
> If this is a man's life, is there any life
> But a dog's life?
>
> > [*CPl* 675]

Harmony collapses. The stichomythia disintegrates rhythmically in Aedh's lackadaisical replies. The energy is exhausted. Not even the dog is vigorous enough to scratch its own parasites. Nevertheless the cycles must keep turning. There can be no stable equilibrium:

> Our fifty battles had made us friends;
> And there are fifty more to come.
> New weapons, a new leader will be found
> And everything begin again.
>
> [*CPl* 660]

The appearance of gentility — in another context, 'Meditations in Time of Civil War' [*CP* 225], imaged as an empty sea-shell — descends to the reality of vulgar violence which is no less fatal for being the product of mutual irrational insult, as Congal and Aedh accuse each other. But it is not a scream from Juno's peacock that marks the conception of a new era as control over the will is lost, but, as in *The Player Queen,* the bray of a donkey. The image of a hollow battle, losses matching losses, wound mirroring wound, is echoed by Attracta's image of the Herne begetting himself in the mirror of her spirit. Both forms of self-reduplicating subjectivity, human and divine, are barren. New life requires the interpenetration of opposites.

The second scene sets up a pair of opposites, Congal and Attracta, but not until Corney and his life-size toy donkey have continued the reductive tone by foreshadowing in his reference to metempsychosis Congal's possible transformation into a donkey. Who is Corney? An easy-going guardian of Attracta's shrine, and subservient to authority, he seems to suggest a kind of piety. To him the Hernery is 'holy' even if it is 'queer', and the theft of the eggs sacrilegious. He will not hear the bride of the Great Herne defamed; he is terrified of the divine thunder; he does not accept Congal's version of the rape. The fact that he is unarmed suggests that he has no quarrel with the Great Herne. On the other hand he seems unaware of the symbolic quality of the Herne's eggs: to him they are ordinary eggs that can be boiled and kept in a larder. Is he *l'homme moyen religieux?* Both he and Attracta respond initially to Congal's demand for eggs with an appeal to custom. Custom will permit him to summon the Herne — provided he is suitably tipped — and custom will forbid the removal of the eggs. Does this suggest that just as the stylized battles of Aedh and Congal represent the emptiness of an effete tradition, so spirituality is no more than empty formalism?

Congal and Aedh's decision to have Herne's eggs to celebrate their temporary peace before the necessary renewal of hostilities represents an imperious, arbitrary assertion of the individual will directed towards material satisfaction in a purely material object. Similarly Congal is arbitrary in his assertion that it is Aedh who has substituted the hen's egg for the Herne's, and again just as arbitrary in being unable to accept any objective criterion outside his own subjectivity when he identifies himself with the law and constitutes himself as its court of judgement. Ignorant of God's music, he rejects Attracta's denial of any reality other than a spiritual one and interprets her refusal to surrender the eggs as human subjective illusion. He cannot treat her as an agent of God because he does not see the Herne as God or the eggs as anything but eggs. She is simply a neurotic woman in charge of the hernery:

> *Congal:* Refused! Must old campaigners lack
> The one sole dish that takes their fancy,
> My cooks what might have proved their skill,
> Because a woman thinks that she
> Is promised or married to a bird?
>
> [*CPl* 649]

But in spite of his unreasonable stand on these issues, he is curiously convincing in his analysis of Attracta's latent sexuality:

> Women thrown into despair
> By the winter of their virginity
> Take its abominable snow,
> As boys take common snow, and make
> An image of god or bird or beast
> To feed their sensuality.
>
> [*CPl* 649]

What carries conviction in this is the weight of the verse − one of the few passages where it rises above its generally plain, unmetaphorical level. He is convincing too when he counters Attracta's assertion that happiness can only be found in the austere pleasures of the mind divorced from the flesh with the view that

> It may be that life is suffering,
> But youth that has not yet known pleasure
> Has not the right to say so.
>
> [*CPl* 650]

But his reasonableness is immediately destroyed by the ruthless absurdity of the cure which he thinks will free her from all obsession and enable her, as he thinks, to 'live as every woman should' [*CPl* 662]. Similarly his claim that the law stands for measurable rationality, balance and dignity, is demolished by the ludicrous spectacle of his six followers, fortified by Dutch courage, throwing their caps at the Herne's egg to decide in what order they will rape Attracta, and then at the first hint of punishment retracting their claim to have done so. There is nothing in the play to identify them, as Wilson does [*Y&T* 130], with either 'the "six enemies" which in Indian tradition wait upon "passion" ', or with the six deadly sins of Christian tradition that support pride. Even their lust has to be artificially stimulated. Collectively they represent a debased humanity in contrast with which Congal stands out for his heroic courage.

To his adamant assertion that not only is his cure the only cure, but that it was applied and seems to have worked, Attracta opposes her own brand of adamant subjectivity in maintaining to the contrary that the Great Herne is the only reality, that she is his bride, that she has endured the terror of being possessed by him. Up to a point the play can be seen as turning on the conflict of totally different views, one of which, the Great Herne's, emerges victorious. In this view Attracta is not, as Congal would have it, 'a crazed loony / Waiting to be trodden by a bird' [*CPl* 666]. She is possessed by the God and as the God's instrument thwarts His human plan and thus initiates the movement that leads him to his heroic folly, or foolish heroism. She is non-human, a creature of phase 15 in Yeats's system, the phase of the full moon:

> The last time she went away
> The moon was full — she returned
> Before its side had flattened.

> [*CPl* 655]

Called away by her God, she becomes the will-less agent of His power, like a doll on a wire:

> Her human life is gone
> And that is why she seems
> A doll upon a wire.

> [*CPl* 654]

Her mystic marriage with the Great Herne may take her outside the cycles altogether to where 'No woman has gone' [*CPl* 655], into what Yeats called the Thirteenth Cycle 'which may deliver us from the twelve cycles of time and space' [*AV (B)* 210]

> *Kate:* Those leaps may carry her where
> No woman has gone, and he
> Extinguish sun, moon, star.
> No bridal torch can burn
> When his black midnight is there.
> *Agnes:* I have heard her claim that they couple
> In the blazing heart of the sun.
>
> [*CPl* 655]

Here opposites are reconciled, enlightenment and annihilation fused. Such a union implies no desecration: it is a marriage of the soul with God uncontaminated by the flesh, and is more akin to the Stroller's marriage with the Queen of *The King of the Great Clock Tower* than to that of the Swineherd and the Queen in *A Full Moon in March*.

But this view ignores both the clear fact that Congal shifts his ground and also the impression, though this is not so clear, that Attracta does too. Congal begins by being flatly opposed to Attracta and to the Great Herne. His act of stealing the eggs is a defiance of God, parallel to Adam's eating of the forbidden fruit, destructive of pre-lapsarian equilibrium, an assertion of the human will, a Faustian declaration of independence. But it is not long before Congal begins to consider whether there can be any independence from the Great Herne, who may be behind everything:

> Maybe the Great Herne's curse has done it.
>
> [*CPl* 660]

When Attracta enters in a trance carrying the egg, Congal acknowledges that the Herne is a god and therefore unassailable.

> I had forgotten
> That all she does he makes her do,
> But he is a god and out of reach.
>
> [*CPl* 662]

Nevertheless, like Satan, he is determined to carry the war to him by attacking his bride:

> Nor stone can bruise, nor a sword pierce him,
> And yet through his betrothed, his bride,
> I have the power to make him suffer.
>
> [*CPl* 662]

He does this in full knowledge of the potentially tragic consequences
to himself:

> His curse has given me the right,
> I am to play the fool and die
> At a fool's hands.

[*CPl* 662]

Like Faustus reaffirming his choice of magic, Congal reaffirms his
pact with himself. Even if he is under a curse in all he does or seems
to do, he will follow his path *jusqu'au bout,* at his own choice. In
the final scene he meets Tom Fool, ludicrously armed and whistling
the god's *leit-motif,* who was decreed to be his killer as God's agent.
But Congal disarms him and plans to find his freedom from the
endless moon-crazed and moon-blind round of fighting a succession
of whatever Fools the Great Herne may send against him by killing
himself.

   This, as we have seen, can be interpreted as Congal's final
humiliation at the hands of the Great Herne in that he does not realize
that this too is part of the God's plan, and that he is himself playing
the fool and thus fulfilling the Great Herne's will. Whatever we do
is bound to be conditioned by the limitations the ˙Great Herne
imposes. But this view underestimates the dramatic impact of Congal.
It is Congal who initiates the dramatic action, who feels himself to
be free, even if only to play the Fool in his own chosen way:

> For the Great Herne may beat me in the end.
> Here I must sit through the full moon,
> And he will send up Fools against me,
> Meandering, roaring, yelling,
> Whispering Fools, then chattering Fools,
> And after that morose, melancholy,
> Sluggish, fat, silent Fools;
> And I, moon-crazed, moon-blind,
> Fighting and wounded, wounded and fighting.
> I never thought of such an end. . . .
>
> If I should give myself a wound,
> Let life run away, I'd win the bout.

[*CPl* 675]

When destiny is freely chosen, or when chance becomes identified
with choice, temporal limitations are transcended. In the serious plays
this moment is reached by an act of passionate assertion of the self,
as is the case with Cuchulain in *On Baile's Strand,* Deirdre in

Deirdre, Emer in *The Only Jealously of Emer.* It is typical of this play's reductive tone that here it is reached in a fit of hysteria, as Congal almost screams in his excitement 'Fool! Am I myself a Fool?' [*CPl* 675]. Congal's 'heroic' gesture of defiance is mocked by the terms in which it is expressed. Mockery runs through the play. The stealing of an egg leads to an ignominious drunken quarrel and the loss of the vestiges of civilized conduct. Conflict is stripped of its dignified trappings: first, helmets and shields give way to skull-caps; then the skull-caps are parodied by saucepan and lid; heroic sword becomes ignominious kitchen-spit. Again the visual effect qualifies the verbal. Congal's defiant assertion of his independent identity:

> I am King Congal of Connacht and of Tara,
> That wise, victorious, voluble, unlucky,
> Blasphemous, famous, infamous man
>
> [*CPl* 676]

splendid and hubristic on the page, becomes comically distanced when it is followed by his mimed death on a kitchen spit that does not even touch him.

Congal's movement from Coriolanus-like utter disregard of anything but his own authority to a grudging acceptance of something other than that, is clear enough. What is not so clear is whether Attracta makes a parallel movement, from pure spirit to womanhood, thus implying the incompleteness of her mystic experience symbolized by marriage to the Great Herne. But there is much to suggest that this is what Yeats meant to convey. Her purity, her detachment from the flesh and from the natural life, her absorption in the Godhead, is expressed throughout the play in the image of carnal intercourse (not the disembodied intercourse of Angels) whose climactic joy is represented in phallic terms:

> *Agnes;* When he comes − will he? −
> *Attracta:* Child, ask what you please.
> *Agnes:* Do all that a man does?
> *Attracta:* Strong sinew and soft flesh
> Are foliage round the shaft
> Before the arrowsmith
> Has stripped it, and I pray
> That I, all foliage gone,
> May shoot into my joy. . . .
>
> [*CPl* 653–4]

Through him she will lose not only the coldness but the childishness of her virginity and put on perfection and a woman's name. It is

difficult to see anything in the scene with Mary, Agnes and Kate,
itself a mockery of the three Wise Men bringing gifts to another
Child, other than the impression of their silliness. Even when they
differ on the question of whether Attracta and the Great Herne
couple in the blue-black midnight or in the blazing heart of the sun,
they are reduced to the playground level of 'It is — it isn't, shall
— shan't'. Her own song, 'When I take a beast to my joyful breast'
[*CPl* 664], looks forward to the experience with an almost
masochistic pleasure. Passages like these tend to confirm Congal's
diagnosis of suppressed sexuality. Is she going to be changed by her
experience? Again her song suggests that she might be:

> When beak and claw their work begin
> Shall horror stir in the roots of my hair?
> *Sang the bride of the Herne, and the Great Herne's bride.*
> And who lie there in the cold dawn
> When all that terror has come and gone?
> Shall I be the woman lying there?
>
> [*CPl* 664–5]

After scene 4 a night passes, the night of the consummation of her
marriage, or of her rape. Thus, when she enters at the beginning
of scene 5, we wonder whether she has in fact been changed. Congal,
of course, maintains that his cure has worked, and that she is now
'all woman, all sensible woman' [*CPl* 666], and it is arguable that
she is, that she should come in as a kind of spiritual housewife,
complete with frilly apron and mob-cap, packing away the uneaten
or unbroken eggs, her 'thoughts upon the cupboard and the larder'
[*CPl* 666]. But if she has, she has not moved far, since she continues
to stand by her own version of events, in which there has been no
physical rape. If there has been congress it has been between purity
and purity, which has left her with knowledge (though this is
incomplete since she does not know the Great Herne's intentions with
regard to Congal) but not with power, a view that the thunder
corroborates:

> *Attracta:* I share his knowledge, and I know
> Every punishment decreed.
> He will come when you are dead,
> Push you down a step or two
> Into cat or rat or bat,
> Into dog or wolf or goose.
> Everybody in his new shape I can see,
> But Congal there stands in a cloud
> Because his fate is not yet settled.

> Speak out, Great Herne, and make it known
> That everything I have said is true.'
> > *(Thunder . . .)*
>
> > > [*CPl* 668–9]

At the end of the scene, her marriage to a god will be acknowledged
by gods and by Congal on the traditionally sacred mountain-top in
the light of the full moon, phase 15 of Yeats's system, the phase
of complete beauty.

> *Attracta:*   Upon the holy mountain,
> Upon Slieve Fuadh, there we meet again
> Just as the moon comes round the hill.
> There all the gods must visit me,
> Acknowledging my marriage to a god.
>
> > > [*CPl* 669–70]

But what sort of beauty and what sort of meeting with gods and
human is it that is illuminated by *'the moon of comic tradition, a
round smiling face'* [*CPl* 671]? The whole episode is characterized
by deflation. Once again Attracta sings her question, 'Was I the
woman lying there?' The effect is to give support to Congal's
assertion that

> I and the Herne have had three bouts,
> He won the first, I won the second,
> Six men and I possessed his wife.
>
> > > [*CPl* 673]

The next time we see her she is prepared to protect Congal at the
cost of her own purity by copulating with Corney. Spiritual congress
with the Great Herne was one thing, but there is another:

> there's a work
> That should be done, and that work needs
> No bird's beak nor claw, but a man,
> The imperfection of a man.
>
> > > [*CPl* 677]

Yeats leaves it uncertain as to what the relation between these two
experiences is. Are they parallel, or is one inferior to the other? And
if so, which? Has Attracta discovered in the night that spirit is
incomplete unless it descends into nature, that the Great Herne's
truth is inadequate? And finally, when the braying of a donkey, as
in *The Player Queen,* announces the end of a cycle, in this case

Congal's life, do Corney's lines imply that Congal's 'heroic' gesture, and beyond that heroism itself, is not worth the effort? In essence does this play mean that human gestures are futile, that humanity is mocked, but also that God is mocked too?

> All that trouble and nothing to show for it,
> Nothing but just another donkey.

[*CPl* 678]

Purgatory

This is one of Yeats's most accessible plays, as well as one of the best. As is the case with *The Words Upon the Window-Pane* and *The Dreaming of the Bones,* with which it has much in common, little, if any, special knowledge needs to be brought to it. What esoteric doctrines it contains are explained, indeed acted out in the play itself. Awareness of the history behind the contemporary situation in Ireland will, of course, deepen and extend appreciation, but even without that the play stands on its own feet. Although it has the compression of a Noh play, it has little of its stylization. There is no need to relate the Old Man's attempt to rescue his mother's spirit from purgatory to either *Nishikigi* or *Motomezuke*. The binding metaphors are there, in the form of lighted ruined house and tree, but these have antecedents in Yeats's own writings and in Irish tradition, and further, are given emphasis by un-Noh-like scenery and lighting-effects. There are no Musicians, the choric element being fully integrated into the dialogue. Of all the verse plays of his maturity and final period, it moves on a level closest to naturalism, though its naturalism is heightened by the masterly verse-structure, so well analysed by David Clark in *W. B. Yeats and the Theatre of Desolate Reality,* which enables Yeats to move effortlessly from circumstantial verisimilitude to a deeper reality.

As all the concerns of the play are mediated through the only two characters and their interaction, they are most easily approached through a study of the Old Man and the Boy. Yeats wrote to Lady Dorothy Wellesley, correcting the misreporting in the press of a remark of his to the effect that he had put nothing into the play because it seemed picturesque, and that he had put there his 'own conviction about this world and the next' [*L* 913]. He elaborated on this in an interview published in the *Irish Independent* on 13 August 1938, in which he answered questions put by Father Connolly, an American priest, at a lecture on Yeats given by F. R. Higgins two days before:

Father Connolly said that my plot is perfectly clear but that he does not understand my meaning. My plot is my meaning. I think the dead suffer remorse and re-create their old lives just as I have described. There are medieval Japanese plays about it, and much in the folk-lore of all countries.

In my play, a spirit suffers because of its share, when alive, in the destruction of an honoured house; that destruction is taking place all over Ireland today. Sometimes it is the result of poverty, but more often because a new individualistic generation has lost interest in the ancient sanctities.

I know of old houses, old pictures, old furniture that have been sold without apparent regret. In some few cases a house has been destroyed by a mesalliance. I have founded my play on this exceptional case, partly because of my interest in certain problems of eugenics, partly because it enables me to depict more vividly than would otherwise be possible the tragedy of the house . . . The problem is not Irish, but European, though it is perhaps more acute here than elsewhere.

[*Y&GI* 357–8]

These words show clearly that certain subjects in which we know that Yeats was personally interested do appear in the play, notably eugenics, the decline of the Big House and of the aristocratic temperament generally, regarded as a symptom of the degeneracy which he claimed was eroding the traditional sanctities of Irish and European civilization, and his own beliefs about the after-life. The Old Man enacts Yeats's views about purgatory; he and his son epitomize in what they are and do Yeats's own views on personal and social degeneracy. Like Yeats, the Old Man has strong views on eugenics:

> I killed that lad because had he grown up
> He would have struck a woman's fancy,
> Begot, and passed pollution on.

[*CPl* 688]

But it does not follow that the Old Man is Yeats, as some, notably Bloom, would have us believe. I doubt if Yeats himself, however much he deplored them, would advocate the systematic extermination of the base-born products of base beds, not even with a changeless sword, and certainly not on a jack-knife. There is a parallel here with Shaw. Captain Shotover and Undershaft, for example, can both be shown as voicing some opinions known to have been held by Shaw himself, but this does not make them into Shaw. They, like the Old Man, must be treated as figures with a dramatic life of their own. As Peter Ure rightly pointed out, Yeats's convictions as philosopher are dissolved into the life of the protagonist: attention is fixed upon the Old Man's story and his divided nature.

[*YTP* 112]

The story he has to tell encompasses the life in time of himself, his ancestors and his sole descendant, as well as the life of the spirit in eternity. Torchiana has brilliantly illuminated the historical symbolism by relating it both to the original scenario of the play, which has the Old Man begotten 63 years before the time of the play, 1938 – which puts the riving of the symbolic tree just before Parnell was rejected in 1889 – and to Yeats's view of Irish history as given in his Commentary on 'A Parnellite at Parnell's Funeral' [*VP* 832–5]. This he sees as divided into four periods, each marked by the tolling of a bell symbolizing

the war that ended in the Flight of the Earls; the Battle of the Boyne; the coming of French influence among our peasants; the beginning of our own age; events that closed the sixteenth, seventeenth, eighteenth and nineteenth centuries.

On this basis, the Old Man's mother represents the second period, from the battles of the Boyne (1690) and Aughrim (1691), which established a Protestant Ascendancy upon Catholic Ireland, to the French Revolution. She betrays the values of her class origins by coupling with a groom and so initiates the process of degeneration. Historically Ireland moves from the Protestant Ascendancy to the Garrison, to that 'democratic bonhomie' that seems to 'grin through a horse-collar' [*VP* 835]. The Old Man is pathetically caught between the consciousness of his aristocratic past and the degeneracy of his own father, who in burning down the house symbolically burns his Protestant past at the very moment when Ireland, in rejecting Parnell, rejects its aristocratic future. In this scheme the Boy, even more degenerate than his father, is born in 1922, the same year in which modern Ireland in the shape of the Irish Free State was born. Sixteen years later – and one cannot help agreeing with Moore [*MLD* 327] that the repetition of 'sixteen' is intended to set up an ironic echo of the Easter 1916 rising – the historical process of decline is set before our eyes in the action of the play, first performed in August 1938.

But neither eugenics nor socio-political matters are the play's central concern, however much that gains by being put in the context of a contemporary Ireland in which poverty and eloquence go hand in hand, an Ireland whose landscape is disfigured with the insignia of its past – the roofless shells of abandoned buildings, whether these are the product of rural decay hastened by the famine years, or of the kind of violence that erupted during the Civil War years of 1922–3 when so many Big Houses were burned down, including Renvyle House, Oliver St John Gogarty's home in Connemara where Yeats had stayed. Torchiana himself, for all his emphasis on the relevance of the play to the Ireland of its time, warns us not to take the Old Man allegorically, since 'he suggests so much more' than an historical period. Behind the historical allegory is the concept of a man who is caught in the grip of necessity and whose efforts to escape from it and to help others escape from it only tighten its bonds around him. Necessity takes the curiously Ibsenish form of the inescapability of the past, in the shape of an amalgam of historical and psychological forces, of cause working itself out inexorably in terms of consequence.

The opening interchanges between the Old Man and the Boy establish not only the differences between them but the horror of their inescapable position. The Boy's first speech reflects the smouldering resentment of his father that flares up later in the attempt to steal the money-bag and the threat to kill him:

> Half-door, hall door
> Hither and thither day and night,
> Hill or hollow, shouldering this pack,
> Hearing you talk.
>
> [*CPl* 681]

The resentment is audible in the rhythm of the lines. It also defines the trap in which the Old Man is caught – between peasant cabin and aristocratic Big House. He is a mixture of half-educated peasant and landowner, last representative of a doomed tradition. The Old Man's response, 'Study that house', at once establishes the gap between them. The Boy in himself is a more brutalized version of his father, so bemired by particulars that he is incapable of following the Old Man into abstraction or symbolism. He can see the ruins of the mansion but not the ruination of the house. To him, metaphor, meditation and vision are all madness. His values are those of his grandfather – possession of the girl and the money, the chance to wear grand clothes and ride a grand horse. His attempt to get even with his father is merely a baser echo of his father's muddled gesture. His threat to kill remains a threat, lacking the conviction of action. For him, the path that they have come merely defines the aimless wanderings of a travelling pedlar. Just as his interjections do not penetrate the Old Man's internal musings, as Lady Macbeth's cannot Macbeth's, so he cannot even trespass on the path which for the Old Man is an endless treadmill of the stricken conscience. Viewed externally the Boy embodies a progressive decline, not only the decadence of the individual soul, the drying of the marrow from the bones, but the desiccation of the sap in the life of the nation, which stands like a tree withered and bare in the cold light of the future. The decline had its source, even before the thunderbolt struck, in its

> Green leaves, ripe leaves, leaves thick as butter,
> Fat, greasy life.
>
> [*CPl* 682]

These are images, not of fruition, but of incipient decay.

The Old Man's 'Study that house' also establishes his authority, maintained throughout by his peremptory imperatives:

— Study that tree	[*CPl* 681
— Stand there and look	682
— Sit there upon that stone	682
— Look at the window	685
— Go fetch Tertullian	686
— Come back! Come back!	686
— Give me that bag	687]

This authority is not only one of will backed by physical strength – 'I will break your fingers' [*CPl* 687] – but one of imagination too, as the Old Man imposes his vision on the Boy.

These opening exchanges also establish the distinction between them in respect of knowledge, education, understanding, sensibility and perception, reflected in the range of the Old Man's vocabulary. This is wide enough to accommodate such subtleties as 'The intricate passages of the house' [*CPl* 683], and 'I here declare a capital offence' [*CPl* 683], and 'There's nothing leaning in the window / But the impression upon my mother's mind' [*CPl* 687–8], and 'she must animate that dead night' [*CPl* 689], phrases which reflect the vestiges of 'aristocratic' qualities inherited from his grandmother. At the same time his speech is punctured by brutal phrases that are a reflection of the degeneracy in him – 'I stuck him with a knife' [*CPl* 684].

The Old Man's personal tragedy is rooted in the conflict of contradictory strains in his mixed nature. In the sixteen years of his upbringing he acquired a rudimentary sense of values, aesthetic and

moral, inherited from his grandmother, who 'did right' [*CPl* 683]
in refusing to speak to his mother after she had degraded herself
and the traditions that the house stands for by marrying his father.
He also acquired the sensibility with which to appreciate those
traditions and to resent their betrayal by his parents. But these
acquisitions are only superficial and are undermined by the traits
inherited from his father. His education taught him something, but
not enough. Rajan amusingly suggests that it must have included
not only Tertullian and Rossetti but also Book 3 of Yeats's *A Vision,*
since he shows a knowledge of Yeats's own views of purgatory. But
the references to Tertullian and Rossetti are surely best regarded in
the dramatic context of the Old Man's upbringing as relics of
information recalled under stress, a name and a passage imperfectly
remembered (the line from Rossetti is a misquotation) from a
haphazard contact with culture. If we require justification for his
knowledge of Yeats's purgatorial beliefs, we can find it in the same
source that the Young Man in *The Dreaming of the Bones* finds it
– folk-belief:

> My Grandam
> Would have it they did penance everywhere;
> Some lived through their old lives again.
>
> [*CPl* 436]

He knows that

> The souls in Purgatory that come back
> To habitations and familiar spots . . . re-live
> Their transgressions, and that not once
> But many times; they know at last
> The consequence of those transgressions
> Whether upon others or themselves;
> Upon others, others may bring help,
> For when the consequence is at an end
> The dream must end; if upon themselves,
> There is no help but in themselves
> And in the mercy of God.
>
> [*CPl* 682]

If he knows this then he should know no act of his can help his
mother, and if he fears that his mother's remorse will not purge her
crime because it is inevitably bound up with pleasure, why, then,
does he kill his son? Because, like Caliban, although he has
knowledge, he lacks understanding, and because of the inherited
brutalization of his nature, which compels him to attempt to stop

the consequences upon others by the very act, the brutal murder of
his son, that perpetuates them, even if it is performed out of
compassion for his mother's tortured spirit, and out of his horror
at the realization that his son's motive for attempting to kill him
is even more degenerate than his own for killing his father. The Old
Man at least recognized his father as base; his son is blind to moral
values and would kill simply because he is his father's son. The Boy
is wrong in saying

> You killed my grand-dad
> Because you were young and he was old.
>
> [*CPl* 687]

The Old Man killed his grand-dad not because he was old but because
he was degrading the house. But what else could the Boy say?
Altogether more degenerate, he is blind to such considerations, and
to let him live, in the Old Man's half-deranged mind, is to risk
spreading a worse stain even further. The Old Man as a boy did not
feel for his father any of the ambivalent feelings he has for his
mother:

> Better-looking, those sixteen years . . . Younger – and yet
> She should have known he was not her kind.
>
> [*CPl* 687]

He killed his father ruthlessly but with cunning – and not even
cunning has descended to his son – and his confession to his son
is in a sense a step in his purgation of the deed. But the very
expression of it shows him to be inextricably locked in his own
brutality:

> I stuck him with a knife,
> That knife that cuts my dinner now.
>
> [*CPl* 684]

Similarly his attempt to free his mother's spirit from continuing
remorse if the pollution is passed on confirms the brutality – it is
emphasized in words and action:

> My father and my son on the same jack-knife!
> That finishes – there – there – there –
> *(He stabs again and again.)*
>
> [*CPl* 698]

His condition, trapped in the contradictory elements of his own nature, is at once dramatized as his brutality dissolves into a complex of emotions in which there can be observed the unbalancing pressures on his mind, tenderness for his mother, and the sense of his own pathetic inability to cope with the situation:

> 'Hush-a-bye baby, thy father's a knight,
> Thy mother a lady, lovely and bright.'
> No, that is something that I read in a book,
> And if I sing it must be to my mother,
> And I lack rhyme.
>
> [*CPl* 688]

This is a crucial passage for the actor since the language here shows the Old Man slipping over the edge of sanity into the mental derangement which is the keynote of his character. His intensity borders on hysteria, his sensibility conflicts with his brutality, his knowledge, such as it is, with passion. The Boy does indeed have some justification for calling him a silly old man and for exclaiming that his wits are out again. This aspect of the Old Man's character must be established in his very first speeches.

It is his incomplete nature that arouses his appreciation of the past traditions of the house expressed in the passage beginning 'Great people lived and died in this house . . .' [*CPl* 683] and yet leaves him unaware of his self-condemnation when he declares:

> to kill a house
> Where great men grew up, married, died,
> I here declare a capital offence.
>
> [*CPl* 683]

The same quality permits him with one side of his nature to appreciate

> old books and books made fine
> By eighteenth-century French binding, books
> Modern and ancient,
>
> [*CPl* 684]

and yet in the same breath to value them not for their content but for their weight:

> books by the ton.
>
> [*CPl* 684]

This is the language of true poetic drama, as it works simultaneously outwards towards the expression of theme and inwards to the delineation of character. The pressure of his own misery and the intensity of his own infected moral sense, which impel him to retrace the path of his own crime and to explore its antecedents in the spirit-life of his dead mother, drive him also to the edge of insanity and into the recognition that although he can see the dead he cannot influence them:

> Do not let him touch you! It is not true
> That drunken men cannot beget,
> And if he touch he must beget
> And you must bear his murderer!
> Deaf! Both deaf! If I should throw
> A stick or a stone they would not hear;
> And that's a proof my wits are out.
>
> [*CPl* 686]

Although for one brief and superbly effective dramatic moment life in time and life in eternity meet as the Old Man sees in the deeps of his mind his mother and father lying upon the mattress begetting himself, and as he forces that vision upon the Boy, the union is bound to be barren. The Boy, who bears the future in him, is blind to the life of the spirit and can see nothing but matter, 'A dead, living, murdered man!' [*CPl* 687] and

> A body that was a bundle of old bones
> Before I was born.
>
> [*CPl* 688]

The Old Man, who is aware of the life of the spirit, is nevertheless deluded into thinking that he can finish all that consequence. For the spirit of his mother is itself flawed, since in the act of re-living her past she re-animates the pleasure that makes it impossible for her to be alone in what the Old Man imagines is nothing but her remorse. He is deluded too in thinking that his mother's soul is purified. The tree, symbolizing both his mother's soul and the spirit of Ireland, which he thinks has been purified, remains riven. Since he cannot, and the mother's spirit will not, break the chain of the consequence of those transgressions, then there is nothing left for him, as he foresaw, but to invoke the mercy of God. His father's lassitude after coition becomes the bride-sleep of Adam, the father of mankind. Degeneracy is built into the human condition. In that case only a prayer to God can be effective, but it is the prayer of the Old Man as a dramatic character in the setting of Roman Catholic Ireland, not the prayer of William Butler Yeats. But God is silent. It is the silence that is Yeats's.

'No tragedy', wrote Yeats, 'is legitimate unless it leads some great character to his final joy' [*E* 448], but there is no joy here. The Old Man has achieved nothing except the damming of the stream of pollution that might have flowed from his son. His act leaves his mother where she was, not so much in purgatory as in hell, since her spirit is incapable of escaping from what Yeats in Book 3 of *A Vision* calls the dreaming-back process by tracing 'every passionate event to its cause until all are related and understood, turned into knowledge, made a part of itself' [*AV(B)* 226] and in that process purging 'pain and joy'. She remains trapped between remorse and pleasure. In relation to her his gesture is pointless:

> Twice a murderer and all for nothing.
> [*CPl* 688]

Moore has the excellent idea [*MLD* 324] that the Boy, in covering his eyes at the vision of his grandfather in the window, leaning there 'like some tired beast', is as good as offering himself as sacrifice, and that the Old Man, seeing the 'likeness (perhaps even the identity) of his father and son . . . does what he can: he stabs the Boy'. The idea could be strengthened in performance by having the father cover his eyes too in a gesture of tiredness. But the sacrifice turns out to be murder. Death, heroic or ritualized, which in the earlier plays such as *The King's Threshold, Deirdre, On Baile's Strand, A Full Moon in March,* had brought transcendence of human limitation, is here reduced to its sordid particulars:

> My father and my son on the same jack-knife!
> [*CPl* 688]

Two positives, however, lighten the prevailing gloom. The Old Man's energy of mind, however flawed, drives him like a second-rate Oedipus to know and to act. As the action temporarily recedes into the deeps of the mind, he succeeds in making his son see what he could not see before, a glimpse of the life of eternity, something outside knowledge and order – the window lit up and the father standing there on floorboards that are not there – even though what he sees is determined by his own limited capacity for vision. That same energy takes him to the point of anagnorisis, a Lear-like recognition of his own guilt and vulnerability:

> I am a wretched foul old man
> And therefore harmless.
>
> [*CPl* 688]

It takes him, too, to a Lear-like compassion for the sufferings of others, a grandeur that enlarges him to a symbol of mankind, and compels us to see and confront a universal condition. At the same time it takes him to a childlike acceptance of his powerlessness in the face of necessity:

> O God,
> Release my mother's soul from its dream.
> Mankind can do no more. Appease
> The misery of the living and the remorse of the dead.
>
> [*CPl* 689]

The Death of Cuchulain

Reading this play, coming as it does at the end of Yeats's career as a dramatist, we are conscious of the forms of so many Yeatsian concerns emerging and receding like figures seen through the gauze curtain of its action and tableaux. It is the dramatic equivalent of those many poems that he wrote in his last periòd, which look back over his artistic career and which are illuminated by it. But, unrevised at his death, it has too many uncertainties to have the cold but passionate clarity of, for example, 'The Circus Animals' Desertion' [*CP* 391]. Nevertheless its meanings can only emerge, however dimly, in relation to the poet and his past work. As soon as the Old Man comes in, the pattern of the play and its resonances are established. Yeats presents to us in the contemporary world of Dublin – though the play was not actually performed until six years after his death – the Old Man as producer, and by implication author, of *The Death of Cuchulain*, 'the last of a series of plays which has for theme his life and death' [*CPl* 693]. The Old Man sets up in effect, in the manner of the earlier Noh-like Musicians, a framework within which the legendary material is acted out and which is completed by the Singer, who returns us to that contemporary world. The legendary figures, all images fashioned in the mind of Yeats himself, since they are all defined in terms of the plays in which they first appeared and with which the audience is expected to be familiar, creatures of myth in the heroic past, have their being in the deeps of the living mind. Then the Morrigu inducts us into the timeless world of the spirit, which is once again evoked in the unheroic and sordid present by the Singer's concluding song. This is the controlling dramatic rhythm of the play – from the temporal world to the timeless, then back to the temporal world, only this time it is a temporal world that has been illuminated by the timeless.

Since it was Yeats who wrote the plays in which these figures are defined, it seems reasonable to conclude, as many critics have done, that the Old Man is Yeats himself, in his seventy-fourth year when he wrote the play. Indeed the Old Man presents visually one aspect of the play's theme – the ageing process leading to the death of the body — a theme which in various forms appears in so many of Yeats's works. His 'guiding principles' [*CPl* 693] bear a remarkable resemblance, even if some of them are taken to extremes, to principles laid down, for example, in the essay, 'Certain Noble Plays of Japan'. His dislike of 'opinionated bitches' [*CPl* 694], the introduction of musicians and a dance, the fondness for severed heads, the reference to Talma, can all be paralleled in Yeats's own writings, and, of course, the action does make more sense to those who know 'the old epics and Mr. Yeats's plays' [*CPl* 693]. The roles of Eithne and Emer become more intelligible if we know *The Only Jealousy of Emer*. Indeed, as the play stands, the character of Emer is only identifiable *if* we know the earlier play. Aoife refers us back to *At the Hawk's Well* and *On Baile's Strand*. The Blind Man is specifically identified [*CPl* 701] as the Blind Man of *On Baile's Strand*. Eithne's reference to ladle and spit [*CPl* 698] evokes the comic mood of *The Green Helmet,* and the way in which past subjective greatness is succeeded by the ignoble objective present recalls *Purgatory* and *The Herne's Egg*. We can imagine not only the Old Man but, in view of Yeats's known preoccupation with the hero, Cuchulain made up to resemble Yeats himself. But too close a personal resemblance would destroy the generalized properties of the Old Man, who, like the Fool in *King Lear,* disappears from Yeats's play in so far as he is absorbed into the image of hero dying into the timeless life of myth. He belongs to mythology and, as Yeats directs [*CPl* 693], he must look like something out of mythology. The Old Man is a product of the creative imagination — in this case Yeats's — just as myths and the figures that appear in them are. He acts only within the limits set for him by his creator, who has created him to 'produce a play called *The Death of Cuchulain*' [*CPl* 693], and left him free, as a dramatic character in his own right, to produce it in the way that he, the Old Man, chooses, according to his own aesthetic principles, however extreme and out of fashion these may be and however much reviled by his audience. It is difficult to imagine Yeats himself treating his own ideal audience of 'personal friends and a few score people of good taste' [*CNPlJ, E&I* 222] with the Old Man's contempt, or that Yeats with his known advocacy of 'the sovereignty of words' [*E* 108] is speaking through the Old Man with his 'I wanted a dance because where there are no words there is less to spoil' [*CPl* 694], a *reductio* of drama that leads logically to the wordless ballet. The Old Man is not so much a paradigm of Yeatsian subjectivity [Friedman, *ADM* 132], as a parody of it. He retains the freedom to spit in the face of history and aesthetic naturalism in the same way that Yeats's Old Pensioner, another fictional character, spits in the face of time − it is the only gesture left to him, the only deed that can isolate his character. In the same way Cuchulain, as dramatic character, although he has to dance to The Morrigu's tune, is left free to decide his own steps. There is an echo here both of Deirdre, who, though trapped by fate, chooses the manner of her death, and of Judas in *Calvary*:

> It was decreed that somebody betray you −
> I'd thought of that − but not that I should do it,
> I the man Judas, born on such a day,
> In such a village, such and such his parents;
> Nor that I'd go with my old coat upon me
> To the High Priest, and chuckle to myself
> As people chuckle when alone, and do it
> For thirty pieces and no more, no less,
> And neither with a nod nor a sent message,
> But with a kiss upon your cheek. I did it,
> I, Judas, and no other man . . .

> [*CPl* 454]

That The Morrigu does not control the action is demonstrated dramatically by the fact that, even before Cuchulain discovers the letter from Emer put into Eithne's hand while she was under the influence of The Morrigu working through Maeve, he had already determined on the course of action that leads to his death. If she were the controlling deity of the action she would have been brought on right at the beginning. As it is, she is merely the presiding deity of the play. Like Apollo in *Oedipus Rex,* or God in *Paradise Lost,* who predict but do not determine events, she sets the scene [*CPl* 695] and arranges the dance [*CPl* 703]. Within that pattern Cuchulain is free to assert himself, and this is what the first scene shows him doing. It is he, not the Morrigu, who uncovers the letter from Emer, he who has taken the decision to go out and fight:

> I am for the fight,
> I and my handful are set upon the fight.

> [*CPl* 696]

Like Oedipus the King he wilfully blinds himself to the truth, and for all his energy and intelligence repeatedly draws the wrong conclusions from the evidence before him. He does not see that Eithne is not behaving naturally, that up to The Morrigu's exit she is in a trance. Her movements, like those of a somnambulist, should make this clear to an audience. He blinds himself also to the presence of The Morrigu. He imagines that Eithne is plotting his death out of desire for a younger man, and that she exults in its approach. He ignores Emer's warning letter – her last attempt to save him from the consequences of his own self-will. Having convinced himself of the 'truth' of Eithne's motives he then in a show of magnanimity 'forgives' her and suggests a way of saving her from the consequences of her own disavowal of treachery by imperiously consigning her to Conall Caernach 'because the women / Have called him a good lover' [*CPl* 698]. This is heroic assertion scaled up to hubristic illusion, selfless magnanimity reduced to childish egoism – 'I make the truth' [*CPl* 698]. But in the event it is Cuchulain who is more adult than Eithne, in that he accepts the fact that like all other sublunary things he is about to die, whereas she, fruitlessly striving to preserve that passion which may be necessary to life but is inappropriate to the dying, would not have him go gently into that good night. In order to preserve the image of what he has meant to her in the past, she would immolate herself in a sacrifice whose manner, with its echo of the reductively anti-heroic *The Herne's Egg*, ironically devalues it:

> When you are gone
> I shall denounce myself to all your cooks,
> Scullions, armourers, bed-makers and messengers
> Until they hammer me with a ladle, cut me with a knife,
> Impale me upon a spit, put me to death
> By what foul way best please their fancy.
>
> [*CPl* 697–8]

It is foolish for middle-age (logically Eithne as a figure from the past must have aged with Cuchulain and Aoife), once what she called in *The Only Jealously of Emer* 'the violent hour' has 'passed over' [*CPl* 285], to attempt to preserve the kind of passion appropriate to superseded youth. Her rigidity of attitude proves her rather than him monstrous; his flexibility shows him to be human. The dancer must learn a new dance turn.

Such a lesson, however, need not be a humiliation. The scene between Cuchulain and Aoife, which seems to recede even further into the deeps of the mind, has something of the quality of trance as it brings Cuchulain to the farthest threshold of consciousness. His passionately human confrontation with Eithne gives way to an almost ritualized calm. What Aoife has to do she does. The winding of the veil about the weakening Cuchulain has a stylized, almost balletic tenderness, which leads up to the mood in which Cuchulain embraces the felicity of his death. There is no recrimination between them, as each, in language in which all passion has been burnt up, relives the past and prepares for its consequences upon themselves. Bodily decrepitude, brought on him by 'wounds and toil' [*CPl* 289] and on her by the debilitating process of ageing, has taught not only wisdom but dignity. Cuchulain's body is too weak to complete his gesture of heroic defiance in vertical death; his eyes can barely recognize in the erect white-haired old lady the 'pale, amorous woman' [*CPl* 276] whom he had loved as a young man; his mind is approaching the limit of understanding. The next stage will be the extinction of the body. After that there is left only the wisdom that is the property of the dead, the conviction of the prophet – 'I say it is about to sing' [*CPl* 703]. Cuchulain has reached the limits of knowledge; there is nothing left for him to do but to embody the truth. This is what is dramatized as the mummified Cuchulain dies into the life of the spirit from which, as timeless Image, he can illuminate and perhaps inspire the times to come.

I find it difficult to believe that the reasons for Aoife's *exit* would have remained unchanged had Yeats lived to revise the play. Ure justified it as a 'masterstroke which draws attention to what is being done by the dramatist' [*YTP* 81]. But the device is extremely clumsy. It may indeed draw attention to what is being done, but masterstroke it is not. What is being done is the denial of a majestic pattern. Aoife ought to have the strength to avenge the death of her son on Cuchulain, but she too is a victim of bodily decrepitude. Cuchulain ought to go out at the hands of a worthy antagonist, but instead his head is ignominiously severed by a Blind Man whose motives recall the materialism of the Fools in *The Hour Glass* and *The Herne's Egg*. To die at the hands of a Blind Man-cum-Fool who does not have the knowledge which Cuchulain in his blindness attributes to him, but merely the 'good sense' [*CPl* 702] that is content to value a hero's head at twelve pence, and to remove it from his body with a knife that suggests the implement with which the debased Old Man of *Purgatory* killed his father and son and cut his dinner [*CPl* 684], far from adding to the hero's dignity, reduces it:

> *Cuchulain:* I think that you know everything, Blind Man.
> My mother or my nurse said that the blind
> Know everything.
> *Blind Man:* No, but they have good sense.
> How could I have got twelve pennies for your head
> If I had not good sense?
>
> [*CPl* 702]

Nevertheless Cuchulain's gesture is heroic. Embracing his fate he rises superior to it. He creates the image of the opposite into which he is dying, and quietly, serenely, asserts its vitality:

> There floats out there
> The shape that I shall take when I am dead,
> My soul's first shape, a soft feathery shape.
> And is not that a strange shape for the soul
> Of a great fighting-man?
>
> [*CPl* 702]

The moment of his passing from life to death actualizes that condition of reverie in which 'the persons upon the stage . . . greaten', not so much into 'humanity itself' [*E&I* 245], but in this instance into an Image that will illuminate the future.

The dying Cuchulain asserts that his soul will sing. This is true — it does sing, but what sort of song do we actually get? The movement of the play suggests that Cuchulain's assertion should be followed by the actual song itself set in the contemporary world which both rejects and yet needs the heroic Image. In the end the bird-song of the spirit is drowned in the 'music of some Irish Fair of our day' [*CPl* 704], and Yeats's ear hears only its coarseness. But before this happens Yeats inserts the ungainly episode of The Morrigu and Emer's dance.

By informing us that she speaks to the dead, The Morrigu places the episode in the spirit world Cuchulain has just entered. His body and those of his enemies have lost their substance and in the shape of parallelograms have become mere symbols, on the way to turning into abstract concepts, to be recreated in the minds of those who in later years 'thought Cuchulain' [*CPl* 705] till it seemed he stood where those who stood in the Post Office with Pearse and Connolly fought and died. Her claim 'I arranged the dance' [*CPl* 703] confirms her position as the deity of the play who presides not only over individual life but also over history. What we have witnessed is both the decline of a hero and the declension of an era. Cuchulain may have completed his subjective being but his Image survives into an objective era which is basically alien to him.

Emer's dance, which follows, also seems to suffer from the play's lack of revision. In the first place she is given two entries, and secondly, in the absence of either any introduction or any link with her attempt eight pages back to save Cuchulain from his chosen end, she simply cannot be identified by a theatre audience. It is left uncertain whether Yeats intends her to be unidentified, relying on our knowledge of his own plays, or whether this is an oversight

which he would have corrected. Taylor may be right in suggesting
that in her dance she rages against his progressive decline as physical
man yet celebrates also the triumph of pure spirit [*DWBY* 190],
but it is difficult to see how that can be conveyed to a theatre audience
in mime. Even more difficult to convey is Wilson's Platonic
interpretation, namely that she dances conflicting responses to the
fact of death: 'adoration, because death is the beginning of reality;
and horror because it is life's opposite' [*Y&T* 174]. It seems more
likely that she rages because she has finally lost the battle that she
seemed to have won, though Pyrrhically, in *The Only Jealousy of
Emer.* Then, she saved Cuchulain for humanity by rescuing him from
Fand, from union with and transformation into an inhuman Image.
Now, she is defeated: he has become that Image and her sacrifice
has proved worthless. First she rages against those who appear to
have robbed him of his life, then she dances in adoration or triumph
as she recognizes that his transformation is his own choice. She
responds to the bird-notes that symbolize his transfiguration. But
in either case this kind of meaning cannot be conveyed by dance.
The dance here is a superimposition on meaning not an extension
of it.

However it is interpreted, what the dance does do is to focus
attention on the centrality of Cuchulain to the era in which he has
his being. Nathan noted [*TD* 197] that the plotting of the play is
somewhat in the manner of *Samson Agonistes* and Yeats's own *The
King's Threshold,* in that the protagonist is confronted with a series
of antagonists. But the relationship of Cuchulain to the other
characters is more than a matter of plotting. What it expresses is
that their identity is only established in relation to him. All have had
a relation with him in the past which still animates the present. In
Eithne he still evokes passion and a vision of his now superseded
past. In Aoife he evokes the mother's vengeance for her dead son
and also the memory of Cuchulain's physical power and sexual
mastery:

> I seemed invulnerable; you took my sword,
> You threw me on the ground and left me there.
> I searched the mountain for your sleeping-place
> And laid my virgin body at your side,
> And yet, because you had left me, hated you,
> And thought that I would kill you in your sleep,
> And yet begot a son that night between
> Two black thorn-trees.

                                                [*CPl* 700–1]

Even though he takes decisions and goes out to fight, in essence, just by being passively what he is, he evokes action and reaction in those who are involved with him. Whereas in the past the young Cuchulain was the innovator of action, now in his old age, his active gestures, of his own making, are based upon illusion and lead to failure and defeat. After his decision to fight and his subsequent defeat, he initiates no further action. He awaits events. In his defeat he becomes powerless − physically he has to be helped to his heroic gesture of dying on his feet, and thereafter, tied to the stone by Aoife's veil, he is passive. He submits to Aoife and he submits to Blind Man. But this very submission and passivity become activity in that the way in which the characters revolve around him is an enactment of his effect upon his own era, just as the Image that he makes of himself is going to have an impact upon a later era. Moreover that submission and that passivity, because consciously adopted, become his strength. As Yeats wrote in *Mythologies,* the hero makes his mask in defeat [*M* 337].

The Death of Cuchulain helps to explain the appeal that Sophocles's *Oedipus at Colonus* held for Yeats. In both plays spiritual authority is born out of physical weakness..Oedipus, blind, infirm, powerless against the brute force of Creon, is paralleled by Cuchulain tied to a stone by the womanish stuff of an old lady's veil. Both plays enact the hero's transition from human to non-human status. In the case of Oedipus the status is that of divinity, achieved through the growth of spiritual authority until he who was once no more than a 'blind old ragged, rambling beggar-man' [*CPl* 567] in the end 'proclaims God's will' [*CPl* 569] and will exert his authority 'from the tomb' [*CPl* 534]. In both plays the heroes re-live their lives, Oedipus by having to repeat to the Chorus the whole horrible story of his past [*CPl* 538-9], Cuchulain in the scenes with Eithne and Aoife. In his prayer to the Furies Oedipus regards himself as in effect already dead:

Dear daughters of ancient darkness, and Athens, most honoured among cities, have mercy upon this ghost of Oedipus, for the man Oedipus is dead, the man men knew.

[*CPl* 524]

So too Cuchulain, as Eithne and Aoife between them remind us five times, is under sentence of death. In both plays the action takes the heroes from life to the inevitability of death. Oedipus's destiny is in the hands of Apollo, Cuchulain's in The Morrigu's. Both have to die, but each in his way masters his fate: Oedipus by the assertion

of his humanity which finally makes him equal to the Gods, and
Cuchulain by what Moore calls his 'own self-possessed, almost
serene, mastery of circumstance' [*MLD* 332]. Finally, in both plays
the action takes the heroes beyond death to the renewal of life in
their continuing authority from the grave. In the case of Cuchulain
the status finally achieved is that of divine Image. As Moore says,
the play asserts 'the permanence of myth in defiance of what the
ravages of time can do' [*MLD* 329].

The major difference between them is that whereas Oedipus's
authority is unambiguous, Cuchulain's is not. His Image survives
— if indeed it survives at all, since the mode of the play's ending
is closer to question than to affirmation — debased, into a debased
world of harlot and beggarman. There is nothing of the regenerative
matrix in the Harlot. Her vision of the heroic past is expressed in
terms of sexuality and cleverness. Cleverness never was a Yeatsian
value, and for him sexuality without spirituality is incomplete. The
Harlot is confronted by the heroic world of the past, the spiritual
world of the imagination, but cannot make contact with it. She can
only make contact with the ignoble present, with the material world.
Yet at the same time she is aware of the difference between the two
and is caught up in the conflicting responses of attraction and
repulsion towards this materiality. Is materiality everything?

> Are those things that men adore and loathe
> Their sole reality?
> What stood in the Post Office
> With Pearse and Connolly?
> What comes out of the mountain
> Where men first shed their blood?
> Who thought Cuchulain till it seemed
> He stood where they had stood?
>
> [*CPl* 704–5]

His Image survives too in the imagination of a frenetic old man
scornful of

> the sort now growing up,
> All out of shape from toe to top.
>
> [*CP* 400]

Not even Pearse and Connolly, whose heroic gesture in the Post
Office may have been inspired by the Image of Cuchulain, measure
up to his stature:

No body like his body
Has modern woman borne.

[*CPl* 705]

Oedipus's transfiguration is unequivocal; in accordance with the mood of bitterness and doubt reflected in works of his last period, such as *The Words Upon the Window-Pane, The Herne's Egg, Purgatory,* and, among the poems,' The Man and the Echo', Cuchulain's apotheosis is qualified. The voice of the Old Man sounds through the concluding song. Majesty is mocked, there is loathing, there is rage, there is debasement, decrepitude, decline and ultimately death, but there is also a kind of unquenchable grandeur, renewal, recognition, adoration even, of the undying Image:

. . . upon the same neck love and loathing, life and death.

[*CPl* 694]

Perhaps some comfort is to be found in that statue 'By Oliver Sheppard done' [*CPl* 705], symbolic breakwater against the filthy modern tide.

EPILOGUE

In the end, after a survey of Yeats's entire dramatic *œuvre,* excluding his 'translations', the nagging doubt remains. Is he a major dramatist, did he contribute anything of significance to the European dramatic tradition, or was he a playwright whose appeal will never extend outside a coterie of *aficionados?* The answer must depend primarily on the degree to which his plays are given adequate performance. The capacity of audiences to digest drama is always being increased. What was thought of as un-dramatic in one era is accepted in the next − witness the acceptance of Ibsen and more recently of Shaw. But Shaw had to fight for recognition and establish the style of acting that his plays required. Yeats has not yet received this public, professional recognition. Katharine Worth has shown (*IDE* chap. 8) not only that the influence of Yeats has permeated modern drama, but also that there has been an increased interest in him as a dramatist in his own right, witnessed by the growing number of performances of his plays. But he is still for the most part the property of well-intentioned amateurs in societies or academic institutions which inevitably, and through no fault of their own, lack the training, the money and the resources to do justice to his dramatic ideals. These include the co-ordination within a unified aesthetic vision of all the components of the dramatic vocabulary: speech, movement, costume, décor, music, dance. But dance, his distinctive contribution to the dramatic norm, as has been said, must not be conceived as an extra, as something superimposed: it must emerge naturally as an extension of the mode of movement that is normal for the play. These things require professionalism, time and money. Acting, as Yeats knew, is an art basically, but not exclusively, of the body. It is almost impossible that amateurs should achieve the degree of physical control that his plays need in the time that is usually available to them for preparation and rehearsal. The same kind of consideration applies to costume, décor, masks and music. These should all be meticulously designed. They comprise the visual part of the overall conception of the play and require more talent than is generally available in, for example, the art-mistress from the local school, or the friends of the producer who can strum chords on a zither, clash a pair of cymbals, beat a drum or blow a flute. And into this overall realization of the play as a visual experience must be fitted the sonic pattern of the play − its different levels of voice, variety of speech rhythms, its music, its sounds and its silences − and finally its kinetic component, realized in the actors' gestures, their movements, their moments of stillness and, where required, their dance movements, as well as in the correlation of these movements in significant groupings within the stage space. This is a tall order, even for professionals, yet if we are to arrive at a fair assessment of Yeats as a dramatist, it should be met. The achievement of any dramatist can only be realized within the material demands of his art. Drama is not to be measured solely from the printed page, as if it were acted in some abstract theatre of mind. It needs a performance, which itself requires a material setting of an appropriate kind. Yeats has so far not received this treatment.

The reasons for this are twofold. His plays appear on the surface to be esoteric, remote from human life as we experience it, both in manner and in content. But this is not so. As regards the manner, the use of poetry chorus and mask is well established in the European dramatic tradition. What does seem odd and idiosyncratic, such as the ritual of the folding of the cloth, which he evolved for the dance plays designed for a drawing-room, is in fact no more odd than the lowering and raising of a curtain, and indeed is inappropriate when these plays are performed in a theatre already equipped with stage-curtains.

More serious are the charges that his plays deal with experiences with which the average audience cannot make contact, and that they deal with them in terms of a mythology which they cannot share. There is a certain amount of truth in these charges, but their justification depends largely on expectations. Many of Yeats's plays deal with psychic essences, whose conflicts occur in a world of the spirit which, because of its very nature, cannot be expressed in terms of temporal and spatial illusion. In these cases, therefore, an audience must reject the expectations aroused by normal drama − whether of character, speech or action. Equally, performances must induce in the audience a mood of almost ritualistic involvement. Nevertheless Yeats is at pains to establish points from which the audience's attention can be led from identification with naturalistic phenomena to the spiritual essences he is concerned with. These phenomena may take the form of figures drawn from an alien mythology, who appear to have an esoteric significance, but in fact they are, for the most part, easily identifiable aspects of common human experience. Deirdre, the Cuchulain and Conchubar of *On Baile's Strand,* Emer, Eithne Inguba, Fand and the Cuchulain of *The Only Jealousy of Emer* are familiar human types; the Queen and the Swineherd of *A Full Moon in March* are recognizable archetypes. Occasionally, as in *At the Hawk's Well* and *The Death of Cuchulain,* the full significance of the action is only apparent to those whose knowledge extends beyond the framework of the actual dramatic experience. This is a weakness, in the earlier plays due to inexperience, in the later to carelessness or lack of revision. The full impact, for example, of the young Cuchulain's rejection of immortality at the well in preference to a life of heroic activity cannot be realised unless we are aware of the consequences of his choice – his meeting with Aoife, which is to end in the killing of his own son, something which is not part of our dramatic experience. Similarly, in *The Death of Cuchulain,* the full significance of Eithne, Aoife and Emer cannot be felt by those who do not know 'the old epics and Mr. Yeats's plays about them' [*CPl* 693–4]. But for the most part, the plays are comprehensible in their own terms. It is true that some make demands of concentration on the audience, demands which are sometimes excessive, as for example the opening and closing lyrics of *The Only Jealousy of Emer, Calvary* and *The Resurrection,* but even so, given the kind of controlled theatrical expression that they require, his plays are capable of exciting a theatrical experience that is as profound as the subject-matter they deal with. Even when inadequately performed, they can produce a powerful, elemental impact. This is because in them we are brought face to face with psychic forces that lie at the roots of human behaviour. They provoke responses that are both sensuous, in that they engage our capacity for visual appreciation, and also consciously intellectual, in that they engage our capacity for analysis. But at the same time, as in visionary experience, they evoke responses that seem to have their origin in some area that lies below the conscious mind. In his most original work Yeats is a dramatist of vision, and the dramatic form he used, involving the full resources of his dramatic vocabulary – aural, visual and kinetic – was his way of making that vision accessible in theatrical terms.

If the plays are adequately performed, if due weight is given to all the components of his dramatic vocabulary – speech, song, music, gesture, dance, costume, décor – all directed towards the expression of a totality of dramatic meaning, it is difficult to believe that Yeats's mature plays will not have a profound and moving impact in the theatre. But that impact will not be achieved until the analyses of the scholars have been brought to life by the creative imagination of the interpreters. Between the reader and a novel or a poem there stands nothing except his own sensitivity, knowledge and general experience of literature and life, but between the audience and a play there stand the actors, the producer, the scene-designer, the costume-designer, and so on – in fact the whole apparatus of theatrical representation. A dramatic script is like a musical score: it has to be brought to life by the interpreters. In all interpretative arts, acting, dancing, music, it is the function of the interpreter to recreate by an act of informed, intelligent, but above all imaginative identification what he supposes to have been the intention of the creative artist, and in that act of imaginative identification, the interpreter must remain the servant of the creative artist. In the theatre his job is to correlate speech, movement, décor, lighting, costume, music into a significant whole, the theatrical experience, which shall not only be faithful to the text but vivify and illuminate it. A performance of, for example, *The Only Jealousy of Emer, A Full Moon in March, Calvary, The Dreaming of the Bones,* should exact from an audience a response that would approach that condition of reverie, almost the intensity of trance, in which the mind becomes conscious of the eternal beyond the temporal, the spiritual beyond the material, the essential beyond the phenomenal, and of the relation between them.

In a letter written to John Quinn at the beginning of his career as a dramatist, Yeats said:

. . . if Finvara, that ancient God, now king of Faery whose sacred hill I passed the other day in the railway train, were to come into the room with all his host of the Sidhe behind him and offer me some gift, I know right well the gift I should ask. I would say, 'Let my plays be acted . . .'

[*L* 406]

Now, eighty years later, in spite of, and perhaps because of the recognition that Yeats has received as a major poet, his wish is still largely unrealised. This book has been written in the hope that it will help in the granting of that gift.